HOLLYWOOD AND

HOLLYWOOD AND THE MOB

Movies, Mafia, Sex and Death

Tim Adler

BLOOMSBURY

First published in Great Britain in 2007
This paperback edition published 2008

Copyright © 2007 by Tim Adler

The moral right of the author has been asserted

No part of this book may be used or reproduced in any manner whatsover
without written permission from the Publisher except in the case of
brief quotations embodied in critical articles or reviews

Bloomsbury Publishing Plc,
36 Soho Square,
London W1D 3QY

www.bloomsbury.com

Bloomsbury Publishing, London, New York and Berlin

A CIP catalogue record for this book
is available from the British Library

ISBN 978 0 7475 7350 0

10 9 8 7 6 5 4 3 2 1

Typeset by Hewer Text UK Ltd, Edinburgh
Printed in Great Britain by Clays Ltd, St Ives plc

All papers used by Bloomsbury Publishing are natural,
recyclable products made from wood grown in well-managed
forests. The manufacturing processes conform to the
environmental regulations of the country of origin.

For Jack and Theo

'Harry, the guy's a crook.'
'So? This town he should fit right in.'

Hollywood producer Harry Zimm
referring to mob loan shark Chili Palmer
in Elmore Leonard's *Get Shorty*.

Contents

Introduction

When my mother and father first visited New York in 1957 there was such a commotion outside their hotel one morning that, at first, my mother thought Marilyn Monroe had arrived. Then, through a window to the left of the hotel lobby, she caught a glimpse of a dead man sprawled in a barber's chair. What my mother had witnessed was the murder of Mafia gangster Albert Anastasia.

Anastasia's nicknames in the Mafia were 'the Executioner' and 'the Mad Hatter'. Comedian Jerry Lewis remembered playing the Copacabana Club in New York in the 1950s, and making fun of a man in the audience. What Lewis did not realise was that his victim was Anastasia. Dean Martin stepped in to cut his pal off before he said something stupid. Years later, Lewis remembered being on-stage that night – although he could not see him, the comedian could feel, as he put it, the gangster's cold steel eyes hitting him like bullets.

The gangster's wealth came from his control of Brooklyn's docks, at the time the entry point for almost all imports into the USA (and most exports leaving it). The forty thousand dock-workers (longshoremen) who operated the three hundred deep-water ports along the Brooklyn waterfront were ultimately under Anastasia's control. Dockworkers took what they wanted – or 'boosted', in Mafia parlance – before loading goods onto ships, passing loot back up to their Mafia overseers. *On the Waterfront*

(1954) exposed Mafia intimidation of dockworkers, deciding who could or could not work on a particular day. However, Anastasia wanted to be more than just the capo, or street boss, of the docks. He murdered his own don, Vincent Mangano, and became enforcer to Frank Costello, head of the five Mafia families in New York.

Now Anastasia became embroiled in a power struggle within the Mafia. Vito Genovese was vying for control of the New York mob, or Syndicate as people called it. Genovese was determined to replace Costello – he of the wheezy, gravelly voice who was one of the inspirations behind Marlon Brando's character in *The Godfather* – to become *capo di tutti capi*, or boss of bosses. He persuaded Carlo Gambino, Anastasia's second in command – another inspiration for Brando's character – to join him. But first, Genovese would not only have to get Costello out of the way, but Anastasia as well.

Gambino justified Anastasia's murder to the Commission – or board of directors of the five families – because the waterfront boss was guilty of charging initiates a $40,000 fee for inducting them into the Mafia, a break with tradition which appalled the dons. Gambino thus assembled a trio of assassins, the Gallo brothers – Joe ('Crazy Joe'), Larry ('Kid Twist') and Albert ('Kid Blast') – to murder the Brooklyn gangster.

On 25 October 1957 two men walked into the Park Sheraton Hotel as Anastasia sat back in the barber's chair. Towels had been draped over his face. They shot the gangster in the back of the head several times. Anastasia's foot kicked so hard that it broke the footrest.

Ever since my mother first told me as a child that story of mistaking the crowd outside the Park Sheraton for the arrival of Marilyn Monroe, I have had the idea that somehow Hollywood and the Mafia are intertwined.

Delving deeper, one realises that not only has the mob run through the history of the movies like letters through a stick of rock, but, in some cases, the Mafia actually *was* Hollywood. The dream factory has always been grounded in a criminal reality. The

Mafia has intimidated actors and producers with threats and violence from the 1930s – when the mob was extorting the studios for $1.5 million a year (the equivalent of $14 million today) – right up to the present day, with members of the Gambino crime family in prison for threatening actor Steven Seagal.

After all, Hollywood and the mob are both, to an extent, in the same business. The theatre has had a dubious moral reputation for centuries. Wandering minstrels, fairground barkers, exploitative impresarios and various conmen have always peopled entertainment. Both Hollywood and organised crime offer people what they want. One peddles escape through flickering images, while the other sells oblivion through drugs and sex and gambling. 'The boys had always been involved in the entertainment things, it was a natural,' said union organiser and Mafia associate Max 'the Butcher' Block.

Film historian David Thomson has pointed out that Hollywood moguls in the Golden Age often behaved like gangsters. It was a way of acting tough and showing off to each other. MGM boss Louis B. Mayer was bosom pals with gangster-turned-agent Frank Orsatti, while Chicago mobster Johnny Rosselli was so close to Columbia Studios boss Harry Cohn that they wore identical rings. Frank Renzulli, one of the executive producers of *The Sopranos*, says producers have liked to be associated with gangsters throughout the history of show business. Hollywood has come to believe its own mythmaking, seeing gangsters as glamorous rather than merely as thugs and extortionists. Brooklyn gangster Henry Hill, the character Ray Liotta played in *GoodFellas* (1990), said, 'All the movie people want to schmooze the hoods. The hoods are like some prized piece of jewellery you parade around with at a party.' Hollywood gossip columnist Hedda Hopper pointed out the opposite is also true – that criminals enjoy hanging around celebrities.

After all, Hollywood has taught gangsters how to dress and how to behave. In person, gangsters were mostly uncouth and stupid. Johnny Rosselli, for many years the Outfit's man on the West Coast and a movie producer himself, could not even read. But movie gangsters such as Humphrey Bogart and George Raft, who in real life was under the wing of the Mafia and whose best friend was Benjamin 'Bugsy' Siegel, the gangster who controlled Hollywood's extras' union, were stylish and laconic. Raft taught the boys how to dress – white tie with black shirt – while Bogart taught them how to speak. As Raymond Chandler noted in *The Big Sleep*, 'his voice was the elaborately casual voice of the tough guy in pictures . . . pictures have made them all like that'. British gangster Reggie Kray modelled himself on Raft, asking his tailor to copy the actor's double-breasted blue suits. In turn, Raft based his screen persona on Joey Adonis, a New York gangster associate of Charles 'Lucky' Luciano. After *The Godfather*, Mafiosi started calling each other godfather – a term invented by the author Mario Puzo – and revived archaic customs such as kissing the don's ring. One Sicilian don even played the theme music of the movie at his daughter's wedding.

Of course, there are financial reasons why the Mafia has been attracted to Hollywood. Movies are ideal for laundering cash – unlike manufacturing businesses, which need time to equip factories before they start to wash money. Film production requires vast amounts of money quickly. Today, the average Hollywood film costs $96 million to produce and publicise. Most revenue flows back within a couple of years of a film's release, once it has been in cinemas and on video. As one Hollywood source told the *New York Times*, there has been a constant flow of mob money finding its way into movies. Hank Messick, a veteran crime reporter, concluded that organised crime has thoroughly corrupted much of show business. He argued that show business is not unique in being corrupted, but it has been a key conquest by what he called 'the fast-buck boys'.

On the other hand, Hollywood has used the same methods as the mob to intimidate actors and steal money from shareholders. In 1958, Columbia's Harry Cohn, who first bought the studio with Mafia money, threatened to blind Sammy Davis Jr and break both his legs unless he stopped seeing Kim Novak. Up until the Second World War, the heads of both Metro-Goldwyn-Mayer and 20th

Century Fox were stealing millions of dollars from box office cash boxes in much the same way as the Mafia 'skimmed' cash from Las Vegas casinos in the 1960s. 'Nobody can skim as well as Las Vegas because they invented it,' said director Richard Brooks, 'but Hollywood is second.'

In the late 1970s it was known for studios owing actors hundreds of thousands of dollars to pay up half of what they owed – and then tell the actor to sue them for the rest. The studio knew that the actor would never sue for fear of never working again. 'Morally, that's exactly the same as sticking a gun in a man's gut and stealing a hundred thousand dollars from him,' wrote television chat show host and anti-corruption campaigner Steve Allen.

Chandler's novels, in which private eye everyman Philip Marlowe battles gangsters, corrupt police and the parasitic rich who employ him, could be seen as a metaphor of the novelist's own relationship with Hollywood. Chandler, writing to a friend in May 1949, noticed the similarity between Hollywood executives and Mafiosi:

Once looking out of Joe Sistrom's window on the [Universal] lot, I happened to see the big boys strolling back from lunch in the exec dining room in a loose group. I was transfixed with a sinister delight. They looked so exactly like a bunch of topflight Chicago gangsters moving in to read the death sentence on a beaten competitor. It brought home to me in a flash the strange psychological and spiritual kinship between the operations of big money business and the rackets. Same faces, same expressions, same manners. Same way of dressing and same exaggerated leisure of movement.

Moguls, gangsters and stars often originated from the same places. Like gangsters, Hollywood moguls were either immigrants or sons of immigrants: the Cohn brothers were sons of a German tailor, while all four Warner brothers were sons of a Polish cobbler. Louis B. Mayer and Meyer Lansky, financier of the Syndicate, both fled from Russia, while Los Angeles gangster Mickey Cohen was born to Russian Jewish parents in New York. Frank Sinatra's grandfather lived in the same Sicilian village as Lucky Luciano. Danny Kaye grew up in the same Brooklyn neighbourhood as Bugsy Siegel.

Just as working-class Sicilians formed the Mafia to give themselves a sense of togetherness and protect themselves from bullying landowners, so the Jews who created Hollywood did so partly as a buffer against the Protestant elite. Hollywood would become, as author Neal Gabler has pointed out, a kingdom of their own. And, like Sicilian immigrants, the first-generation studio bosses decided to police themselves rather than let outsiders in. As Celia Brady, narrator of Scott Fitzgerald's novel *The Last Tycoon*, remarks, 'We don't go for outsiders much in Hollywood.' So, when newspapers called for the government to regulate the industry during the Fatty Arbuckle scandal in 1920, Hollywood appointed censor Will Hays as its enforcer. The idea was that Hollywood, like the Mafia, would have a respectable front. As Arbuckle's biographer David Yallop wrote, 'Bootlegging had operated successfully behind a front of dry cleaning establishments – why couldn't the movies?'

Mafia and the studios have sometimes structured themselves in the same way, with a nominal chief executive acting as a lightning rod – deflecting attention away from a powerful board. Therefore, Louis B. Mayer may have been the public face of MGM – and, for many years, the highest-paid executive in America – but its real boss was Nick Schenck, chairman of holding company Loew's in New York. In much the same way, Frank Nitti was the supposed head of the Chicago Outfit, but the real power lay with board members Joe 'Batters' Accardo and Murray 'the Camel' Humphreys.

Chicago gangster Johnny Rosselli once compared getting to the truth to peeling an onion. 'What you perceive to be true isn't true,' he said. 'You have to keep peeling it until you get to the core.' One of the best observations made about drilling down deep to get to the truth about anything was made during the Watergate scandal of the 1970s – follow the money. Perhaps the real reason why, at the peak of the Mafia's influence, Hollywood moguls such as Harry Cohn and Lew Wasserman were so close to gangsters was because the mob was prepared to invest in movies. Rosselli and fellow mobster Mickey Cohen are both known to have put money into films. The mob had the capital, controlled the unions and was prepared to take a bigger risk for greater reward than Wall Street. Conservative bankers saw Hollywood as volatile, unable to produce a consistent return on investment and, frankly, 'Jewish' to boot. Ironically, the Bank of Italy was the only bank which would lend to the moguls. Perhaps the gangsters agreed with Bank of America's chief film lender, A.P. Gianinni, who said: 'They who control the cinema can control the thought of the world.' Even today, bankers are wary of lending money to an industry that is more of a roulette game than a quantifiable business. But as the Western economy becomes increasingly based on entertainment in many forms – from television to personal therapy – it could be argued that the Mafia was just as visionary about Hollywood as it was about Las Vegas.

Even today, there are similarities between Hollywood and the Mafia. Although there are few barriers to entry into the movie business, at the higher levels Hollywood becomes Cosa Nostra, literally translated as 'This Thing of Ours'. One of the most famous lines in *The Godfather* is 'keep your friends close and your enemies closer'. So today's studio heads attend each other's charity dinners, celebrity golf matches and even go on holiday together. When former agent Brad Grey took over Paramount in 2005, one of the first things he did was pay his respects to the other studio bosses – the new godfather doing the rounds of the other dons. Kevin Smith, director of *Clerks*, has compared the speciality arms of the studios to the five families – Sony Classics, Focus Features, Paramount Classics, Fine Line and Miramax. *Variety*, Hollywood's daily newspaper, refers to studio production executives as 'capos', an abbreviation of the Mafia term *capo regime*, or street boss. How one becomes a fully-fledged Hollywood insider, or 'made', is unspoken and mysterious.

Perhaps the best way of looking at it is the Sicilian expression which translates as 'one hand washes another'. Only when one understands this favour-for-a-favour mentality is one inducted into the higher reaches of the industry – or any business for that matter. So when agent Mike Ovitz threatened to destroy screenwriter Joe Eszterhas's career after he tried to defect to a rival agency (Ovitz threatened Eszterhas that his 'foot soldiers who go up and down Wilshire Boulevard each day will blow your brains out'), producer Ray Stark interceded, offering to lend the writer $2 million to make sure he did not lose his home. Eszterhas declined the offer, perhaps not wanting to be in thrall to Stark. After all, a Mafia don never offers help without expecting something in return.

One gangster who moved into the entertainment business said that Hollywood was a much tougher racket. As Henry Hill put it, 'On the surface, this world seems as far away from the gangster life as you can imagine. But the slime below the surface is sickening. It recently occurred to me that my adventures [as a gangster] prepared me nicely for swimming with the sharks on Wilshire Boulevard.'

Author Mario Puzo added: 'Motion pictures are the most crooked business that I've ever had any experience with. You can get a better shake in Vegas than you can get in Hollywood.'

Therefore, perhaps one reason why there have been so many gangster movies, from *Scarface* to *GoodFellas*, is because gangsterism is a *modus operandi*. Hollywood has bullied employees, forced actors to hand over most of their salaries when loaned out to other studios and destroyed the careers of those who do not agree with it politically.

But the key resemblance between Hollywood and the Mafia is that both are to an extent secret societies, whose members never speak to outsiders. In Mafia parlance, the inner circle has sworn to keep *omerta*. Don Corleone tells his son never to let anybody outside the family know what he is thinking. In much the same way, Hollywood expels those who break the Sacred Code of Silence. When producer Julia Phillips, who won an Academy Award for *The Sting*, wrote an autobiography, *You'll Never Eat*

Lunch in This Town Again, ridiculing studio executives, the community shunned her. Phillips died of cancer in 2002. Columbia Pictures boss Dawn Steel, on the other hand, kept *omerta* in her autobiography and her peers – including David Geffen, one of those made fun of in Phillips's book – funded medical research to help her. She subsequently died of a brain tumour in 1997.

If Hollywood behaves like Cosa Nostra, then film historian Peter Biskind has compared independent film companies outside of the studios to the Russian mob. In both cases, says Biskind, the bad guys bump off the good guys, but in Hollywood they at least do it with a certain finesse – sending a basket of fruit afterwards to the victim's assistant, say. The indies, says Biskind, just whack you – and your wife and kids for good measure.

The legend of the Mafia has become America's most potent myth, underlining the importance of family at a time when families are breaking up. Mafia also taps into people's fantasies of omnipotence: what man would not like to be a king like *The Godfather's* Michael Corleone? Or have extramarital affairs with impunity, like Tony Soprano? But Mafia history has reached the point where it is becoming myth rather than legend. Each generation projects its own concerns onto the Mafia story. Therefore, on one level, Michael Corleone's vengeance at the end of *The Godfather Part II* is a metaphor for American foreign policy in Vietnam (director Francis Ford Coppola has said as much), just as *The Sopranos* reflects our own unease in the twenty-first century. Tony Soprano sums up the end-of-something theme in the first episode, when he says that lately he has the feeling the best has gone, to which his therapist replies that many Americans feel the same.

In attempting to write a history of Mafia corruption in Hollywood, one realises that source materials are a palimpsest of exaggeration, half-truths and lies. One is tempted to say, like John Milius, screenwriter of *Dillinger* (1973), that if this story is not the way it was – then it is the way it should have been. Source material

– be it testimony given at the 1951 Mafia hearings or the 1986 grand jury investigation into organised crime in Hollywood – has become almost threadbare with constant fingering, so stretched and worn that it frays to the very touch.

CHAPTER ONE

Al Capone Visits Hollywood

One night in 1917 an incident took place, which, although insignificant at the time, would trigger a fault line – and eventually a schism – between gangsters in Chicago and New York. Ultimately, its aftershocks would still be felt twenty years later in Hollywood as rival groups battled for control of organised crime in the movie industry.

Despite its grand name, the Harvard Inn bar and restaurant in Coney Island, New York, was a modest establishment. The name was a dig at a rival restaurant, the College Inn, whose pianist, Jimmy Durante, played for its resident Charleston dancer George Raft. The Harvard Inn was a nondescript bungalow on Seaside Walk. Its most interesting feature was the bar, which was 20 foot long and ran the length of one wall. There was also a small dance floor with room for a band. Francesco Ioele, better known as Frankie Yale, owned the restaurant. Yale was a gangster who had been involved in various schemes, including a laundry business and a cigar-manufacturing company – threatening shopkeepers unless they stocked his cigars.

That night, his seventeen-year-old barman, bouncer and general factotum was serving a table occupied by a couple about his own age. His job was also to beat up hookers not kicking back enough money to the restaurant. Alphonse Capone had been working at the Harvard Inn for about a year. He could not take his eyes off the girl. She was Italian with a lovely figure. He hovered near the table before finally leaning down and saying, 'Honey, you have a nice ass and I mean that as a compliment.' Immediately, the man sitting next to her stood up. He was the girl's brother and he was drunk. Frank Gallucio was not about to have anybody insult his sister. Gallucio threw a punch at Capone. The blow enraged Capone but then Gallucio pulled a four-inch knife from his pocket. Other customers scrambled out of the way. Gallucio slashed at Capone's face three times. There was blood everywhere. Gallucio grabbed his sister and fled the building.

Gallucio left a four-inch scar down Capone's left cheek from ear to jaw, a smaller two-inch scar across the jaw and a third below the left ear. No hair would subsequently grow through the scar tissue. Later, Capone would apply coats of talcum powder to cover the scars, and he became so self-conscious about them that he even considered plastic surgery. Capone would present his right, un-scarred, cheek to the camera when having his photograph taken. He hated the nickname the press gave him – 'Scarface'.

Capone made it known that he wanted revenge on Gallucio. Gallucio asked a criminal called Albert Altierri for help. In turn, Altierri went to see another gangster, Salvatore Luciana, later better known as Lucky Luciano. Luciano had been at school with Capone. They had also belonged to the same teenage gang. On hearing the story of the knife fight, however, Luciano, who was only two years older than Capone, sided with Gallucio. Nobody should insult a man's sister like that. Luciano proposed a summit between all parties to settle differences. One night, after the Harvard Inn had closed up, Capone, Gallucio, Luciano and Yale sat down to determine what should happen next. Yale told Capone that he must apologise to Gallucio. They would kill Capone if he tried to exact revenge. One can imagine how this must have stuck in Capone's craw. However, Luciano already had a reputation as somebody to fear, whereas Capone was nobody, a mop boy in a Coney Island bar.

Alphonse Capone was born in New York on 17 January 1899, the son of Gabriele and Teresina 'Theresa' Capone. His parents had escaped the slums of Naples for the slums of New York City.

Between 1901 and 1903, more than one million Sicilians alone immigrated to the USA, slightly less than 25 per cent of the island's population. On arrival in Manhattan, Italians scrabbled to find employment. Some would make a quick buck helping street criminals. Immigrants found ghetto politics similar to politics back home. The Democratic Party organisation, known as Tammany Hall, farmed votes in exchange for favours, a practice known as *'maccheroni* politics'. This favour-for-a-favour mentality was the way things worked in Naples or Sicily. In southern Italy, organised crime went by different names. In Naples, where the Capones came from, it was the Camorra. In Sicily, it was the Mafia. Mafiosi called themselves 'men of respect', or just 'the Organisation'. In America, organised crime groups went by a variety of names: in Chicago, the Outfit; in New York, the Syndicate – overall, the mob or Cosa Nostra.

The Capones lived in a slum on Navy Street in Brooklyn, the centre of the largest Italian ghetto in New York. Gabriele Capone was a barber and, as such, slightly better off than most usually illiterate immigrants. Capone started going to school when he was five. Both Capone and Luciano had the same teacher, one Miss Mulvaney, at Public School 7 on Adams Street, Brooklyn. It is possible they fought together in the playground, given the enmity between Sicilians and Neapolitans.

By now, Capone had moved to 38 Garfield Place, Brooklyn. At school, Capone averaged a B grade until he was twelve. However, when he started playing truant his marks fell. One day, during his second year in sixth grade, the thirteen-year-old Capone punched a teacher. The school principal beat Capone for his insubordination. Capone dropped out of school and never went back.

Instead, he drifted into a job in a candy store, before getting a job setting pins in a bowling alley. After that, he worked as a paper cutter in a bookbindery. However, by now, Capone had started bullying schoolchildren for their lunch money.

He had now also met Johnny Torrio, the man who would organise crime in Chicago and, later, New York and, by extension, Los Angeles. Born in Orsara, southern Italy, in 1882, Torrio's

parents immigrated to the Lower East Side of New York City when
he was two. Torrio had his own gang when he was a teenager.
When Capone met him, he was also running a youth club, the John
Torrio Association, which was really a recruiting office for teenage
gangs. Torrio introduced Capone to the Five Pointers, one of many
gangs roaming the Lower East Side of Manhattan, the other end of
Brooklyn Bridge. The Five Pointers got their name from an intersection between Broadway and the Bowery. Its leader was a former
boxer named Paolo Antonini Vacarelli. Like many Italian boxers,
Vacaralli had assumed an Irish name, Paul Kelly, to defy anti-
Italian prejudice. The gang had its headquarters in the New
Brighton Dance Hall, owned by Kelly, in Great Jones Street. Kelly
commanded some 1500 Five Pointer thugs and offered a number of
services – $2 for punching; $4 for both eyes blackened; $10 for
nose and jaw broken; $15 for beating somebody unconscious; $19
for a broken arm or leg; $25 for a shot in the leg; $25 for a
stabbing; and $100 for murder. Tammany Hall protected Kelly in
exchange for his farming votes at election time. Later, Luciano
would remember Capone as 'just a great big lug . . . but he was
strong and useful, and Johnny Torrio sure brought him up fast'.

In the ghetto, Italian and Irish communities kept to themselves.
However, Italian boys expected to marry early, whereas Irish boys
preferred to wait until they were more established. Therefore, Irish
girls eager for marriage were attracted to Italian boys. In spring
1918, Capone – by now calling himself Al Brown – met an Irish girl
named Mae Coughlin at a teenage cellar club. Capone married
Coughlin within weeks of their meeting, on 18 May 1918. Mae
gave birth to their first and only child, Albert Francis Capone,
nicknamed Sonny, one year later. Johnny Torrio was the boy's
godfather.

That same year, 1919, also saw Congress pass legislation ban-
ning the sale of alcohol. Congress gave in to the temperance lobby,
which had campaigned for the ban. It passed the Volstead Act on
27 October 1919 and the Prohibition Amendment became law on
20 January 1920. Prohibition had the effect of drops of stimulant
on organised crime. At the height of Prohibition, Americans would

spend about $5 billion a year on alcohol, the equivalent of $56 billion today. Gangsters such as Capone and Luciano helped slake the nation's thirst. The mob would generate the equivalent of about 5 per cent of gross national product through bootlegging. Gangsterism also gained a degree of respectability, as cocking a snook at Prohibition became fashionable. Even President Harding served bootleg whisky in the White House. However, at first, gangsters were slow to realise the implications of the alcohol ban.

Over in Chicago, described by H.G. Wells as a 'dark smear under the sky', blackmailers were extorting 'Big Jim' Colosimo, the city's crime boss. They wanted Colosimo, who was earning about $600,000 a year (the equivalent of $10 million today) through ownership of some two hundred brothels and collecting bribes for local politicians, to hand over $50,000 – an unconscionable sum for the time. Colosimo's wife Vittoria was Johnny Torrio's cousin. She suggested her husband call her cousin for help. After all, New York was only twenty hours away by train. Torrio imported some rival extortionists to murder the blackmailers. In 1920, he called for Capone, plus two of Capone's supposed cousins – Charlie and Rocco Fischetti, who would later introduce Frank Sinatra to Luciano. For a brief time, all four lived at the same address on South Wabash Avenue, Chicago.

Torrio became Colosimo's second in command, while Capone became Torrio's enforcer. Chicago's gangs were fighting each other, district by district, for control of bootlegging. Colosimo, however, distracted by a love affair with a young singer, seemed oblivious of the threat to his business. Presumably, Torrio decided Colosimo was a brake on his ambitions. On 11 May 1922, Torrio telephoned Colosimo. He apparently told his boss that two alcohol shipments were arriving that afternoon at Colosimo's Café. Colosimo turned up at the all but empty restaurant at 4 p.m., where cleaners were preparing for the evening. Colosimo waited for half an hour before walking back into the lobby. There an assassin stepped out and shot him dead with a .38 revolver. The bullet destroyed Colosimo's right ear and entered his brain. Police questioned thirty people, including Torrio, but never made an arrest.

The authorities' chief suspect, however, was Capone's old boss, Frankie Yale. Torrio was supposed to have paid Yale, or somebody, $10,000 to murder Colosimo. The murder was later dramatised in Howard Hawks's 1932 film, *Scarface*. However, one witness, Colosimo's secretary Frank Camilla, described the assassin as a heavyset man with scars down the left side of his face.

Johnny Torrio was now Chicago's new boss of bosses. Al Capone was his right-hand man. Torrio began by smoothing out differences between gangs. The best way forward, he reasoned, was to carve up the city between them. One gang, however, led by Dion O'Banion, rubbed up against the emollient Torrio. O'Banion started hijacking Torrio's booze trucks and even had the gang boss arrested in a raid on a jointly owned brewery. On 10 November 1924, a car pulled up outside Schofield florists, from where O'Banion ran his organisation. O'Banion was in the shop as three men stepped out of a Cadillac. O'Banion extended his hand to greet one of them. The assassin grabbed the Irishman in a bear hug. His companion shot O'Banion several times in the back of the head. (Again, *Scarface* refers to the off-screen assassination.)

O'Banion's murder sparked a street war across the city. What alarmed Torrio was that he had not ordered O'Banion's murder – that had come from Capone. Torrio tried to make peace but the war claimed more than five hundred lives. On 25 January 1925, Torrio was helping his wife and chauffeur carry packages from their car to their house when another car pulled up. Two men jumped out with machine guns. The assassins sprayed Torrio with bullets in the face, chest, groin and arms. Torrio, however, survived. Presumably, he now realised that his attempt to rationalise organised crime in Chicago had been a failure. After three weeks in hospital, Torrio left for New York, where he would amalgamate East Coast gangsterism into a single organisation, the Syndicate. In doing so, he established two rival organisations with conflicting interests. Unwittingly, he also set New York and Chicago on a collision course, like axes of a graph converging years in the future – a battle for control of trade unions in Hollywood.

With Torrio gone, foot soldiers assumed Capone was in charge.

They began asking him questions. By default, Capone had become crime boss of Chicago. According to one eyewitness, Luis Kutner, the former bouncer never had any leadership ambitions. Nor did he have the ability to handle money – he would squander millions of dollars and eventually die penniless. However, life is often about timing and Capone was lucky to be in Chicago in 1925. The city had become a three-dimensional jigsaw puzzle of self-interest. Gangsters patrolled district polls on election day, ensuring the right politicians were elected; these politicians appointed police captains, who in turn ensured their men left gangs alone; and gangsters extorted the workers – the green grease which lubricated the machine – taking their cut before kicking cash back upstairs to politicians. Capone was paying more than $30 million a year to Chicago police, half of whom were taking bribes. They would line up to collect money at warehouses. Overall, Capone's operation was costing $300,000 a week in overheads – mostly consisting of meeting his one-thousand-man payroll. On the other hand, about $10 million a week was pouring into Capone's coffers from alcohol, gambling and prostitution.

One employee on Capone's payroll was his driver, Filippo Sacco. Capone himself suggested that Sacco change his name to the more American-sounding Johnny Rosselli. After one particularly biting Chicago winter, Rosselli was diagnosed with incipient tuberculosis. Capone dispatched his driver to California to look out for opportunities in the growing movie industry. Once in Los Angeles, Rosselli hung around the studios getting work as a movie extra. In time, Rosselli would become the Outfit's *capo regime*, or street boss, in Hollywood.

Capone established his headquarters in Chicago's Lexington Hotel, where he appropriated between fifty and sixty rooms over two floors. The gang had its own private lift, bar and wine cellar, spending about $1500 per day at the hotel. To gain an audience with Capone, one had to run a gauntlet of bodyguards with, in the words of one journalist, 'eyes as expressionless as a dead mackerel's'. Capone presided in an Italianate, high-backed throne – a prop taken from a local cinema – resting his hands on lions' heads protruding from each arm. Behind him were photographs of his favourite movie stars, Fatty Arbuckle and Theda Bara.

Al Capone was now a twenty-five-year-old tycoon, albeit one embroiled in a nasty gang war with Earl 'Hymie' Weiss, who had taken over O'Banion's organisation. (Capone's volatility – elation followed by despair – was probably due to his increasing cocaine abuse.) Chicago became so violent that even Luciano called it 'a real goddam crazy place. Nobody's safe in the streets.' There were two hundred unsolved murders over a four-year period during the 1920s. By this time, the city's reputation for anarchy had even reached the Soviet Union. Soviet film director Sergei Eisenstein (*Battleship Potemkin*) asked a detective to take him on a tour of gangland when he visited Chicago. The director was disappointed to find all the gangsters had gone into hiding following a recent murder.

Another source of revenue was forcing workers to join unions and then pocketing membership fees. Capone concentrated on unions that controlled factories, bars and trucking companies, among other things. His second in command, Frank 'the Enforcer' Nitti, would lead his men into factories and warehouses and force workers to join the union at gunpoint.

With unions generating so much cash, it is somewhat surprising that Capone ignored the Motion Picture Operators' Union, the Local 110, supposedly considering control of movie theatres – still seen as mainly a working-class diversion – as somehow beneath him. Chicago was, after all, one of the film centres of America. During the 1920s, Chicago produced one-fifth of all films made in the USA. Hollywood moguls who came from the city included Carl Laemmle, founder of Universal; Adolph Zukor, founder of Paramount; and Leo Spitz, president of RKO. Laemmle and Zukor had both run studios in Chicago's North Side before moving to California. Chicago's bad weather made it impossible to shoot westerns outside the city.

Instead, Tommy Maloy, an Irish gangster born in Chicago in 1893, controlled the Local 110, itself a subsidiary of a bigger union, the International Alliance of Theatrical Stage Employees

(IATSE), which represented everybody in the movie business – from art directors, cinematographers and electricians to laboratory staff and projectionists. Maloy – a never-convicted suspect in nine murders, including one which took place right in his own office – was the protégé of Maurice 'Mossy' Enright, a union boss who controlled builders and garbage workers. Enright had begun his career as an enforcer for Dion O'Banion. He later bombed the premises of one business that stood up to him. Maloy became Enright's chauffeur, squiring the union leader around in a car known as 'the Gray Ghost'. However, Maloy found himself out of a job when Enright became the victim of Chicago's first drive-by shooting in February 1920.

Maloy found employment as a cinema projectionist, while at the same time organising gambling under the theatre stage. He then got a job as an enforcer working for Jack Miller, head of the Local 110. Maloy inherited the union leadership after Miller was murdered and his first meeting as head of the union in 1924 turned violent when members complained about Maloy's takeover. Thugs fired several rounds of machine-gun fire into the ceiling to restore order.

Membership of the projectionists' union grew under Maloy's leadership, however. This is partly because Maloy's soldiers threatened projectionists with violence unless they joined. In any case, most projectionists were happy to join because it made economic sense to do so. Being a cinema projectionist in Chicago was a well-paid job: many could earn up to $95 per week. Maloy charged members union dues of $4 a week – $3 to the Local 110 and another dollar to IATSE (presumably lining Maloy's pocket). However, non-members, whom cinemas would hire by the day, had to hand over up to 10 per cent of their salary to the union. Therefore, it was cheaper to join the Local 110. (Even as late as the mid-1990s, Chicago projectionists earned far more than their counterparts elsewhere, being paid ten times the national average of $10–15 per hour.)

Chicago's most prosperous cinema chain was that of Balaban & Katz, owned by Barney Balaban and Stan Katz. Balaban later ran Paramount Pictures with his brother, while Katz was a future vice-president of MGM. They opened their first cinema in 1908 and by the mid-1920s owned dozens of sites – grandiose movie palaces with names such as the Riviera, the Valencia and the Tivoli. Balaban & Katz's empire depended on projectionists, and, by extension, the Motion Picture Operators' Union. Maloy extorted cash from Balaban & Katz, among other chains, in exchange for union tranquillity. In addition, Maloy squeezed small wage increases out of exhibitors to keep his members placated. As with other union rackets, Maloy threw crumbs to the membership to keep them happy while at the same time defrauding them.

Union members also contributed to a separate Maloy 'special assessments' fund, which he dipped into on top of his $25,000 annual salary. Maloy used this cash to pay for, among other things, a $22,000 European holiday with his mistress, and a $5000 bar and $4000 bathroom installed in his house – ostensibly so that he could conduct union business at home. Investigators later estimated that Maloy plundered at least $500,000 from members.

Warner Bros released the first 'talkie', *The Jazz Singer*, in October 1927. Maloy used the introduction of sound to increase his income even further. In the early days of sound gramophone records had to be played in synchronisation with the film. Maloy insisted cinema owners install a second man, known as the 'fader', in the projectionist booth to play records. Then, when sound became part of celluloid itself, Maloy forced exhibitors to hand over $1100 for each fader they made redundant. Exhibitors paid up because it was still cheaper than keeping the faders on.

Meanwhile, in Chicago, the press was calling for authorities to investigate systematic corruption in the city. Mayor William 'Big Bill' Thompson – who was himself on Capone's payroll – felt the pressure and ordered police to clamp down on organised crime. Thompson aspired to become president one day and Chief of Police Hughes advised Capone to get out of Chicago until things cooled down.

Capone made his first visit to Los Angeles at the end of 1927. Los Angeles was booming, as people who had failed back east drifted to the city, drawn by the climate, the promise of easy money, or the

Hollywood dream – as addictive and illusory as silky cocaine. Hollywood had become the fourth largest business in America with capital assets in the form of cinemas, studios and offices worth $1.5 billion. This didn't include other intangible assets such as film libraries, which, in time, would become the studios' most valuable property. About one hundred million Americans were going to the cinema each week, buying tickets at one of 21,000 movie houses. Trade association Motion Picture Producers and Distributors claimed that Hollywood used more silver to print film stock than the Treasury used to mint coins. Wall Street was evaluating studios as being worth astronomical figures for the time. The holding company that owned Warner Bros, for example, was valued at $160 million (the equivalent of $1.8 billion today).

Capone's gang funnelled several hundred million dollars into southern California property using supposedly legitimate business-men to front for them.

The gang is also thought to have lent money to Joseph P. Kennedy, father of future president John F. Kennedy, to buy a Hollywood studio. He was now trying to build Hollywood's first vertically integrated company, comprising production, distribution and exhibition – a business model which all studios would even-tually follow. Kennedy was also partners with the New York mob in the bootlegging business, smuggling alcohol into America through Canada.

Born in 1888, the son of a bar owner whose own father had fled the Irish potato famine, Kennedy grew up in Boston. Protestants dominated the city, having founded it four hundred years before, although there were Catholic ghettoes. Kennedy graduated from Harvard in 1912 and decided to become a banker. He saw banking as a platform from which he could jump into any number of careers. Kennedy got a job as a clerk in a small bank, the Columbia Trust. Within a few months, he was calling himself the first Irish Catholic bank examiner in Massachusetts. A rival bank attempted to buy the single-branch Columbia Trust, but Kennedy saw off the hostile takeover. The board was so grateful that it made him president.

In 1919, Kennedy joined rival banker and stockbroker Hayden,

Stone and Company. He became convinced movies were the key to making his fortune. Few lenders took Hollywood seriously as a business. For a start, immigrants and women made up a large proportion of those working in the industry, which consisted of hundreds of small companies. Consolidation had yet to occur. Only Amadeo Giannini, founder of the Bank of Italy (later the Bank of America), was prepared to lend money to showmen, for example helping Louis B. Mayer – the film executive Kennedy referred to as 'that kike junkman'. Most films were financed with profits from previous ones – a volatile way of doing things which alarmed risk-averse bankers. However, this was precisely what attracted Kennedy, who became Hayden, Stone's lender to movie companies. Soon, dozens of companies were petitioning Kennedy for loans. What applicants did not know was that the lender himself was planning to enter the business.

Kennedy decided it made more sense to invest in an established studio than build up a company himself. In short, let somebody else do the work and then step in. He put together a group of investors who became shareholders in Hallmark Pictures, a company consolidated from several smaller ones. Hallmark itself merged with Robertson-Cole/Film Booking Offices, a distributor which supplied movies to cinemas across America. Robertson-Cole had emerged out of a British car dealership that distributed British Rohmer Automobiles throughout the States. The company built a studio in Hollywood in 1920 and renamed itself Film Booking Office of America (FBO). The newly merged FBO released low-budget westerns and serials with relatively unknown actors, which it either produced itself or acquired from other Hollywood producers. However, by 1920 FBO was having cash-flow problems. Distribution revenue was trickling in too slowly to finance production. Rufus Cole, president of RC/FBO, came to see Kennedy asking for more money. Kennedy turned him down.

British banking firm Graham's of London stepped in to buy FBO for $7 million. Graham's put Major H.C.S. Thomson in charge but the former soldier knew little about the movie business. In 1921, Graham's decided to sell the company and appointed Kennedy to handle the sale, putting him on the board of directors. Kennedy wrote to Frank Joseph Godsol, chairman of Goldwyn Pictures, proposing a merger between FBO, Goldwyn, Cosmopolitan Pictures – the production company of newspaper magnate William Randolph Hearst – Metro and Selznick. The banker was convinced that unless all these small companies consolidated they would go bankrupt as the market matured. However, Hearst's Cosmopolitan Pictures was just a vehicle for films starring his mistress, Marion Davies. Having rejected an offer from Paramount, Hearst saw little attraction in merging with the unknown Kennedy. Eventually, Hearst would make a deal to have Davies's films distributed by Metro-Goldwyn-Mayer, a studio created in a 1924 merger along the lines Kennedy envisaged three years earlier. The banker's analysis had been correct but ahead of its time. By 1924, FBO was still unsold despite Kennedy earning $18,000 a year for handling the sale. The banker submitted his resignation, which was 'regrettably accepted and understood' by the board.

However, one year later, in the summer of 1925, Kennedy arrived in London with an offer to buy FBO. The studio was now in the equivalent of receivership. Graham's found it could only borrow cash at an interest rate of 18 per cent – closer to usury than debt. Presumably, its English owners were seething once they realised Kennedy had soured any sale in order to buy it himself. Nevertheless, Kennedy's was the only offer on the table. After several months of debate, the bankers agreed to sell FBO (the company had dropped the RC from its name) to Kennedy for $1.1 million – $400,000 less than their asking price five years before. Kennedy is thought to have borrowed money from Chicago gangsters Ricca, Humphreys and Frank 'the Enforcer' Nitti – Capone's successor as head of the Outfit – to finance the deal.

Hollywood studio chiefs in the mid-1920s were almost all immigrants, men such as Carl Laemmle of Universal, Louis B. Mayer and Marcus Loew of MGM, and Adolph Zukor of Paramount. These men, all Jews, had grown up with the movies, having started out running slot-machine amusement arcades, nickelodeons or burlesque theatres. Therefore, when the *New*

York Times reported, 'Boston Banker Buys British Film Concern', there was some consternation. 'A banker?' Marcus Loew is supposed to have said. 'I thought this business was for furriers.' For his part, Kennedy apparently told a colleague, 'Look at that bunch of pants pressers in Hollywood making themselves millionaires. I could take the whole business away from them.'

FBO's films were not screened in cities – they were aimed at the rural circuit. But Kennedy persuaded a New York cinema to show one of the studio's cowboy movies. It became a box office success. FBO grossed $9 million during its first year under new ownership.

Kennedy's strategy was to increase production to fifty low-budget movies each year. No film was to cost more than $30,000 or take more than seven days to shoot. By comparison, MGM productions such as *The Big Parade* or *Ben-Hur* cost up to $700,000 each with shooting running into months.

Kennedy then brought in leading companies from outside the industry, such as General Electric, to become shareholders and board members. This had never happened before in Hollywood.

At the same time, Kennedy forged friendships with William Randolph Hearst and industry regulator and censor Will Hays. One of Kennedy's Hollywood friends was Hearst's mistress, silent movie actress Marion Davies. Davies supposedly used Kennedy as her bootlegging connection when he visited their home, San Simeon. Drink was smuggled into the castle without Hearst's knowledge: the newspaper tycoon disapproved of alcohol. According to Kennedy's biographer Ted Schwarz, Joe Kennedy used Al Capone's men to deliver booze to Davies and her guests, who included Charlie Chaplin. Kennedy, who was married, also began an affair with Gloria Swanson, the biggest film star of the time.

Frank Costello was Kennedy's bootlegging partner, importing Scottish and Irish whisky into New England and New York. Owney Madden, leader of the Gopher Gang also said that he was in the bootlegging business with Kennedy. When Kennedy's Harvard class of 1912 met for their annual reunion in June 1922, class secretary Ralph Cowell described Kennedy as 'our chief bootlegger'. John Kohlert, a musician Capone had taken under his wing, was present at a 1926 meeting between Kennedy and Capone where they discussed bootlegging. Kennedy's name appeared alongside those of Capone and Outfit accountant Jake 'Greasy Thumb' Guzik as whisky importers in Canadian Customs documents that same year.

However, Jewish gangsters put a contract out on Kennedy's life when he tried selling alcohol in Detroit. The so-called Purple Gang controlled bootlegging in the city and did not want anybody cutting into its business. Kennedy begged two of Capone's lieutenants, Paul 'the Waiter' Ricca and Murray 'the Camel' Humphreys – the gang's political fixer – to intercede. The Purple Gang called off the murder.

Kennedy accelerated the introduction of sound into movies. Although many in the industry dismissed talking films as a gimmick, Kennedy was convinced they were the future. In October 1927, two months before Capone's visit to Los Angeles, Kennedy met David Sarnoff, the thirty-six-year-old owner of the Radio Corporation of America, in the Oyster Bar of New York's Grand Central Station. Warner Bros had just released *The Jazz Singer*. Sarnoff, who had founded the National Broadcasting Company – the first national radio network – the year before, had the equipment and expertise to add sound. Kennedy was bringing production facilities and a distribution network to the table. Sarnoff agreed to buy $400,000 worth of stock in FBO. All they needed now was somewhere to show their talking pictures.

Keith-Albee-Orpheum was a chain of about three hundred vaudeville theatres that still showed live acts. Edward Albee, grandfather of the playwright of the same name, had owned the company for years. Kennedy went behind Albee's back, buying shares from the proprietor's right-hand man, John Murdock. Kennedy then launched a hostile takeover bid for Keith-Albee-Orpheum, backed by various Wall Street banks, including Lehman Brothers and Chase National Bank. Albee found himself painted into a corner and sold the company to Kennedy for $4.2 million. On the face of it, buying a chain of old-fashioned theatres had little to do with the movie business, a misperception Kennedy was keen to encourage. Writing to Louis B. Mayer, Kennedy explained that he had gone into vaudeville because movies were just not exciting enough. Kennedy became chairman of Keith-Albee-Orpheum, retaining Albee as president. A few months later, Albee was talking to his new chairman when Kennedy told him, 'Didn't you know, Ed? You're washed up, you're through.' Albee resigned and died sixteen months later.

Kennedy and his still secret partner David Sarnoff now had studios, sound equipment and theatres to convert to sound. He brought in his own people to help run FBO and Keith-Albee-Orpheum. E.B. Derr, Edward Moore, Charles 'Pat' Sullivan and Pat Scollard formed a praetorian guard around Kennedy. What Kennedy valued in them was their willingness to 'take the gloves off and get down in the gutter and fight', as Derr wrote to Scollard. Like a Mafia family, they called him 'the boss' and themselves 'the gang'. With their loud ties, at least one secretary thought they looked like gangsters when they walked into a room.

Sarnoff bought FBO and Keith-Albee-Orpheum on 23 October 1928. The three companies merged to form Radio-Keith-Orpheum, or RKO, the first studio created just to produce talking pictures. Kennedy pocketed $5 million out of the deal, presumably having repaid Chicago the $1.1 million he had borrowed plus a healthy premium.

However, Kennedy was not through with the movies. Pathé, the French company, called him in to try to salvage its finances. Kennedy launched a complicated share issue, rewarding himself with stock worth $80 a share while ordinary investors made do with $1.50 shares. Eventually, many small shareholders lost their life savings while Kennedy walked away $5 million the richer.

In 1929, Kennedy tried to buy the California-based Pantages cinema chain, which consisted of sixty sites stretching along the West Coast from Mexico to Canada. However, Alexander Pantages, who owned the chain, did not want to sell to Kennedy. Then, on 9 August 1929, Eunice Pringle, a seventeen-year-old dancer from Garden Grove, California, accused Pantages of rape. At his trial, Pantages's lawyer Jerry Giesler – who would later defend

Bugsy Siegel, Charlie Chaplin and Marilyn Monroe – argued that the cinema owner was innocent, but Pantages was found guilty and sentenced to fifty years in prison. Kennedy bought the by now discredited Pantages chain for much less than its market value. Giesler appealed the case in the California Supreme Court and the verdict was overturned. The lawyer argued that the court should hear about the morals of the plaintiff, even though she was underage – thereby setting legal precedent. Four years later, Pringle admitted Kennedy had schemed to obtain the cinema circuit. Promising to make her a movie star, Kennedy had paid the dancer $10,000 to accuse Pantages of rape. Overcome by remorse, the twenty-one-year-old died suddenly, apparently of cyanide poisoning.

Kennedy legitimised his alcohol business after Prohibition was repealed, going into competition against Canada's Seagram, another business with bootlegging connections. Seagram would years later buy Universal Pictures. One source estimates that the Bronfman family, which owns Seagram, supplied the mob with half of its alcohol between 1920 and 1933. In 1946, Kennedy sold his alcohol business, Somerset Importers, to New Jersey mob boss Longy Zwillman and his partner Joe Reinfeld, another former bootlegger.

In Los Angeles on Sunday 11 December 1927, Capone checked in to the Biltmore Hotel for his Hollywood visit. He had become hooked on something far more addictive and warping than cocaine – the drug of self-publicity. According to Kutner, Capone was the original gangster showman, who 'threw press conferences like confetti'. The local press crammed into his suite, firing questions. Did Capone sanction the murder of men he considered his rivals? Capone replied that he was a businessman and having people murdered was not good business. Capone laughed and the press laughed with him – he made for good copy and he enjoyed the newspapermen's attention.

In 1927, Los Angeles was 'an open city' – unlike, for example, Detroit, where no single organisation dominated organised crime. Police would greet gangsters arriving by train, escort them around the back of Union Station, give them a beating and then send them back home as a warning. After the press had left, detectives turned up, sent by 'the Combination'. The Combination, although not Mafia, represented organised crime in Los Angeles. This group paid off police and criminal judges, providing protection for illegal activity, from gambling to prostitution. In exchange, brothels and casinos paid about $50 million each year to the organisation. Many government officials elected to stamp out corruption turned a blind eye in exchange for a payoff. The Combination had some links with gangs in New York and Chicago, but mostly it remained independent. Now its members were terrified that Chicago had designs on its rackets. Capone greeted the detectives warmly and offered them coffee. He said he knew whom the detectives represented and reassured them he was just a tourist.

Capone spent the second day of his visit to Los Angeles touring a movie studio. 'I never saw them make pictures before,' said Capone, 'that's a grand racket.' He went on a tour of the stars' houses, notably Pickfair, home of Mary Pickford and Douglas Fairbanks.

However, police were swarming over the Biltmore by the time Capone got back. The authorities told Capone to leave. Johnny Rosselli, the Outfit's man in Hollywood, acted as mediator between the gangster, police and reporters. He offered to have Capone and his entourage stay at his house but the police rejected the offer. Instead, Detective 'Roughhouse' Brown escorted Capone, his cousin Charlie Fischetti and a bodyguard to Sante Fe Station on the night of 12 December and put them on a train back to Chicago. Up until now, Capone had shown no interest in the movie business as a racket, although film stars had always fascinated him. Now he talked about moving to Los Angeles permanently. After all, Hollywood had potential for any number of shakedowns. 'I have a lot of money to spend that I made in Chicago,' Capone told the Los Angeles Times. 'I'm all burned up, but you can't keep me away . . . I am coming back pretty soon.'

Capone never did move to Los Angeles, however, mainly because on his return to Chicago he became preoccupied with taming the North Siders, with George 'Bugs' Moran now running the

O'Banion gang. Instead, Capone sent his brother Ralph out to Los Angeles to explore bootlegging opportunities. Movie moguls and stars were spending thousands of dollars on eating out. Restaurants were opening all over Hollywood. Ralph Capone intimidated restaurant owners into selling their businesses to him cheap.

Back in Chicago, Al Capone decided the only way to rid himself of Moran was to dispose of his gang in one go. On 14 February 1929, two police officers walked into Moran's headquarters in a garage on 2122 North Clark Street. They ordered seven of Moran's henchmen to line up against one wall. The gangsters did what they were told, thinking this was just another police shakedown. Three other men in street clothes accompanying the police officers opened fire with machine guns. One of the fake police officers is thought to have been Sam Giancana, like Charlie Fischetti another friend of Sinatra's. W.R. Burnett, author of the gangster novel *Little Caesar* – filmed two years later with Edward G. Robinson as the Capone character – glimpsed the St Valentine's Day Massacre, but could not bring himself to walk into the garage. 'I saw, I just saw it. It was a slaughterhouse – blood all over the wall and guys lying around on the floor. I got one look and I said, "Uh uh." I didn't want any of that.'

Billy Wilder played the group murder for laughs in *Some Like It Hot* (1959). Roger Corman hired Chicago reporter Harold Browne to write the script for his 1967 history of the Capone/O' Banion/ Moran power struggle, *The St. Valentine's Day Massacre*. Corman described *The St. Valentine's Day Massacre* as the most accurate gangster movie ever. 20th Century Fox vetoed Orson Welles starring as Capone; instead, tall, slim Jason Robards played the gangster. Although *The St. Valentine's Day Massacre* only cost $1 million, it looked much bigger because Corman used sets left over from other Fox productions. For example, a ballroom created for *The Sound of Music* (1965) became Capone's mansion.

At first, the press thought the St Valentine's Day Massacre was the work of police double-crossed in some bribery deal. When Capone emerged as its instigator, public pressure to do *something* about gangsterism grew.

Capone's wiping out of the North Side gang also alarmed his colleagues in New York. Luciano, Capone's teenage enemy, was by now head of what would become the New York Syndicate. Like Johnny Torrio, he wanted to modernise organised crime and outlaw killings like the St Valentine's Day Massacre. Luciano and Torrio invited all prominent gangsters to a meeting at the Hotel President in Atlantic City from 13 to 16 May 1930. Invitees included Capone, Albert Anastasia, Bugsy Siegel and Longy Zwillman. Gangsters considered Atlantic City to be neutral ground: it was the weekend retreat for heads of movie studios, all of which at this time were controlled from New York. The purpose of the meeting – again, lampooned in *Some Like It Hot* but moved to Miami, Florida – was to curb Capone's excesses.

That first night the crime lords sat in the hotel conference room at mahogany tables under a crystal chandelier. The New York delegation sat at one end, headed by Lucky Luciano. Johnny Torrio, Frank Costello and Bugsy Siegel flanked Luciano. Al Capone and his delegation – Frank Nitti, Jake 'Greasy Thumb' Guzik and Frank Rio – sat near the other end. Torrio and Costello spoke first, appealing for unity, putting things on a business footing. In particular, the Chicago gang war must stop. Then Luciano got up to speak. He called for a national commission with every family represented. From now on, the commission would first approve any murders. 'If we keep the fireworks going, we'll all be out of business in a year,' Luciano finished before sitting down. (Gangsters were so pleased with themselves they gave daily briefings to the press.)

Torrio rose to speak again and asked Capone to volunteer to go to jail, at least until things calmed down. Capone started shouting obscenities. He got to his feet, throwing his chair to the floor. 'I'll let you know,' he said. Capone walked out with his boys close behind. However, after consulting his fellow gangsters, Capone realised Luciano had once again left him no option but to accede to his wishes, that he had to go to jail. Once he had calmed down, however, he may have seen prison as an opportunity. He had, after all, said he wanted to quit when he was in Los Angeles. Two days after the Atlantic City summit, detectives James Malone and John Creedon arrested Capone and Rio in Philadelphia for carrying guns. Malone and Creedon were both on the Outfit's payroll, having stayed with Capone in Florida. Capone tipped them $20,000 for making the arrest. Rio and Capone were sentenced to a year in jail for carrying concealed weapons. Capone was sent to Eastern State Penitentiary, Philadelphia. He was well looked after. His cell had carpet, a telephone with which to make long-distance calls, and a cabinet radio and matching chest of drawers. Asked whether he wanted a stock market ticker-tape machine installed, Capone demurred, saying he never gambled.

Capone spent ten months in jail between May 1929 and March 1930. His brother Ralph was put in charge of the gang. However, Prohibition agents had tapped Ralph's phone. Agents raided three of Capone's secret breweries. The officer in charge of the investigation was Eliot Ness, a federal agent immortalised as Capone's nemesis on television and on film. Ness raided one brewery by ramming the entrance with a snowplough, an event recreated by Brian De Palma in *The Untouchables* (1987).

Eliot Ness was born in Chicago in 1903. His parents were Norwegian and lived on Prairie Avenue, where, by coincidence, Al Capone's family also lived. Ness graduated from the University of Chicago and joined the Bureau of Prohibition in 1928, working under district attorney George E.Q. Johnson. Ness began by working undercover, posing as a corrupt official. The operation resulted in the indictment of eighty-one men and the breaking up of a bootlegging ring worth $36 million a year. Ness now turned his attention to the Chicago suburb of Cicero, which Capone controlled. However, the Prohibition Bureau was so corrupt it was making little headway against bootlegging. Ness selected a team of nine agents whom he knew to be honest. Their resistance to bribery by the Capone organisation led to the press dubbing them 'the Untouchables'. By tracing beer barrels on their journey back from speakeasy to brewery, the Untouchables smashed six Capone breweries and five distribution plants. They impounded twenty-five delivery trucks and confiscated beer worth $9 million. Capone was, by now, out of prison. To humiliate Capone, Ness paraded beer trucks down Michigan Avenue past the Lexington Hotel – after first calling Capone to tell him to look out of the window.

Capone was clearly rattled by Ness, who had damaged the infrastructure of his organisation. Ness survived several attempts on his life, including a bomb planted in his car. A 1931 grand jury investigation – the US legal system presents evidence to a jury, which then decides whether to go to full trial – indicted Capone and sixty-eight gang members with five thousand offences under the Volstead Act. However, several prosecution witnesses were murdered – again recreated in the 1987 film. The movie climaxes with Ness taunting Capone in court. In reality, though, the two men never met. The prosecution abandoned the trial because of witness intimidation.

Ness moved to Cleveland, Ohio, where he became director of public safety. Ness purged the city's corrupt police department and fought organised crime. However, his failure to catch a serial killer dented his reputation, and he failed to become mayor in 1947. This failure, combined with the collapse of his marriage, triggered Ness's alcoholism. United Press International sports reporter Oscar Fraley met Ness in 1956 and in two weeks wrote a book based on Ness's memories of Capone. Ness had just finished reading the proofs when he went into the kitchen to get a glass of water. He dropped dead of a heart attack. Ness was fifty-four years old, $9000 in debt and, as Fraley put it, had just missed witnessing his own immortality.

Fraley's book *The Untouchables* sold 1.5 million copies. Desi Arnaz, the actor who co-starred with his wife Lucille Ball in the television comedy *I Love Lucy*, owned a production company, Desilu Productions. Arnaz bought the book from children's publisher Julian Messner and in 1959 he adapted it into a $600,000, two-part programme for *Desilu Playhouse*, the anthology drama series Desilu made for ABC. Retitled *The Scarface Mob*, the two shows starred Robert Stack as Ness and Neville Brand as Capone. Columnist Walter Winchall was the narrator. They were such ratings winners that Arnaz and his producer, Quinn Martin, stitched them together and released them in Europe as a feature film.

ABC was so pleased with *The Scarface Mob* that it commissioned Desilu to create a series for its 1959/60 autumn schedule. *The Untouchables* was first broadcast in October 1959. It generated huge audiences. In its first season, *The Untouchables* won Emmy Awards for best actor, cinematography, editing, art direction and production design.

However, the series antagonised both Edgar J. Hoover for crediting Ness with FBI successes and Capone's widow, Mae, who unsuccessfully tried to sue for defamation. Mafioso Jimmy 'the Weasel' Fratiano later testified that Sam Giancana, head of the Chicago mob, had thought about having Arnaz murdered. According to Fratiano, Giancana ordered Frank 'Bomp' Bompensiero to murder Arnaz but then changed his mind.

The Untouchables also angered Italian-American groups, who complained about ethnic stereotyping. Every villain on the show was, after all, Italian. Frank Sinatra and Senator John Pastore, chairman of the Senate Communications Committee, started exerting pressure on Arnaz to drop Italian names. ABC executives met the Federation of Italian-American Democratic Organizations and agreed to introduce villains from other ethnic backgrounds. One Russian mobster in the show's final season was the improbably named Joe Vodka.

Meanwhile, the Mafia warned the show's sponsor, Liggett and Meyers (L&M), that it would hurt the tobacco company's business if it continued to support *The Untouchables*. Albert Anastasia's younger brother Anthony 'Tough Tony' Anastasia of the New York Longshoreman's Union told L&M that his members would not handle its cigarettes in US and Canadian ports unless it cancelled its sponsorship. 'You play ball with us and we'll play ball with you,' Anastasia said. L&M duly announced it was cancelling sponsorship of the show. Its press release claimed this was because ABC was moving *The Untouchables* from 9.30 p.m. to 10 p.m.

However, in the end it was neither the Mafia, Italian-American groups nor deserting sponsors which killed off the series. ABC finally cancelled the show after a rival music programme started getting higher ratings. The last episode of *The Untouchables* was broadcast on 10 September 1963, having run for 118 episodes.

Twenty years later, Paramount, which owned the rights, persuaded producer Art Linson and Brian De Palma to remake the series as a feature film. Neither man had any affection for the original series. De Palma was attracted, however, to telling a simple story in a classical way. He saw *The Untouchables* as the triumph of a man of principle over the system. Usually his films were much darker, leaving the hero cynical (*Blow Out* (1981)) or facing death (*Body Double* (1984)).

Robert De Niro agreed to play Capone. According to De Niro, Capone was not just purely evil; he had to be a politician, an administrator. 'He had to have something going for him other than just fear,' De Niro told *Newsweek*. 'He must have a certain crazy charm.'

Al Wolff, the last surviving member of Ness's team of agents, was brought on board as technical adviser – although De Palma did not want to tell the truth so much as 'print the legend'. The director of *Dressed to Kill* and *Blow Out* wanted Chicago to look opulent, like Nazi Germany. 'Corruption looks great,' he said. 'It's a slick world, a world run by money.'

One scene based on truth, however, is when Capone repeatedly smashes the head of a traitor with a baseball bat. The movie tones down the violence of what actually happened. In reality, Capone took a baseball bat to three gangsters – Albert Anselmi, Joseph Guinta and John Scalise – at a banquet. He suspected the trio of allying themselves with another gang.

The movie blurs Ness's exploits with the real reason for Capone's downfall – income tax evasion. In the film, one of Ness's agents, Oscar Wallace – a character based on accountant Frank Wilson – convinces Ness (Kevin Costner) that the only way to send Capone to jail is for evading income tax. By 1931, income tax evasion had become the government's favourite tool for convicting gangsters. Income tax had only been in existence for eighteen years.

Just 7 per cent of the US population earned enough to pay any tax at all. Mafia folklore has it that the flashpoint for the government going after Capone was when President Hoover stayed next to the gangster's compound in Miami Beach, Florida. Hoover is supposed to have seen naked women dancing round a fire, with gangsters firing off live rounds into the night sky. Hoover decided then and there that something had to be done about Capone. District attorney Johnson instructed special prosecutor Dwight H. Green to investigate Capone's gang for unpaid taxes. Johnson, Green and Elmer Irey, head of the Internal Revenue Service (IRS), began with Frank Nitti, Capone's heir apparent. Nitti had spent at least $624,888 in the last three years without submitting a return. The gangster was sentenced to eighteen months in prison and fined $10,000. Ralph Capone was next in line. He was also fined $10,000 and sentenced to three years in Leavenworth Penitentiary, Kansas, described by one prisoner as a 'giant mausoleum adrift in a great sea of nothingness'. However, the Justice Department had just been warming up for Capone himself.

Capone was by now worth an estimated $40 million with his Outfit earning $6 million a week. IRS officials combed stores in Chicago and Miami calculating the cost of Capone's cutlery, furniture, rugs and even his underwear. After interviewing hundreds of people, it was clear that Capone's income was much greater than he stated. According to the IRS, he owed at least $1 million in unpaid tax. On 5 June 1931 the IRS indicted Capone on twenty-two counts of income tax evasion. Capone offered to pay off the tax, but the IRS rejected his offer. Insiders whispered that Capone's own men had given the IRS financial records that sealed his fate.

Meanwhile, producer Howard Hughes had bought the rights to the novel *Scarface*. Written by Maurice Coons under the pseudonym Armitage Trail, *Scarface* was published in 1930. The novel followed two brothers, one of whom becomes a gangster and the other a cop. Having lost money in the movie business, Hughes decided gangster films were the nearest thing to a guaranteed profit. He hired various writers, including W.R. Burnett, to adapt the novel. Then he offered Howard Hawks $25,000 to direct the film. However, Hawks, who had known several gangsters in Chicago, came up with a more original angle. He had heard the story of Capone clubbing three gangsters to death. It occurred to him that Capone was the equivalent of a modern-day Cesare Borgia, the son of Rodrigo Borgia, Pope Alexander VI, who murdered papal prisoners. Which got him thinking – what if Capone was having an incestuous relationship with his sister, just as Borgia was supposed to have had? Hawks approached Ben Hecht, former Chicago newspaperman and co-author of *The Front Page*, to write the script. At first, Hecht said no. He had won the first-ever Academy Award for Best Original Story for another gangster movie, *Underworld* (1927). He did not want to repeat himself.

However, Hecht's agent, Myron Selznick, concocted a publicity stunt whereby Hughes would pay Hecht $1000 in cash for each day he worked on *Scarface*. Selznick had already coined the nickname 'the Shakespeare of movies' for his client. What the press did not know was that Hecht's salary was capped at $15,000. Hecht wrote a sixty-page treatment in eleven days.

Somehow, Capone heard that Hollywood was making a film about him. One night there was a knock on the door of Hecht's hotel room. Standing outside were, according to Hecht, two 'hard-eyed' strangers, one of whom was holding a copy of his treatment. The gangster asked Hecht whether he had written the draft screenplay. Hecht admitted he had. 'We've read it,' said the gangster. Hecht asked them what they thought of it. 'Is this stuff about Al Capone?' asked one. Hecht lied and said the script was really about other gangsters, such as Dion O'Banion. 'Okay, then. We'll tell Al this stuff you wrote is about them other guys.' As they started to leave, one of them had an afterthought: 'If this stuff isn't about Al Capone, why are you calling it *Scarface*? Everybody'll think it's him.' Hecht came up with some nonsense about tricking people into believing they were seeing a movie about Al Capone, when in fact they weren't. It was all part, said Hecht, of the show-business racket. 'I'll tell Al. Who's this fella Howard Hughes?' Hecht said he was the sucker with the money. 'Okay. The hell with him.' The gangsters walked off, satisfied.

Paul Muni was cast as Camonte/Capone and Ann Dvorak was given the part of his sister, based on Lucrezia Borgia. Hecht, who had met Capone, said Muni's performance was more like Hitler than the Chicago gangster, who in real life was voluble rather than baleful, the way Muni played him.

Hawks hired former dancer George Raft for the part of Camonte/Capone's enforcer, based on Capone's bodyguard Frank Rio. Raft's father was German and his mother Italian. His real name was George Ranfft, but he dropped the 'n' and the second 'f' to make the name easier to say – and for the press to spell. Raft had ties to the New York mob and was the protégé of Owney Madden. Television presenter Ed Sullivan later compared knowing Madden in the 1920s to being friendly with the mayor. Madden had introduced Raft to Capone in Delmonico's restaurant in New York. Other gangsters Raft had met during his career as a dancer included Lucky Luciano, Meyer Lansky and Bugsy Siegel. Raft would frequent Arnold Rothstein's gambling club off Broadway, where the police once caught him in a craps game. Raft did not use his own name, the police did not bother to fingerprint him and the charges were dismissed. One night the police raided a Third Avenue speakeasy where Raft was having something to eat following a late show at a nightclub. Dutch Schultz, the New Jersey bootlegger, got up from his table and put his gun underneath Raft's coat. He waited for the police to go and, without saying a word, retrieved it.

Raft admitted that when he was younger he would much rather have become a gangster than an actor. 'When I became a movie star and was asked about tough guys I knew, I said: "I think they're the greatest guys in the world",' Raft told his biographer:

These fellows – [Bugsy] Siegel, Costello, Adonis, Luciano and Madden – were gods to me. They all had 16-cylinder Cadillacs, and, like somebody said, when there is money around you might step on it. Wherever they went there were police captains and politicians bowing to them. I thought, these fellows can't be really doing anything wrong. Why shouldn't I be like them? I wanted to follow them.

Hawks thought that Raft had a 'marvellous impassive quality' that made him just right for Guido Renaldo. Raft based some of his mannerisms on New York gangster Joe Adonis. He noticed how the gangster used his hands, how he talked and how he held his chin at a certain angle. Adonis was so flattered by Raft's imitation that, in 1951, he asked for the actor's coaching help when called to testify before the televised hearings of the Kefauver committee crime investigation.

Scarface is often thought of as being Raft's first screen role. In fact, it was his twelfth. Until now, he had usually appeared on screen dancing, having toured America and Europe in stage musicals. Hawks had heard a story about Capone gang member Jack McGurn – real name Vincenzo DeMora – who would leave a measly nickel in the palms of murder victims as a sign of disrespect. Hawks had Raft always flipping a coin – a mannerism picked up by would-be gangsters. During the 1940s, Raft became best friends with Bugsy Siegel. In the 1950s he lampooned himself, playing the Mafia boss 'Spats' Columbo in *Some Like It Hot*. (In a wink to the audience, Raft stops one gangster irritatingly flipping a coin in his face by growling, 'Where did you learn that stupid trick?') In 1967, when Raft was living in London, the British government deported him for fronting the Colony Club, a Mafia-backed casino in London.

The censor warned Hughes and Hawks he would block *Scarface* from release should they be foolish enough to make it. 'The American public and all conscientious state boards of censorship find mobsters and hoodlums repellent,' said deputy censor Colonel Jason Joy. 'Gangsterism must not be mentioned in the cinema.' Rather than scrap the movie, Hughes sent Hawks a note: 'Screw the Hays Office. Start the picture and make it as realistic, as exciting, as grisly as possible.'

Chicago Tribune crime reporter Fred Paisley was hired as

consultant to make sure the film was accurate. One day, a man calling himself George White turned up on set. White asked if he could watch filming. Hawks sent a telegram to a friend in Chicago asking him to find out more about this George White. It turned out that George White was really Whitney Krokower alias of Puggy White, a member of Capone's gang. His sister Estelle was married to Bugsy Siegel. When White turned up the next morning, Hawks confronted him. He told White he knew he was a pimp who had killed a dozen men. White admitted to being a murderer, but objected to being called a pimp. White began advising Hawks on how to make scenes more realistic. For example, the scene where gangsters bring flowers to an enemy in hospital and pull out guns from the bouquet to shoot him dead actually happened.

Various film historians have Capone turning up in Hollywood to watch filming. Hawks himself said that he invited Capone, who was in Los Angeles at the time, to view the film's rushes. He said more gangsters turned up during editing, saying, 'The boss wants us to look at the picture.' One anecdote has Capone throwing a cocktail party in Chicago for Hawks at the Lexington Hotel. Hawks was struck, apparently, by how cordial and polite everybody was. The high point of the evening supposedly came when Capone, dressed in morning coat and striped trousers, presented Hawks with a small machine gun as a memento. Another story has Capone summoning Raft to the Lexington on the night of *Scarface*'s Chicago premiere – which couldn't have happened as Capone was in prison at the time.

Scarface begins with title cards justifying the mayhem the audience is about to watch: 'This picture is an indictment of gang rule in America and of the callous indifference of the government to the constantly increasing menace to our safety and liberty. Every incident in this picture is the reproduction of an actual occurrence, and the purpose of this picture is to demand of the government: "What are you going to do about it?"'

Hawks fades in to the aftermath of a party given by 'Big Louis' Costillo, a character based on 'Big Jim' Colosimo. A gunman in silhouette murders the gang boss in his restaurant foyer. The gunman is Tony Camonte, the Capone character. When a detective asks Camonte how he got his scar, the gangster, like Capone, claims it is a First World War battle wound. The editor of the city's newspaper predicts gangsters will shoot each other like rabbits for control of Chicago's beer business. Costillo's successor, Johnny Lovo (the John Torrio character), appoints Camonte as his enforcer. Like Torrio, Lovo wants to organise bootlegging along business lines. Camonte, backed by his henchman Guido Renaldo (George Raft), murders rival gangsters and blows up their restaurants until Lovo takes control of South Side bootlegging.

Camonte is obsessed by his sister Cesca, whose purity he wants to protect (or keep for himself). The sister, however, has her own strong sexual appetite. Spotting Renaldo resting against the bonnet of his car outside her house, she flips him a coin, which he pockets.

However, Camonte has designs both on Lovo's girlfriend, Poppy (a bit of fiction dreamt up by Hecht and Hawks), and on the North Side beer business as well. O'Hara, the Dion O'Banion character, is the leader of the North Side gang. Camonte has him murdered in his flower shop. War breaks out again, but the North Siders have tommy guns smuggled across the state line. A convoy of North Siders strafe the restaurant where Camonte is eating, but the gangster escapes unharmed – just like the botched attempt on Capone's life on 20 September 1926. In retaliation, seven North Siders are machine-gunned to death in a warehouse – a re-creation of the St Valentine's Day Massacre.

Now Tom Gabney (Boris Karloff) – a composite character based on Earl 'Hymie' Weiss, the Polish gangster who took control of the North Siders, and his successor, George 'Bugs' Moran – goes into hiding, fearing for his life. But Camonte tracks Gabney down in a bowling alley and shoots him dead. (Each time a murder takes place an 'X' appears on screen – Camonte's X-shaped scar – from shadows cast by a streetlamp to criss-crossed barn girders and a full strike on a bowling alley scorecard.)

One Capone-inspired scene that was written but never shot showed Scarface lolling about on his yacht in Florida surrounded by artists, including a female novelist, and the Establishment.

Hawks dropped the scene because it showed how well crime paid for somebody like Capone during the Depression.

In the film public opposition to gang war grows. Camonte beats up a man dancing with his sister in a nightclub. He also takes possession of Lovo's girl. Lovo arranges to have his protégé murdered, but Camonte escapes again and, instead, takes revenge on his mentor.

Wounded from the attempt on his life, Camonte tracks down Renaldo. Then he discovers that Guido has married his sister. Insane with jealousy, he murders his best friend and flees to a safe house. However, the police have the building surrounded. His sister joins him inside the barricaded apartment. Camonte is manic, firing a machine gun down into the street. But he loses his nerve when his sister is killed. He pleads for his life but the police open fire. Camonte dies sprawled on the pavement underneath a neon sign that reads 'The World Is Yours'.

Scarface remains, as it was in 1932, the last word on Chicago gangsterism of the 1920s, the smartest, cleverest, punchiest portrait of an individual mobster's rise and fall. According to Hawks's biographer Todd McCarthy, '*Scarface* would still emerge as the most potent film about organised crime Hollywood would produce for decades.' It would remain Hawks's favourite film; he went on to make *To Have and Have Not* (1944) and *The Big Sleep* (1946). Depicting forty-three murders, *Scarface* still carries a '15' certificate seventy years after its release. It is, in computer game parlance, a marvellous shoot 'em up, dominated by Muni's performance. In the same scene, Muni will switch from post-cocaine binge depression to hysterical laughter. He captures some of, in the words of one eyewitness, Capone's likeable goofiness, turning on the flip of a coin into a lurching, pop-eyed Frankenstein monster.

Scarface's violence so infuriated the Hays Office that it ordered Hawks to add the subtitle *The Shame of the Nation* to tell the audience what to think. It also forced Hawks to tack on a sermonising ending. Camonte listens to a 'crime does not pay' speech before hanging. The censor also insisted on another scene, where a group of concerned citizens, including one

Italian-American, berate a newspaper publisher for publicising gang warfare. The publisher, in turn, talks straight to camera, admonishing the audience to fight gangsterism. Richard Rosson directed both these scenes as Hawks had moved on to *The Crowd Roars* (1932). Muni would have nothing to do with the revised ending. A stand-in plays Camonte with his back to the camera. When United Artists released the film in April 1932, two different versions played across the country. The sermonising version toured rural areas, while the original screened in cities.

Scarface's original budget had been $600,000, but all the additional shooting and editing had pushed its cost to $700,000. The film did fairly well at the box office, grossing $905,298 for United Artists between its debut in 1932 and its final run in 1935. By comparison, Hughes's biggest hit, *Hell's Angels*, grossed $2,361,125. Hughes kept 75 per cent of the cash *Scarface* took at the box office. The film also did well in Britain. Astor Films released *Scarface* in 1936. It grossed an additional $297,934, pushing worldwide theatrical earnings up to $1,203,233.

Author Maurice Coons never saw the finished film. Coons, who weighed more than 300 pounds, dropped dead of a heart attack in 1931 having moved to Hollywood to become a screenwriter.

Brian De Palma's *Scarface* remake, made fifty years later, with Al Pacino in the Capone role, adds little to the original – unless one counts Ferdinando Scarfiotti's kitsch design or Giorgio Moroder's syrupy synthesiser score. The plot is roughly the same. Dedicated to Ben Hecht, the script – by Oliver Stone and an uncredited De Palma – updates the Capone story to the 1980s. At the time, the Cuban government was sending boatloads of political prisoners, criminals and other 'undesirables' to America. One of these exiles is Tony Montana, who rises to the top of Florida's cocaine business. Michelle Pfeiffer, playing the moll, is vapid by comparison with Karen Morely. Mary Elizabeth Mastrantonio, playing the sister, is screechy rather than slinky like Dvorak. Only the scene where Pacino rips open a bag of cocaine, plunges his head into it and fires a rocket launcher at gang members coming to kill him has the chutzpah of the original. Like the first *Scarface*, the remake ran into trouble with the censor. However, Universal resubmitted the film with minor cuts and the Motion Picture Association of America (MPAA) (successor to the Hays Office) certified it 'R' for theatrical release.

Seven months before the original *Scarface* was released, Capone went on trial for income tax evasion. Somebody who watched the publicity circus surrounding the trial was Jules Stein, a music agent whose office was opposite the Dearborn Street courthouse. Stein's booking agency, Music Corporation of America (MCA), would one day acquire Universal Pictures. Stein would become chairman of the Hollywood studio. Stein and Capone each owned a percentage of the Chez Paree nightclub, Chicago's hottest nightspot, and a meeting place for the Outfit. Several of Stein's jazz bands played in Outfit speakeasies. He also used Capone's men to force clubs to book his acts. The Capone that Stein knew was not so bloodthirsty or evil as newspapers portrayed him. Actually, he was kind of a likeable goof. The overweight man in gaudy clothes who Stein saw showing up each day at court resembled a well-fed Wall Street banker. Stein concluded that Capone's crimes were not so much murder or mayhem, but conspicuous wealth during the Depression.

Over the course of the four-day trial, the government demonstrated that between 1924 and 1929 Capone had earned at least $1,038,654.84. Therefore, he owed $215,080.48 in unpaid tax. After deliberating for eight hours, the jury returned a guilty verdict. On 17 October 1931, Capone was found guilty of three counts of tax evasion and two counts of not filing a return. At his sentencing a week later, Capone was sent to jail for eleven years. In addition, he had to pay a $50,000 fine plus $30,000 in court costs.

Soon after arriving in Atlanta Penitentiary in spring 1932, Capone was diagnosed with syphilis, gonorrhoea and a perforated septum due to cocaine abuse. He was only thirty-three years old. Capone was moved to Alcatraz in 1934, where he was placed in a mental ward. His mental health continued to deteriorate. He got into a faeces-throwing battle with another patient in an adjacent cage. Capone was next moved to Terminal Island Federal Correctional Institution near Los Angeles in January 1939. That November he was released into the care of his wife. He spent the next eight years as a recluse, paranoid about being murdered. He died from a brain haemorrhage on 27 January 1947.

Capone never moved to Los Angeles as he planned. Distracted by gang warfare, he failed to make inroads into Hollywood unions, extorting studios and skimming membership fees. This was not an opportunity missed by his successors, however. Once Prohibition was repealed on 5 December 1933, the Outfit needed to find new ways to make money. Indeed, the Outfit would soon be earning $1.5 million a year from extorting Hollywood. Within a few years, Capone's gang planned to own the studios themselves.

CHAPTER TWO

Once Corrupted, Always Controlled

Making inroads into Hollywood set the Outfit on a collision course with rival gangsters. The New York Syndicate had been supplying Hollywood with drugs for years. It was alarmed at the prospect of the Outfit muscling in on its narcotics and gambling operations. The man who had no qualms about supplying Hollywood with drugs was Lucky Luciano.

Raymond Chandler once described Luciano as having a soft voice, a patient, sad face and being extremely courteous in every way. He was born Salvatore Luciana on 24 November 1897 in Lercara Friddi, a village near Palermo, Sicily. Luciana's family immigrated to America in the spring of 1906 when he was nine. On 26 June 1916 Luciana was sentenced to one year at the New Hampshire Farms Correctional Institute for heroin dealing. He was released after six months. He was now calling himself Charlie Luciana. About this time, Luciana was inducted into the Mafia family of Giuseppe (Joe) Masseria.

Luciana first met fellow gangsters Meyer Lansky and Bugsy Siegel in 1917. Lansky was so adept at mental arithmetic that, later on, he would hire a maths tutor to play numbers games with him. Siegel, on the other hand, was a thug who spent Jewish holidays breaking into stores when he knew their owners were in synagogue. As an adolescent, he began his criminal career snatching purses and pickpocketing drunks. He stole from blind men's cups – not only coins but pencils too. Lansky and Siegel formed a gang, ostensibly to protect Jewish children from attacks by the Irish. Within two years, their 'Bugs [Siegel] and Meyer [Lansky]' gang had twenty members terrorising East Harlem and Manhattan, robbing banks, stores and warehouses. One gang member was Francesco Castiglia, better known as Frank Costello. When Luciano joined the Bugs and Meyer gang it moved into betting and gambling. In 1921 the gang entered the bootlegging business, operating under cover of a car rental company, supplying vehicles, drivers and gang members for hire.

Luciano first suggested importing drugs into America from Europe and the Middle East at the beginning of the 1920s. At one point, the gang had a factory in the Bronx boiling down heroin from morphine base. New York gangsters had watched the success of Capone's bootlegging operation. Now they decided to emulate it. Capone manufactured and produced his own beer, which he sold mainly to workers. Lansky suggested another strategy. They should import the best spirits available from Britain and Canada and sell them to the rich. That way, they would make more money and gain support from people with influence. After all, for many Americans bootlegging was a victimless crime. About 50 pounds of narcotics, mainly heroin and opium, were included in the very first shipment of twenty thousand cases of whisky from Britain in 1921. Arnold Rothstein, a gangster and shareholder in the Loew's cinema chain, owner of Metro-Goldwyn-Mayer, arranged the shipment, having organised the supply line from Scotland.

Cocaine use had been prevalent in Hollywood since the first studios opened in California. As early as 1916 – the year D.W. Griffith started work on *Intolerance* – self-proclaimed black magician Aleister Crowley described Hollywood as 'a cinema crowd of cocaine-crazed lunatics'. One May 1922 article in Hollywood trade paper *Variety* gives a flavour of how drugs were viewed at the time:

Drugs are not much in evidence as during the more trying months of winter, but they still spread their genial influence at some of the more exclusive functions. Last week, Little Lulu Lenore of the Cuckoo Comedy Co. gave a small house dance for the youngest addicts. 'Will you come to my "Snow-Ball"' read the clever invitations. In one corner of the living room was a miniature 'drugstore' where Otto Everard kept the company in a roar as he dispensed little packages of cocaine, morphine and heroin. The guests at their departure received exquisite hypodermic needles in vanity boxes which may have caused heart-burnings among those who were not invited.

Each member of the Bugs and Meyer gang began to specialise as business grew. Luciano was, in a sense, the overseer, handling recruitment and negotiating with other gangs. Lansky and Siegel organised gangsters to ride shotgun with alcohol shipments. Costello dealt with bribes, or, as he preferred to call them, 'influence payments'. Other racketeers who joined the organisation included Albert Anastasia and Louis 'Lepke' Buchalter. By the mid-1920s, Luciano, Lansky and Siegel were pocketing $4 million a year, having paid out $5 million each year in bribes.

By the mid-1920s also, drugs had become widespread in Hollywood. Cocaine was the drug of choice among the fashionable and wealthy. Flappers wore little spoons around their necks to scoop the so-called 'joy powder'. One addict was silent movie star Barbara La Marr, who kept her cocaine in a gold box on her grand piano; she died of drug abuse aged twenty-eight in 1926. Film stars Wallace Reid and Alma Rubens also died because of drug addiction. Pushers would hang around movie studios, supplying actors with drugs. Luciano was in turn supplying pushers with drugs imported from New York. According to movie lore, drug dealers who used to haunt movie sets were nicknamed 'the Man' at Paramount, 'Mr Fix It' at Fox and 'the Count' at the Mack Sennett Studio. Eventually, Luciano decided to have his own man in Hollywood. The man he chose was Pasquale 'Pat' DiCicco, a talent agent who represented a number of minor actors. DiCicco's cousin Albert R. 'Cubby' Broccoli would go on to produce the James Bond movies.

Luciano's mentor, Joe Masseria, was appalled at his protégé allowing non-Sicilians like Costello and, even worse, Jews into the organisation. Masseria also loathed fellow Sicilians born in the Golfodi Castellammare area. He wanted them all disposed of, especially Salvatore Maranzano, most important of the Castellammare dons. Masseria ordered the murder of Castellammarese leader Tommy Reina on 26 February 1930. War broke out between both sides. Men had to sleep in hideaways on mattresses, afraid to go out into the street (hence, the expression Sonny Corleone uses in *The Godfather*, 'go to the mattresses'). Luciano was contemptuous of the so-called Castellammarese war of 1930–31. For him, this kind of nineteenth-century blood feud had no place in the twentieth century; it interfered with business. He therefore had his mentor murdered on 15 April 1931 in a Coney Island seafood restaurant. On hearing of Masseria's death, Maranzano, the Castellammare leader, anointed himself head of the New York Mafia. Like Frank Pentageli, the character in *The Godfather Part II*, Maranzano was obsessed with Roman history, particularly the life of Julius Caesar. He considered Caesar to be the first *capo di tutti capi*. Maranzano gave Luciano the Masseria family to preside over, but then drew up a list of people he wanted murdered, including Luciano, Capone, Costello, Buchalter, Siegel and about fifty others. On hearing this, Luciano had Maranzano killed on 10 September 1931. Luciano knew that Maranzano's assassination would antagonise old-guard Mafiosi – so-called Moustache Petes – into coming together to avenge his death. Therefore, according to Mafia legend, Luciano decided to attack first: he had about fifty Mafiosi murdered within twenty-four hours of Maranzano's assassination. Nicknamed the Night of Sicilian Vespers, this killing spree inspired the climax of *The Godfather*. However, it may be that the Night of Sicilian Vespers itself is a fiction. Contemporary newspapers do not contain any stories about a glut of killings. As Robert Lacey said in *Little Man: Meyer Lansky and the Gangster Life*, his biography of Lansky, myths are often attempts to explain complicated phenomena in simple terms. It may be that the Night of Sicilian Vespers was a way of explaining power struggles across America as younger rivals supplanted older *padrones*.

By the end of 1932 audiences and box office grosses were beginning to decline as the Depression took hold. The studios were alarmed when President Roosevelt closed the banks – cinema-going was, after all, a cash business. Paramount, Universal, Fox and RKO all went into receivership despite continuing to make movies. Yet the moguls saw no reason to tighten their own belts. Nineteen of the twenty-five highest-paid executives in America were studio executives, prompting Roosevelt to criticise Holly-wood salaries as 'unconscionable'. Instead, the bosses decided to squeeze people in the lowest-paid jobs. MGM ordered a 50 per cent pay cut across the board for at least eight weeks. Actors and writers defected from the in-house Academy of Motion Picture Arts and Sciences to form their own guilds. IATSE complained to producers' organisation the Motion Picture Producers and Distributors of America (MPPDA) – now the MPAA – about its members' wages being halved. But the union was rebuffed by MPPDA union negotiator Pat Casey, a former security guard who had worked for the Schenck brothers in New York. IATSE called its members out on strike on 24 July 1933. Casey – a big, gruff Irishman – turned to the Outfit's man on the West Coast, Johnny Rosselli, for help. Rosselli's job was to import Chicago thugs to protect studio employees crossing picket lines – and to beat up strikers who got in the way. Rosselli, who was hired as a 'labor conciliator', told Casey he did not want to be paid but wanted a full-time job afterwards. As Rosselli later reminisced to a Senate committee investigating organised crime,

At that time, to go back, I didn't have much money. They had a strike in the industry and the unions – that is, the studios – were in difficulty. The unions were trying to get on to this – I don't know whether it was a demand for higher wages or recognition or what it was. There was a little rough play around and the studios naturally didn't want it. They didn't want their workers hurt. They needed some cameramen to go back to work, and they had been threatened

through some people. They had asked if I could help. I said: 'The
only way to help is to fight fire with fire. You don't have to knock
anybody on the head doing it, but you can just get them enough
protection from these fellows so no one will approach them with
any rough play.'

After one ugly, confrontational week, it was all over. The union
caved in. Rosselli was given a full-time job at the producers'
organisation, as he had wanted. 'The girls at the office all seemed
to know him,' one union leader remembered. 'They called him
Johnny and he was quite popular with the ladies – they thought he
was the perfect gentleman.' Studio bosses also embraced Rosselli
and he was seen at their mansions, swimming and flirting with
starlets. Rosselli later boasted about his friendship with producer
Sam Goldwyn, Clark Gable and Charlie Chaplin. Back in Chicago,
the Outfit began calling Rosselli 'the Hollywood kid'. Rosselli
became the moguls' bookmaker. All of the studio heads were
compulsive gamblers, especially David O. Selznick. Rosselli placed
bets and became friendly with Joseph Kennedy, Joe Schenck and,
most importantly, Harry Cohn.

Nicknamed 'White Fang' by Ben Hecht, Harry Cohn was
rapacious, greedy and confrontational – all the qualities needed
to be a successful movie producer. James Bacon, an Associated
Press reporter based in Chicago who moved to Hollywood, said
that he went from covering Al Capone to covering the Columbia
boss, and that Cohn was meaner by far. Cohn admired Benito
Mussolini and based his office on the Italian dictator's. Executives
called the walk up to the raised dais of Cohn's desk 'the last mile'
after the walk the condemned take to the electric chair.

Rosselli was also a frequent guest at Cohn's home, where he
played tennis and swam in the pool. In addition, the gangster spent
weekends at Cohn's second home in Palm Springs. Once Cohn
offered Rosselli a $500 per week job as a producer on the lot but
the gangster turned him down, saying he made more cash as a
bookmaker. Rosselli and Cohn became so close that the gangster
bought two identical rubies and had them set into rings. He gave

one to Cohn, explaining to Los Angeles mob boss Jack Dragna that this was the closest he could come to reproducing the blood-brother Mafia induction ceremony with somebody who was not Italian. Cohn was honoured and wore the ring for several years.

In 1932 Cohn had been struggling for control of Columbia Pictures. Needing $500,000 to buy his brother's share of the company, Cohn contacted Longy Zwillman either through his bookie or Rosselli. According to Zwillman's biographer, the New Jersey mob boss met Cohn at his bungalow in the Hollywood hotel the Garden of Allah, a fashionable address at the beginning of the 1930s. Cohn proposed that Zwillman lend him the $500,000 in exchange for an IOU plus interest. Instead, Zwillman said he would lend Cohn the $500,000 but the mogul would have to hand over the Columbia stock to the gangster until the debt was repaid. In effect, Zwillman would own Columbia Pictures until Cohn repaid the debt.

The authorities knew about the friendship between Cohn and a known gangster. Los Angeles police described Rosselli as Cohn's personal bookmaker, whereas the FBI, which kept Rosselli under surveillance from time to time, concluded the gangster was more Cohn's bodyguard. Rosselli described himself as a producer at Columbia when questioned by police after the murder of a gambling club owner. Columbia distanced itself from Rosselli, telling reporters, 'all anybody around here knows is that he hangs around Hollywood and Vine a lot and talks out of the corner of his mouth'.

President Roosevelt was by now pushing for the repeal of Prohibition, arguing that taxing alcohol would raise $300 million with which to fight the Depression. Congress passed the Twenty-first Amendment, nullifying the Eighteenth, on 20 February 1933. Prohibition was repealed on 5 December 1933. Although gangsters still had gambling and prostitution, they now needed to find new ways of making money.

According to Llewella Humphreys, supposedly the illegitimate daughter of Al Capone, the idea of shaking down Hollywood came from her mother, a movie fan. 'So she mentioned to my father,

"Why don't we go into this business so that I can meet everybody?" '

Of course, the Outfit was aware of the industry's shakedown potential. For years, a number of cinema owners had refused to pay Tommy Maloy to waive his union requirement to have each projection booth manned by two operators. By 1930, exhibitors had had enough. Complaints to local politicians prompted a Cook County state's attorney to investigate Maloy. In desperation, Maloy began bribing officials, spreading cash around the Illinois state capital, Springfield. Consequently, having two operators per booth became law on public safety grounds, long after sound had become part of the filmstrip.

The movies were beginning to bounce back from the Depression. No matter how poor people were, they still needed escapism. People would scrape together 25 cents for the cost of a cinema ticket. One of the most popular genres was the gangster movie, which often portrayed gangsters as modern-day Robin Hoods rather than dead-eyed, fedora-wearing psychopaths. *Little Caesar*, which opened in New York at the Strand Theatre on Broadway and 47th Street in January 1931, was the first movie to tell the story from the gangster's point of view. Audiences assumed Edward G. Robinson based his snarling Italian hood on Capone – even though his staccato way of talking was unlike the gregarious, occasionally affable gangland boss. Some of the movie's dialogue – 'You can dish it out, but you can't take it' and 'Take him for a ride' – entered the language. Author W.R. Burnett described Little Caesar as 'a gutter Macbeth – a composite figure that would indicate how men could rise to prominence or money under the most hazardous conditions, but not much more hazardous than the Renaissance'. At the opening police had to be called after a crowd of nearly three thousand stampeded into the cinema, shattering glass. Publicised as 'the picture gangland defied Hollywood to make', ticket demand was such that the Strand ran eleven shows a day from 9 a.m. to 4.30 the following morning.

The mob was attracted to the movie industry partly because there was plenty of money to be made and partly because of its glamour (gangsters were celebrities themselves, often mentioned in society columns). One could control Hollywood from the bottom up through technicians' unions. Strike action could cripple the industry. Conversely, gangland felt empathy for the moguls themselves. The men who controlled the studios, Harry Warner or Louis B. Mayer, for example, were rough and uncouth, like gangsters. The methods the moguls used to get what they wanted – threatening a cowed workforce – were broadly the same as gangsterdom. In short, gangsters and moguls spoke the same language. After all, they came from the same background. Even Frank Capra, the director whose work was mostly about the American dream, was born in Sicily, the birthplace of Lucky Luciano.

Even before the Outfit and the Syndicate looked to Hollywood, the studios were involved with criminal activity. MGM had its own brothel north of Sunset Strip, run by actress Billie Bennett. The brothel mostly catered for visiting cinema managers and overseas staff. Prostitutes were doubles of famous movie stars. Author Garson Kanin remembered being taken to Mae's, a brothel where the girls bore a close resemblance to real-life film stars. Among the 'stars' on offer were Ginger Rogers, Marlene Dietrich and Joan Crawford. Prostitutes having plastic surgery to look like stars became part of the story of LA Confidential (1997), in which James Ellroy transplanted the MGM brothel from 1930s to 1950s Hollywood.

Studio executives already had links to gangland. Frank Orsatti, right-hand man of MGM head Louis B. Mayer, was a bootlegger and a gangster. According to an FBI summary dated 17 June 1939, Orsatti had a reputation for handling all of MGM's 'dirty work'. MGM production head Eddie Mannix introduced Orsatti to Mayer in 1931. Ava Gardner later described Mannix himself as a gangster. According to Mickey Cohen, Mannix 'knew some pretty nasty people who knew even nastier people'. Orsatti became Mayer's golfing partner and closest friend, supplying him with alcohol and women. Mayer established Orsatti as a talent agent in 1933 after the repeal of Prohibition, having pointed out to him that bootlegging was a dying business. Orsatti should move into agenting, suggested Mayer. After all, he would earn 10 per cent of whatever Mayer's stars at MGM earned. Orsatti's success as an agent was mainly due to his closeness to Mayer. Carter Barron, a political lobbyist who represented MGM's parent company, Loew's, once confronted Mayer about his mob connections. Barron refused to join a dinner table where Mayer was eating with an underworld associate. The lobbyist did not want to sit down with a gangster. 'You're a damn Baptist,' Mayer said. 'Don't you know you've got to know all sorts of people? I use him to do things for me that you wouldn't do.'

The Outfit's most audacious scheme was to extort Hollywood for $1.5 million a year (the equivalent of $20 million today). Al Capone's gang even dreamed of owning studios themselves. How Capone's successors became involved in the biggest scandal ever to shame the industry – in which the president of 20th Century Fox would go to jail as a sacrifice for the other moguls – was due to happenstance: a former pimp and his pal getting drunk one night and bragging how they had just extorted Chicago's leading theatre chain.

Kosher chicken shops once lined one side of Fulton Street in Chicago. Jewish shopkeepers paid protection money to one Willie Bioff – alias William Berg, alias Henry Martin, alias Harry Martin. Bioff, whose real name was actually Morris, promised shopkeepers their shops would not be bombed or burned down, in exchange for a regular fee.

Bioff immigrated to America from Russia when he was five years old. He started his criminal career by pimping at the age of nine. He would sidle up to men walking in the street, telling them his little sister was alone at home. Then he would take them to a nearby brothel full of considerably older prostitutes. Bioff continued pimping after he met his wife, Laurie. The two of them would approach teenage runaway girls, offering them jobs and a place to live. In fact, they were recruiting for their Southside brothel. Bioff would threaten to throw acid in girls' faces if they tried to escape. Some attempted to do so and had their nipples tortured with pliers as punishment. One girl whom Bioff had beaten did escape and sought police protection: Bioff was duly sent to prison for six months for aggravated assault and battery.

On his release, Bioff got a job as a union 'slugger' – threatening to beat people up if they did not join the union – for $35 a week. Although Bioff was only 5 foot 6 inches, he weighed more than 14 stone, most of which was muscle. He was also an alcoholic. The *New York Times* noted that his daily consumption of one hundred bottles of beer meant he smelled of drink. On top of his job as a union slugger, Bioff also began extorting the shopkeepers in Fulton Street.

It was in Fulton Street that Bioff met George Browne, head of the local stagehands' union, Chicago Stagehands Local No. 2. Browne was extorting stores on the other side of the street owned by Gentiles. He had become head of Local No. 2 after beating its previous business manager with a lead pipe. Local No. 2 was a subsidiary of the projectionists' union, Local 110, run by Tommy Maloy. When Browne met Bioff the local Chicago branch of IATSE had four hundred members, 250 of whom were unemployed.

The stagehands' union was already infested with gangsters and hoodlums right across America. Local chapters in Cincinnatti, New York, Newark, St Louis and Southern California all used violence to extort money from cinema owners. 'We are being unmercifully persecuted by a notorious method of racketeering by a gang of inhuman scoundrels,' wrote one cinema owner in Alhambra, California. 'Our theaters are being stench-bombed, teargas bombed. Three have been burned. They are broken into at night and motion picture equipment machines, seats, carpets, draperies are destroyed.'

Browne and Bioff decided to go into business together. One of the first things they did was to raise union membership fees by $5 a week. Bioff bludgeoned one union official who objected so badly with a blackjack that he later died. Another man was murdered while trying to organise a breakaway union. Then, imitating Al Capone, they opened a soup kitchen, the B&B, where unemployed members could go for something to eat. Capone had opened a soup kitchen as a public relations exercise when facing jail.

By 1933, Balaban & Katz was the leading cinema chain in Chicago. However, Balaban & Katz had cut its stagehands' wages by 25 per cent four years earlier. The wage cut was supposed to be temporary but Balaban & Katz had never restored it. Browne and Bioff went to see Barney Balaban and raised the question of restoring Local No. 2's wages to previous levels. Balaban told them to get out of his office.

He then had second thoughts. Possibly thinking Browne was the more biddable of the two, he paid him a visit. Browne was in hospital, having treatment for an ulcer. Balaban made a counter-proposal. For years, he said, he had been paying Maloy $150 a week to waive the two-men-per-projection-booth rule. Would Browne be amenable to the same arrangement if he forgot about any wage increase? Browne, presumably thinking $7200 a year was the best he could hope for, accepted the deal. It is important to note that the impetus to cheat the union came from Balaban, not the gangsters. Balaban would go on to become president of Paramount Pictures.

Bioff was furious when Browne told him about accepting $150 a week. Smelling blood in the water, Bioff decided to apply pressure. If Balaban, the leading exhibitor, caved in then others would follow. Bioff confronted Balaban in his office, telling him the union now wanted $50,000 in cash to cover retroactive pay cuts going back to 1929. Balaban told him to get out again. Bioff left, warning there would be trouble.

It was no empty threat. That night, staff sabotaged every Balaban & Katz theatre. Films were screened upside down. Projectionists mixed up film reels. At the Oriental, a film ran backwards. The musical One Night of Love played without sound at the same theatre. At the Tivoli, the screen went black at a key moment during It Happened One Night. Cinemagoers berated box-office staff, demanding their money back.

Balaban met Katz the next day. Both men were worried. Bioff and Browne had proved more intransigent than expected. Now the exhibitors felt backed into a corner. They agreed to pay off the gangsters $20,000, making the cheque out to the soup kitchen.

Browne and Bioff split $19,000, while Balaban's lawyer, Leo Spitz, pocketed $1000 as a 'carrying charge'. The money was supposed to go to Local No. 2 to restore the 1929 pay cut. Instead, the wage increase was forgotten about. All Bioff and Browne cared about was money – getting their snouts in the trough.

The pair decided to celebrate. Shaking down the biggest theatre chain in Chicago had been easier than anticipated. They decided to go to Club 100, formerly the Yacht Club, on East Superior Street. The decision to celebrate at Club 100 was unfortunate: Al Capone's cousin, Nick Circella – also known as Nicky Dean – ran the bar, which was owned by the Outfit. Bioff and Browne got very drunk and started boasting about their new racket. This new racket was going to make them a fortune, they bragged. Circella listened to them talking. He bought them some more drinks – champagne, bourbon and beer. Then he arranged for two prostitutes to take Bioff and Browne upstairs and made a phone call to Capone's successor as head of the Outfit, Frank Nitti.

Circella met Nitti and Paul 'the Waiter' Ricca for lunch the next day at the Capri restaurant. He told them about the exhibitor shakedown. A phone call woke Browne, who was still sleeping off the previous night's debauch. Gangster Frank Rio told Browne to meet him at a street corner, then drove him around Chicago, intimidating the union boss. Browne, hung-over, started to cry and pleaded for his life.

Two days later, Browne and Bioff were invited to the house of Harry Hochstein, Rio's bodyguard. Hochstein lived next door to Nitti on Riverside. Bioff and Browne assumed they had been invited for lunch. However, when they got there, they realised they had walked into an Outfit business meeting. Others in the room included Ricca, Charlie Fischetti and Lepke Buchalter, from Luciano's gang in New York. It was Mafia custom to eat first and do business afterwards. After a cold buffet, ice cream and espresso, Nitti called the meeting to order. He told Bioff and Browne that the Outfit was taking over their shakedown racket. It wanted half of whatever the pair were making (later, the Outfit would take two-thirds of the money). On the other hand, Nitti knew that

Browne wanted to become president of IATSE. Browne had lost to a rival at the previous year's convention, in 1932. Nitti offered to swing the next year's election in Kentucky. That way, the Outfit could extend the shakedown racket to every movie theatre in the country.

The following March the Outfit convened at Capone's estate in Miami, Florida. Johnny Rosselli joined Nitti, Ricca, Circella and Fischetti from the West Coast. He explained that the studios had neutered Hollywood trade unions, such as IATSE – partly, it should be said, through Rosselli's own doing. However, the studios were still vulnerable to a strong trade union, should one emerge. Despite its weakened state, IATSE members ran nearly every movie theatre in the country. Nitti added that, contrary to popular belief, New York-based theatre chains controlled movie production – not the other way around. MGM, for example, was a subsidiary of the Loew's theatre chain. Hollywood was also a tight-knit community, Nitti said. Barney Balaban's brother John, for example, ran Paramount Pictures. Joseph Schenck, president of 20th Century Fox, was the brother of Nick Schenck, president of Loew's Theatres. Therefore, the studios' Achilles heel was their New York-based cinemas. If the Outfit controlled the technicians' union, it could then hold exhibitors to ransom – and, by extension, Hollywood itself. Circella and Browne would go to New York; Bioff would go to Los Angeles, where Rosselli would be his handler. If nothing else, many stars and producers in Hollywood were either alcoholic or homosexual, making them vulnerable to blackmail. Nitti recalled how Capone had often expressed his desire to move in on Hollywood. He concluded the meeting by declaring the Outfit expected to earn $1 million a year from Hollywood. In short, said Nitti, the goose was in the oven waiting to be cooked.

Nitti then asked Luciano to come to Chicago to see him. The Outfit could not encroach on New York, extorting exhibitors, without the Syndicate's permission. However, Luciano turned up late for the meeting, a snub not lost on Nitti. Chicago and New York were fighting for control of the drugs business in Los Angeles.

Once again, Rosselli explained that New York controlled Holly-wood and that the movie industry was vulnerable to a strong trade union.

Nitti said there was plenty of money to be made, providing everybody worked together under him. Luciano's response was that he was the boss, not Nitti. Then he gave his conditions for giving the Outfit permission to encroach on his territory. First, he wanted Nitti out of his drugs business in Los Angeles. Second, he wanted a share of the revenue from Nitti's Hollywood night-clubs and restaurants. Nitti immediately agreed to dividing cash from the restaurants and nightclubs. The drugs business, however, was more complicated; they should discuss it at a later date, he suggested. Luciano walked out. One week later Luciano sent Nitti a telegram. It read, 'Me Includi [Count me in].'

Nitti next had to deal with Tommy Maloy. Like Browne, Maloy also wanted to become president of IATSE. Maloy went to see Nitti, asking for his help. He owed $81,000 in unpaid income tax and was now facing jail. In addition to the IATSE presidency, Maloy wanted Nitti to use his influence to reduce the prison sentence. Maloy was, however, unaware of the Outfit's plan to install Browne as head of IATSE. Nitti promised to help him in exchange for details about how Local 110 operated – the amount of bribes paid out and to whom, the amount of cash Maloy himself was skimming, that kind of thing. In return, Maloy would only serve six months in jail for tax evasion, and he would become head of IATSE when he got out. In the meantime, Browne would run IATSE in a caretaker capacity. Maloy left Nitti, presumably reassured about his future.

In June 1934 IATSE met for its biennial conference in Louisville, Kentucky. The union had hired the Brown Hotel on Broadway for the conference. However, observers had the impression there were more gangsters than delegates present. Gunmen patrolled the aisles, sat on the dais and lined the room's perimeter. In addition to those from the Outfit, other gangsters included Luciano, Meyer Lansky, Bugsy Siegel and Lepke Buchalter from New York; Longy Zwillman from New

Jersey; 'Big Al' Polizzi from Cleveland; and Johnny Dougherty from St Louis. Unsurprisingly, Browne was anointed president. Delegates were so frightened that nobody else was even nominated. Browne was in tears when he accepted the presidency. He kept thanking 'the boys' for the job, presumably referring to the gangsters rather than union members. Browne was now earning $25,000 a year as president of IATSE on top of the $13,000 he was making as head of Local No. 2. (Later, the Outfit would invoice IATSE to pay for its rooms and travelling expenses.)

Following the Louisville convention, Bioff, Browne and Circella travelled to Manhattan. There they met Ricca. All four then went to the Casino de Paree restaurant, where they had dinner with Luciano, Frank Costello and Jack Dragna, head of the mob in Los Angeles. Bioff and Browne contacted the Association of Motion Picture Producers (AMPP), the New York-based sister association of the MPPDA (now both absorbed into the Motion Picture Association of America, MPAA). They told AMPP they intended to revitalise the technicians' union. Then Circella took Bioff to see Rosselli at the Medical Arts Sanatorium, where he was having treatment for tuberculosis. Circella told Bioff that Rosselli would be his overseer in California.

On his release from jail, Maloy realised he had been double-crossed. On Christmas Eve 1934 the Outfit met and decided to murder Maloy. Nitti told Bioff and Browne that Maloy would not be a problem for much longer. On 4 February 1935, Maloy was driving along Lake Shore Drive when another car drew up alongside him. Two gunmen opened fire on Maloy's Cadillac with shotguns. The FBI believed the murderers were Tony Accardo, future head of the Outfit, and a younger man, Gus Alex. Maloy's funeral was one of the most grandiose in Chicago's history with three hundred cars in the funeral procession. Circella inherited the leadership of Maloy's Chicago projectionists' union, Local 110.

It was now time to move in on the rest of Chicago's movie theatres. The first target was the Warner Bros chain. Bioff went to see area manager James Coston, telling him that his members were insisting on two projectionists in each projection booth, as the law stipulated. Coston protested that such a move would double his projectionists' salary bill. Bioff then tried to make out that he was on Coston's side: his members would forget about the two-men-per-projection-booth rule if Warner Bros paid out $30,000. Coston said he would have to talk to his superiors in New York. Bioff, Browne and Circella accompanied Coston to Manhattan. Warner Bros, realising this was no bluff, agreed to make the payment. The gangsters returned to Chicago with $30,000 in cash. Nitti took half, leaving the rest for the trio to divide between themselves. Circella used his cash to invest in a new nightclub and casino on Chicago's Rush Street, in which Nitti also had a share of the profits.

Next, the Outfit turned the screw on Balaban & Katz again. Bioff and Browne invited John Balaban to lunch. They gave him the same story they had given to James Coston, except this time they asked for $120,000 if their members were to waive the two-men-per-projection-booth law. Balaban was unaware that Coston only had to pay $30,000. However, after talking to his brother, Balaban agreed to pay only $60,000. Having only paid $20,000 at the initial shakedown, the Balabans thought the gangsters' greed excessive.

By the time the Outfit had shaken down all of Chicago's exhibitors, the gangsters had collected $332,000.

The next stage was to take on the New York cinema chains. On 15 July 1935, Browne gave permission for union members to disrupt Loew's and RKO cinemas. Rather than call all IATSE members out on strike – which would have enabled Hollywood to hire non-union projectionists – the gangsters encouraged random disruption. Film stock was set on fire, projectionists were slow to change reels and stink bombs were thrown into audiences. Loew's and RKO caved in after two weeks.

Bioff, Browne and Circella – accompanied by Buchalter – next went to see Leslie Thompson, chairman of RKO. Bioff demanded that RKO give his members a raise. Buchalter stood silent and intimidating in the background. Browne then stepped in as peacemaker. IATSE would call off the strike and forget about any wage demand if RKO paid out $150,000, he said emolliently. Thompson haggled until Browne agreed a fee of $87,000. Thompson gave the gangsters $50,000 in cash that afternoon and another $37,000 the next morning.

Next, the four men called on Nick Schenck, president and chief executive officer of Loew's. The kingpin of the industry, he was so inscrutable that he was nicknamed 'Buddha'. According to director John Huston, Schenck was 'the ruler of rulers . . . Schenck never gets his picture in the papers, and he doesn't go to parties, and he avoids going out in public, but he's the *real* king of the pack.'

Bioff and Schenck might have been brothers. Schenck, like Bioff, had been a penniless immigrant from Russia. He was born on 15 November 1880. His older brother Joseph, with whom Bioff would become friendly in Hollywood, was born four years earlier. Schenck's father had sold vodka to riverboats plying the Volga. The Schenck brothers arrived in New York when Nick was eleven years old. Nick and Joe got a job in a drugstore. Soon the brothers were running the drugstore. One year later, the Schencks owned a chain of drugstores. They also bought a dancehall in Fort George, New Jersey, where they had swum when younger. The dancehall was part of Palisades amusement park. Next, the Schencks opened a Ferris wheel in the park, the largest in the north-east. The attraction proved so popular that they acquired Palisades outright in 1908, renaming it Paradise Park. There they met a nickelodeon operator named Marcus Loew, who persuaded them to buy some cinemas in Hoboken, New Jersey. Eventually, they bought out Loew, while Loew himself moved into production, supplying the Schencks with titles. In 1924, Loew merged his Metro Studio with the Goldwyn Studio and hired Louis B. Mayer to form Metro-Goldwyn-Mayer (MGM).

Bioff told Schenck that he would call off the MGM strike in exchange for $100,000. Schenck, however, was not intimidated. After all, he had known Johnny Rosselli for years. Indeed, Rosselli was just one of many gangsters with whom Schenck was on familiar terms. Screenwriter Anita Loos said that Schenck knew everybody in gangsterdom, from the lowest ranks to the highest echelons. The mob had already offered to kill actor Gilbert Roland a year after Schenck's brother Joe discovered that his wife was having an affair with the star.

Instead, Schenck, speaking on behalf of all the studios, made a counteroffer: would Bioff and Browne take $150,000 if they pledged no strikes for the next seven years? Not only that, but would the gangsters cut IATSE's wage demands by two-thirds? Would they also forget about the union sharing profits with the studios? Of course, Bioff and Browne agreed. In making the offer, Hollywood became just as guilty as Chicago of defrauding the technicians' union. It would also tie the studios' hands when the gangsters came back to extort money the following year. Hollywood had lost any moral high ground in its dealings with gangsters. Or, as the Italians put it, *una volta corrotto, sempre controllato* – once corrupted, always controlled.

However, the studios were afraid people would realise they had come to an illegal agreement too quickly. The Outfit offered to stage a fake strike, allowing producers to pretend to capitulate. If IATSE put on a show of strength, then Hollywood could award it the first 'closed shop' agreement in industry history. Crew would have to join IATSE if they wanted to work on studio backlots.

The flashpoint for the strike came towards the end of 1935. A Paramount Pictures film crew, none of them union members, arrived in New York to shoot aerial footage for ensemble-drama *13 Hours By Air* (1936). A seemingly irate Browne ordered his members to go on strike on Saturday 30 November. From Chicago to New York, IATSE projectionists walked out of more than five hundred Paramount cinemas. Producers and union representatives met for 'emergency' talks at the Union League Club in New York. After supposedly tough negotiations, both sides emerged to make a statement. From now on, said producers, IATSE would be the only union allowed in Hollywood. This supposed Hollywood had the right to enforce a closed shop, which it did not. Later, executives admitted that the mob deal saved studios approximately $15 million in wage demands and profit-sharing arrangements.

Luciano, meanwhile, had still not seen his cut of the shakedown of the Loew's and RKO cinema chains. Apparently, during one conversation, Nitti tried to smooth things over by telling Luciano not to worry – Buchalter was there to represent his interests. Luciano told Nitti that Buchalter did not speak for him.

Nitti's men were still making inroads into his Los Angeles drug business, his dealers undercutting Luciano's on the street. Shipments were being hijacked; Luciano's men were being beaten up, drugged or even murdered. The two men were locked in a curious dance. On the one hand, they were cooperating over the New York cinema shakedown; on the other, they were at each other's throats for control of drugs in Hollywood. Luciano wanted to move in on restaurant extortion. Nitti wanted to get more involved in the drugs business. However, neither man would compromise and give each other a share of revenue.

Bioff arrived in Los Angeles in September 1935. Rosselli and Browne were waiting for him on the quayside as his ship docked. With Bioff as its front, the Outfit established its West Coast headquarters in the penthouse of the twelve-storey Taft Building. Bioff's first priority was to increase IATSE membership, which was low in Hollywood. Thugs imported from Chicago intimidated fellow unions with threats and violence. Chicago began sending artisans with Outfit connections out to Hollywood, where they became part of the IATSE infrastructure. The idea was that even if the leadership were decapitated, the Mafia would still be involved in the movie business. In 1934, there were fewer than two hundred IATSE members in Hollywood but within three years membership had grown to 12,000. Having been awarded the closed-shop agreement by the studios, Bioff presented the people who worked on the soundstages with a choice: either join IATSE and get a 10 per cent pay rise or find themselves out of work.

IATSE ordered members to pay 2 per cent of their wages into a 'war chest' in case the union had to go out on strike. Workers paid about $1.5 million into the hardship fund – two-thirds of which went to the Outfit with Bioff and Browne pocketing the rest.

Bioff also found a new angle by which to extort Hollywood. He went to see Jules Brulator, distributor of Eastman film stock in Los Angeles, who sold film stock to the studios. Unless Eastman appointed Bioff as its 'purchasing agent', its warehouse would be bombed. Bioff collected a 7 per cent commission on all film stock sold. He earned $230,000 over a two-year period through the Eastman swindle – $150,000 of which was kicked back upstairs to Chicago. When reporters teased Bioff for wearing elegant suits and expensive shirts, his standard reply was, 'It's the union that's rich, not Willie Bioff.'

Luciano could see events slipping beyond his grasp. He was losing control in Los Angeles, where Nitti was winning the drugs war. As a warning to Nitti, he wanted Bugsy Siegel to kill Bioff and Browne. Buchalter protested that killing the head of a trade union would have repercussions all the way to the White House. Instead, Luciano decided to have Nitti murdered.

In September 1935, Luciano booked in to the Sherman Hotel in Chicago. According to Mafia lore, he demanded three things from Nitti. First, Luciano wanted his own men on the board of IATSE. Second, he wanted all the money owed to him. Third, from now on Nitti could keep the Hollywood racket to himself, providing he stayed out of Luciano's way when it came to drugs, gambling and prostitution in Los Angeles. Luciano was prepared to go to war if Nitti would not accept these terms. Nitti had until the next day to make up his mind.

Nitti met Luciano for lunch the following afternoon. Apparently, both men were unable to agree and lunch ended abruptly. Nitti had just stepped outside the restaurant when a passing car opened fire. The head of the Outfit survived the drive-by shooting. Following the assassination attempt Nitti agreed to Luciano's terms. The Outfit concentrated on the studio shakedown, while Luciano kept drugs, gambling and prostitution for himself.

Meanwhile, Will Hays, the former chairman of the Republican National Committee and postmaster general in the Warren Harding administration who now ran the MPPDA, asked for Rosselli's help. An amateur gang had obtained a pornographic stag reel MGM was keen to suppress. Titled *The Casting Couch*, the porno reel starred one of the studio's fastest rising stars, Joan Crawford. A document in Crawford's FBI file refers to a 'story from a high police authority' that, shortly after her arrest in Detroit for prostitution in the early 1920s, a pornographic film of Crawford was doing the rounds of stag parties. Crawford herself later wrote that the whole thing was a case of mistaken identity; the reel was shot in 1918 when she would only have been fourteen – the actress in the reel was considerably older. Nevertheless, the blackmailers wanted $100,000 to hand over the negative, but the studio would go no higher than $25,000. Hays asked Rosselli if he could broker a deal. The gangster met the extortionists and explained who he was and for whom he worked. He also made it clear that unless they handed over the negative he would have them all murdered. The blackmailers relinquished the negative and Rosselli pocketed the $25,000. In 1943, Crawford had to pay MGM $50,000 to be released from her contract, despite her departure having been mutually agreed. Her biographer, Fred Lawrence Guiles, suggests Crawford may have had to repay MGM the cash it gave Rosselli to buy back the porno reel. In January 1974 MGM's former head of security, Howard Strickling, told erstwhile colleague Samuel Marx that the studio had to buy up pornographic movies starring Crawford.

On the morning of Thursday 16 April 1936, members of the IATSE hierarchy went to see MGM chairman Nick Schenck in New York. The Outfit had decided to turn the screw again. Orson Welles summed up what happened next: 'A group of industrialists finance a group of gangsters to break trade unionism . . . When the gangsters succeed at what they were paid to do, they turn on the men who paid them . . . [The] puppet masters find their creatures taking on a terrible life of their own.' Browne told Schenck that all the studios must pay a combined $2 million in cash to avoid a strike. Schenck later testified that, at first, he thought Browne had lost his mind. He was so dumbfounded he was unable to speak. Bioff added that unless Hollywood agreed to the payoff, IATSE would cause chaos in cinemas across the country. They gave Schenck a few hours to make up his mind.

Schenck immediately went to see Sidney Kent, president of 20th Century Fox, where Schenck's brother Joe was chairman. Louis B. Mayer had provided $100,000 of seed funding for Twentieth Century Pictures, the production company which merged with Fox in May 1935. Kent begged Schenck not to capitulate, presumably unaware of the secret $150,000 seven-year, no-strike deal the studios had made the year before. Hollywood was now in a hole: it had lost any purchase on the situation, greed having compromised its integrity.

When the gangsters returned that afternoon, Schenck told them the studios could not afford $2 million. Bioff cut him short, saying he would take $1 million. Schenck again tried to bargain but Bioff stood up to leave, saying $1 million was his final offer.

The next day the gang explained how the money was going to be split up. Studio executives present included Austin Keogh, vice-president of Paramount; Leo Spitz, now working for RKO; Hugh Strong, head of personnel at 20th Century Fox; and Albert Warner, vice-president and finance director of Warner Bros. Each of the four major studios – Fox, MGM, Paramount and Warner Bros – would have to pay $50,000 a year, while lesser studios such as Universal, Columbia, RKO and twelve other companies would each pay $25,000. In total, the studios were being extorted for nearly $600,000 a year. In addition, Bioff wanted $100,000 upfront in cash.

Schenck went round to Bioff's hotel with his share of the money on Saturday morning. He laid $50,000 in cash in a brown paper bag down on Bioff's bed. Bioff handed the package to Browne and told him to count it. Schenck stood by the window, smoking and looking thoughtfully out over Manhattan. As Schenck stood and smoked, another visitor arrived at the Warwick Hotel. It was Kent with another cash bundle, which he too placed on the bed. Kent explained he was $25,000 shy but it was the best he could do at such short notice. Bioff told Browne to count that too – adding to the executives' humiliation. 'I've found out that dickering with these picture producers goes about the same all the time,' Bioff testified. 'You get into a room with them and they start yelling and hollering about how they're being held up and robbed. That goes on and on. Me, I'm a busy man and I don't get too much sleep. After a while, it dies down and the quiet wakes me up. Then I say, "All right, gentlemen, do we get the money?"'

Bioff went back to Los Angeles to inform the studio heads of their fate. Louis B. Mayer later testified that he only capitulated after Bioff threatened to murder him. Harry Warner, president of Warner Bros, claimed he was so frightened of Bioff that he hired a bodyguard – which was odd, considering he went to synagogue with the gangster and invited Bioff to stay at his ranch.

Harry Cohn of Columbia was the one studio head immune to extortion because of his existing relationship with the mob. Cohn telephoned Rosselli after Bioff called a strike at Columbia in November 1937. The strike was supposedly over Columbia letting go of some make-up artists but, according to Cohn's biographer Bob Thomas, Bioff was intimidating Cohn into paying up his share of the Outfit's payoff. Rosselli went to see Bioff at the IATSE offices, finding him sitting behind his desk in his hat and coat, a cigar clamped between his teeth and a gun resting on the desktop before him. According to Thomas, Rosselli told Bioff, 'Listen, Willie. I don't know what you're trying to prove, but it isn't going to work.' Rosselli ordered Bioff to telephone Browne. Bioff sullenly did what Rosselli told him. Browne told Rosselli that the Columbia strike had been Bioff's doing. In the end, Bioff telephoned Cohn to apologise for the one-day strike. (Producer Samuel Goldwyn also refused to have anything to do with the racket, supposedly uttering the famous words 'Gentlemen, include me out.')

In some cases, such as the deeply indebted Warner Bros, Bioff had to settle for less than he wanted. Albert Warner cut a deal for $10,000 upfront, plus regular instalment payments. Loss-making Paramount could only pay out $27,000. Nevertheless, the Outfit grossed more than $1.5 million from studio extortion, the no-strike deal and union dues in one year alone.

Studio accountants masked transactions to ensure there was no record of money changing hands. Warner Bros described one $12,000 payment as Christmas presents for critics.

However, Bioff kept the studios sweet by keeping his side of the bargain. Over a four-year period, technicians' wages declined by anything between 15 and 40 per cent. When the breakaway Federation of Motion Picture Craftsmen went on strike in 1937, Bioff imported thugs from Chicago to terrorise its leaders. Although strikers hired dockworkers to protect them from Bioff – and by implication the studios – gangsters with machine guns attacked picket lines. Harry Warner said it was just good business sense to have a relationship with Bioff. By 1938, the once-humiliated Sidney Kent was telling the IATSE convention that relations between Hollywood and its workers were the best out of any industry in America.

The Schenck brothers were also defrauding MGM, employing Bioff as a money courier between New York and Los Angeles. The Schencks were creaming off hundreds of thousands of dollars from box offices. In Mafia parlance, they were 'skimming' their own company. Nick Schenck would send the money to his brother Joe at his house in Hollywood. Bioff made dozens of trips over a six-year period. One such delivery was worth $62,000 alone. Joe Schenck would sometimes count the money by his swimming pool, peeling off $500 from the bundle to cover Bioff's expenses. Clearly, Bioff did not have to corrupt Hollywood. He merely folded smoothly into the environment. Bioff later testified, 'These businessmen are nothing but two-bit whores with clean shirts and a shine.'

Bioff's power became such that once, when an MGM security guard denied him entry to the studio, he ordered Mayer to come down personally and castigate his employee. Helping to ensure that the mob-controlled IATSE enjoyed warm press coverage, Rosselli owned the insurance company that insured trade paper *Hollywood Reporter*, while Bioff controlled its journalists' trade union. Bioff said later that Hollywood was dancing to his tune.

In 1937, Bioff decided he wanted to build a ranch-style house in the Los Angeles suburb of Woodland Hills. He found an 80-acre estate he wanted to buy, intending to call the house Rancho Laurie, after his former-brothel-keeper wife. Their neighbours would include Clark Gable, Barbara Stanwyck and Tyrone Power. One unusual architectural feature would be gun turrets on each corner of the roof.

Bioff's problem was how to pay for it. He thought that by demanding payments in cash he could avoid a paper trail linking him to the shakedown. In the short term, he was correct. However, he could hardly walk into a bank with $100,000 in five-dollar bills to pay the deposit on Rancho Laurie. Sometimes the smallest decision can affect the whole of one's life. Bioff asked Joe Schenck if he would launder the cash. Schenck made out a Fox company cheque for $100,000 to Bioff. The gangster would claim it was his commission on film stock. This favour would unravel the entire studio extortion scheme.

Bioff duly built his house and then asked RKO if he could buy $5000 worth of furniture through the studio's props department. He later testified that he never had any intention of paying for it. Rancho Laurie was furnished with Louis XV furniture and oriental vases. There was also a wood-panelled library, although Bioff himself only read comic books.

In November 1937 the industry began to fight back against mob control. Union members who complained about IATSE taking over their existing organisation either found themselves unemployed or beaten up. Carey McWilliams, a Los Angeles lawyer, convinced a state committee to investigate leadership of the technicians' union. Bioff hired another lawyer, Colonel William Neblett, to represent IATSE. Neblett happened to work for the same law firm as California assembly speaker William Mosley Jones, the man in charge of the investigation. The two days of public hearings were desultory and inconclusive. Nobody asked the right questions. The investigation fizzled out.

However, public attitudes to gangsterism had changed. Most people no longer regarded gangsters as Robin Hoods manqués, almost providing a public service, as they had during Prohibition. Now the press vilified the mob as a cancer eating into America itself. Hollywood reflected the hardening of public attitude. Instead of romanticising gangsters, Hollywood began making films with federal agents as heroes. By 1935, James Cagney, who played a sympathetic gangster in *The Public Enemy* (1932), was working for the FBI (*G Men*).

Indeed, Cagney was instrumental in exposing the studio shakedown – to the point where the Outfit planned to have him murdered as a warning to others. Cagney's wife Willie began receiving anonymous phone calls while Cagney was at Warner Bros making *Each Dawn I Die* (1939). The voice on the phone would tell her Cagney had been in an accident. She would phone the studio to find out it was not true. On one occasion, Willie was told Cagney had been killed in a car crash. However, this psychological torture was supposed to be a build-up to Cagney's eventual murder, so that Willie would one day call the studio to discover this time it was true. According to Cagney, his co-star George Raft heard about the plan and intervened. The Outfit called off the murder. Raft's own version was that he saw Bioff on set regarding Cagney with obvious dislike. Then the union leader stared up at the klieg lights overhead and exchanged a meaningful look with a technician. Bioff later told Raft in New York that he had been ordered to abandon Cagney's murder because it might hurt Raft's own career. 'The studio wasn't going to pay off and we were going to take care of Cagney,' Bioff told Raft. 'We were all set to drop a lamp on him. But I got word to lay off because you were in the picture.' Cagney later said that Raft was the only genuinely tough man he had ever met in show business.

By 1939 Bioff was attempting to take over actors' union the Screen Actors Guild (SAG). Union members would come out of SAG meetings to find their car tyres slashed. SAG officials were threatened or mugged. However, SAG's leadership – under the presidency of Robert Montgomery – refused to be intimidated. Cagney and others were vocal in calling for another investigation into IATSE's leadership.

Montgomery joined forces with Arthur Ungar, editor of trade paper *Variety*, and newspaper columnist Westbrook Pegler to investigate Bioff. The Motion Picture Technicians' Committee had already made a formal complaint against the gangster with the National Labor Relations Board. The SAG investigation un-covered the $100,000 cheque Schenck had made out to Bioff.

Bioff, growing increasingly desperate, began threatening film-makers directly. He went to see director Cecil B. De Mille in hospital. Bioff stood over De Mille's hospital bed and informed him that unless he paid up he might have an accident. De Mille, however, refused to be intimidated. He had already survived one attempt on his life in 1913 when a thug working for a rival film consortium took a shot at him. Despite being in great pain, De Mille struggled out of bed. Did Bioff know why De Mille was still alive? (De Mille had nearly died from acute rheumatic fever years earlier in Paris.) 'Because,' said De Mille, 'I've got God on my side. I was told that I would never stand again. But as you can see, God has made me stand. Do you honestly think you can succeed where all the others have failed? I defy you to cause an accident. God defies you. Now get out of here.'

The Mafia's stranglehold may have been broken but extorting Hollywood had brought gangsters into contact with some of the most fascinating and mythic beauties in the world. Longy Zwill-man, for example, had already had an affair with Jean Harlow – and may have been involved in the murder of her husband, producer Paul Bern. Lucky Luciano is supposed to have had an affair with comedienne Thelma Todd. Several film historians believe he had her murdered after she attempted to tip off the Los Angeles authorities about the Hollywood shakedown.

CHAPTER THREE

A Conspiracy of Evil

The influx of East Coast criminals into Los Angeles at the beginning of the 1930s did not go unnoticed. As Philip Marlowe says in Raymond Chandler's novel *The Little Sister*, 'Now we've got the big money, the sharp shooters, the percentage workers, the fast-dollar boys, the hoodlums out of New York and Chicago . . . riffraff of a big hardboiled city with no more personality than a paper cup.'

Somebody whom Chandler would have categorised as one of the riffraff was Marino Bello. Bello was a Chicago exile on the fringes of gangsterism. He had fled Chicago wanting to save his own skin during the Chicago gang wars. Now he was living off his wife's earnings as a waitress and door-to-door saleswoman. Bello had met Jean Carpenter when she was a single mother living in Kansas. Carpenter's father, a property developer, had put his teenage granddaughter, Harlean, through private school. However, when the school expelled the girl, her grandfather, exasperated with all three of them, packed mother, daughter and Bello off to California. He gave them just enough money to get started. Soon, the three of them were living in a two-bedroom apartment in Los Angeles. Mrs Carpenter called herself Mama Jean and her daughter 'the Baby'. By now, Bello had married Mama Jean and had become infatuated with his stepdaughter. One day, for example, he would sit down beside the teenager and show her how to apply lipstick. Bello refused to get a full-time job. Instead, he decided he wanted to be an actor, and both he and his wife became extras. Jean would occasionally take her daughter with her to casting calls. One agent, Arthur Landau, decided that young Harlean had the makings of a star. He took her to see Hal Roach, the comedy impresario who had launched the careers of Harold Lloyd and Laurel and Hardy. Roach offered Harlean a contract on the spot. Harlean adopted her mother's Christian name. From now on she would be known as Jean Harlow.

Howard Hughes, meanwhile, had spent two years making his first film, *Hell's Angels*, a silent First World War fighter pilot spectacle. *Hell's Angels* starred Ben Lyon and James Hall as two Oxford undergraduates who join the Royal Flying Corps. Greta Nissen, a Norwegian actress, played the English rose who loves them both. However, just when Hughes thought he was finished with the movie, Warner Bros released *The Jazz Singer* in October 1927. Warner made a $3 million profit from its talkie. Hughes decided to reshoot *Hell's Angels* with sound. Although Lyon and Hall could just about pass muster as Oxford undergraduates, Hughes knew that audiences would laugh at Nissen with her thick Norwegian accent. He decided to replace her.

By the late 1920s, Thelma Todd was one of Hollywood's most popular comediennes, best remembered today for her roles in the Marx Brothers' *Monkey Business* (1931) and *Horse Feathers* (1932). She was also under contract to Roach. Todd had collapsed on the set of *All Teed Up* (1930), diagnosed with exhaustion but probably suffering from a crashing depression caused by the amphetamine-based diet pills the studio encouraged her to take. Todd had problems with her weight. She spent several days in bed and then returned to finish the movie. Once shooting was over, Todd went on holiday for three months. She took a cruise to Catalina Island, off the California coast south-west of Los Angeles, where she met Roland West, a forty-four-year-old United Artists executive. United Artists was distributing *Hell's Angels*. West and Todd began an affair. Todd confided to West that she wanted to be taken seriously as an actress, not just a comedienne. West promised her the lead in the new sound version of *Hell's Angels*, a decision beyond his authority. Todd went back to work for Roach. Three weeks later, she heard from West. He asked her to join him for dinner that night at the Brown Derby restaurant. Waiting at the table were Hughes and Joe Schenck, chairman of United Artists. They offered her the part. However, Roach would not release his biggest female star. Although Todd's five-year contract allowed her to work for other studios, Roach had to approve any deal. Hughes and Schenck dropped Todd. Bitter about the way she had been passed over, Todd began drinking heavily. Soon after, she was banned for drink driving.

Meanwhile, Ben Lyon was walking through the Roach studio when he saw Jean Harlow. He decided she would be perfect for the role of the aviators' love interest. Hughes agreed to give her a screen test. Despite misgivings as to whether Harlow could speak with an English accent, Hughes gave her the part – possibly spurred by Harlow's habit of not wearing a brassiere. Roach released Harlow for the movie, presumably to teach Todd a lesson, and Hughes signed Harlow to a three-year contract. Marino Bello then fired Arthur Landau and took over as Harlow's manager. Hughes devoted the rest of 1928 to reshooting *Hell's Angels* with Harlow, spending the whole of 1929 and the spring of 1930 obsessing over its editing. Harlow was farmed out to Warner Bros for gangster movie *The Public Enemy* (1931). *Hell's Angels* was publicised as the most expensive movie ever made. However, the reviews were mocking. The film, which cost $3.8 million to make, left Hughes $1.5 million out of pocket.

Roland West was nonetheless determined to keep his promise to Todd and reinvent her as a serious actress. He wanted to direct her in a drama titled *Corsair*. This time Roach did release Todd. West changed her name to Alison Lloyd, so that, he told the press, 'no taint of comedy might cling to Miss Todd's skirt'. Roach replied that when Todd came back to work for him, he would change her name to Susie Dinkleberry so that 'no taint of drama will cling to her pyjamas'.

Hughes lost interest in Harlow after *Hell's Angels*, eventually loaning her to MGM. The studio sent Harlow on a cross-country tour promoting *Platinum Blonde* (1931), accompanied by Bello. At some point during the 1931 tour, Bello is supposed to have introduced Harlow to New Jersey gangster Longy Zwillman. Bello hoped the mob would reward him for the introduction, possibly running a Manhattan speakeasy. According to Zwillman's biographer, it was Zwillman's friend Joseph 'Doc' Stacher who first saw Harlow on stage at the Adams Theater, New Jersey. After hearing Stacher's description of Harlow – unfunny jokes, cheap dress but glorious blonde hair the colour of eggnog – Zwillman, who like Luciano had already invested in plays, introduced himself to the actress backstage. That night, Zwillman is supposed to have taken Harlow and her mother to dinner in the Oak Room of New York's Plaza Hotel. Over dinner, Harlow complained about the terms of her contract. Hughes had Harlow under contract for $250 a week, despite MGM paying her $3500 each week while she was on tour – Hughes was pocketing the difference. Zwillman told her to pretend to be ill for the next ten days. His own doctor would tell Hughes the actress was unfit to travel. The gangster hired two Broadway cabaret writers to develop a new act for Harlow. The new material would show off her natural comic ability. He also called on gangster friends to make sure Harlow's personal appearances were publicised at each tour stop over the next six weeks. Zwillman planted people in the audience during press conferences asking pre-arranged questions, giving Harlow the chance to come back with snappy, saucy replies. It was during one of these press conferences that Harlow offered to show one reporter her pubic hair in order to prove that she was a natural blonde. The *New York Daily Graphic* picked up the story and soon women all over the country were going 'platinum blonde' in beauty parlours. Zwillman also bumped up the $250 Harlow was getting from Hughes to $1000 a week. It was, he reportedly told Johnny Rosselli, an investment in the future. Zwillman's plan was to get Hughes to release Harlow from her contract. Harlow could then move to Columbia under his pal Harry Cohn, repaying Zwillman's investment in her.

The twenty-one-year-old actress began having an affair with Zwillman, who became a frequent visitor to Los Angeles. Zwillman would meet Harlow at a bungalow in the Garden of Allah, where

F. Scott Fitzgerald lived. The mob rented one of twenty-five bunga-lows grouped round two swimming pools. Later, Costello, Lansky and Siegel would all stay there. Zwillman once told Mafia hitman Abe 'Kid Twist' Reles how agitated Harlow made him feel. It would appear that Harlow was genuinely fond of Zwillman. For the rest of her life, she would wear a platinum charm bracelet he had given her. Among the trinkets hanging from it was a pig – supposedly, a jokey reference to her eating habits. Fan magazines noticed the jewellery and a craze for charm bracelets promptly swept America. In ex-change, she gave Zwillman some strands of pubic hair, which the gangster framed in lockets and gave to gangster friends.

But Joe Schenck persuaded Harlow that Zwillman was about to lose his main source of income. It was inevitable that the govern-ment would repeal Prohibition after the 1932 presidential election. Harlow would be much better off moving to MGM, he argued – owned, incidentally, by his brother – than staying with a small outfit like Columbia. Harlow followed Schenck's advice and moved to MGM, then the leading studio in Hollywood. Hughes sold Harlow for $60,000, retaining the right to use her in two movies on her new MGM salary. MGM signed Harlow to a seven-year contract with an escalating salary, reaching $5000 per week by year seven.

Thelma Todd's career flourished after returning to Roach. The producer paired her with ZaSu Pitts to become a double act, a kind of female Laurel and Hardy. Roach gave a party in May 1931 to celebrate Todd's new $2000-a-week contract and it was at this party that Todd met Pat DiCicco, Luciano's man in Hollywood. They began having an affair. On 18 July 1932, DiCicco and Todd married in Prescott, Arizona. The newlyweds set up home in Brentwood, Los Angeles, but the marriage began to fail almost immediately. Luciano would summon DiCicco at short notice to meet him in New York and DiCicco would often disappear with-out warning, rarely bothering to tell his wife where he was going or what he was doing. Todd had always been a heavy drinker. Triggered by this latest crisis, her drinking spiralled out of control. She became unbalanced, mixing alcohol with diet pills.

At the same time as Harlow was having an affair with Zwillman, she was also seeing forty-two-year-old studio executive Paul Bern. Bern was an assistant to Irving Thalberg, MGM's head of production. Louis B. Mayer's daughter, Irene Mayer Selznick, described Bern as 'probably the single most beloved figure in Hollywood'. He was a sensitive man in a vulgar business. He was especially good at listening. Female film stars felt they could unburden themselves to him.

Bern also had a reputation in Hollywood for having unusually small genitals. Although apparently capable of intercourse, Bern was ashamed of his condition. In her memoirs, screenwriter Frances Marion suggested Bern had a taste for sado-masochism. He was also prone to hysteria. During his affair with actress Barbara La Marr, for example, he became so distraught that he tried to drown himself by sticking his head down a flushing toilet. MGM studio manager Eddie Mannix was of the opinion that all Harlow needed was 'a good cocksman and Paul ain't it'.

Harlow married Bern on 2 July 1932, possibly to escape the influence of her stepfather. Harlow disliked Bello, who, she told Landau, used to beat up Mama Jean. Bello now saw control of the actress's money passing from his hands and into Bern's.

Then, on 5 September 1932, a gardener discovered Bern's body at his home on Easton Drive, off Benedict Canyon. He was lying in front of a full-length bedroom mirror, having apparently shot himself in the head. Bern was still clutching the gun. Harlow was not at home, having stayed the night at her parents' house in Beverly Hills.

One of the first people to arrive at the scene was Louis B. Mayer, accompanied by publicity head Howard Strickling and Whitey Hendry, head of security at MGM. Although Mayer disapproved of Harlow, having learned the story about the gold locket from Mannix – who had in turn heard it from mob associate Eddie Nealis – she was still the property of MGM. Harlow was poised to become the studio's biggest star. A scandal like this could ruin her career. Years later, Hendry said that the moment he saw Bern's corpse he knew he had been murdered. Hendry suggested to Mayer that the murder should be made to look like suicide. The police chief at the crime scene picked up the gun, which was on the other side of the room, and put it in Bern's hand. He also shifted the body fully in front of the mirror, giving the death a narcissistic quality. Mayer's thinking was that making Bern's death look like suicide would be somehow less harmful to Harlow's career than murder, a somewhat theological point lost on those who do not worship in Holy Wood.

Thalberg told staff the next morning that Mayer was already writing the script for the inquest. MGM released to the press an alleged suicide note, which read:

> Dearest Dear,
>   Unfortunately, this is the only way to make good the frightful wrong I have done you, and to wipe out my abject humiliation.
>   I love you.
>   Paul.
>   You understand last night was only a comedy.

The implication was that Bern, humiliated by his impotence, had killed himself. According to Landau, the 'frightful wrong' that Bern referred to was attempting to have sex with Harlow wearing a strap-on dildo. MGM put out the official line that Bern had stripped himself naked, doused himself in Harlow's favourite perfume, stood in front of the mirror and pulled the trigger. Dr Frank Webb, assistant autopsy surgeon of the coroner's office, gave credence to the suicide theory when he said that Bern's genitalia were smaller than average.

Years later, a handwriting expert confirmed that Bern had indeed written the note. However, the note was part of a longer letter, the rest of which was missing. Strickling confessed to author Charles Higham in 1970 that the suicide note was a fraud.

Next, Mayer, Hendry and Strickling had to ensure the District Attorney's office did not probe into Bern's death. Budd Schulberg, author of *On the Waterfront*, saw Hollywood as a law unto itself – a principality like Luxembourg or Liechtenstein. Schulberg grew up under the studio system – his father was Paramount production head B.P. Schulberg. According to Schulberg, studio bosses like Mayer were powerful enough to cover up a murder. Much like the mob, Strickling and Hendry kept a list of officials they bribed to keep the studio out of trouble. They even greased the palm of Los Angeles district attorney Buron Fitts. Ida Koverman, Mayer's political adviser, was present in Mayer's office the day after Bern's body was discovered. According to Koverman, Hendry called Fitt's colleague Blaney Matthews, chief of the bureau of criminal investigations. Their conversation implied that Fitts had agreed to drop the investigation in exchange for a payoff.

The inquest fell into line with MGM's suicide theory. It decided Bern had committed suicide for reasons unknown. The official verdict was 'death by gunshot wound of the head, self-inflicted by the deceased with suicidal intent. Motive undetermined.'

The body of Dorothy Milette, Bern's common-law wife, was pulled from the Sacramento River ten days later. Milette was a schizophrenic who had been a patient at the Blythewood Sanatorium in Connecticut. Bern had supported her for many years but kept her existence secret. Presumably, grief-stricken by Bern's death, Milette too was supposed to have committed suicide. She had been seen taking a ferry from San Francisco the day after Bern's body was found. Sacramento sheriff Don Cox felt that Milette may have been murdered but MGM obstructed his investigation. Just as with Bern, the studio wanted a suicide verdict at the inquest as quickly as possible.

In 1960, Ben Hecht, screenwriter of *Scarface*, wrote an article for *Esquire* magazine maintaining Bern was murdered. One theory is that Bello paid Zwillman to arrange Bern's murder – which, given his jealousy, the gangster was supposedly happy to do. According to Harlow's former agent Arthur Landau, Harlow told him Bern had beaten her up on her wedding night. Possibly Harlow also told Zwillman about the beating, increasing his hatred of Bern. According to this version of events, Zwillman collected Milette from her hotel and drove her to Harlow's home, where he gave her a gun. Harlow was unaware of the other woman's existence. Milette then shot Bern dead. Zwillman drove Milette back to San Francisco to catch the ferry, perhaps even accompanying her to Sacramento and pushing her off the boat himself. After all, why did Milette catch a ferry to Sacramento if she wanted to drown herself? San Francisco sits in a bay, with water all around. On the other hand, even if Bello did want Bern killed so that he could keep control of Harlow's money, why involve a mentally ill woman as assassin?

Harlow's biographer Irving Shulman has suggested that Hecht dreamed up Bern's murder after writing a biopic of Harlow for movie producer Jerry Wald the year before. Often during the 1959 story conferences, Wald would suggest that the property's dramatic value would be doubled if Bern's suicide could be revealed as murder.

Whether or not Zwillman drove Bern's common-law wife to murder him, the New Jersey gangster continued to be involved in the movie business. He spent most of his three-week honeymoon in July 1939 in Hollywood going on private tours of the studios. Zwillman invested in the business through two production companies, Manhattan Productions and Greentree Productions. His contact at 20th Century Fox was executive Sol Wurtzel, who eventually ran the studio's B-picture unit. And Zwillman continued to have affairs with actresses, including starlets Blanche Williams, Alice Irene Sheppard and Suzie Donner.

Thelma Todd's marriage, meanwhile, was fraying. DiCicco again disappeared without warning in February 1933. As the days wore on, Todd called Roland West and arranged to meet him for dinner at the Brown Derby. West had married actress Jewel Carmen after his affair with Todd. The marriage had not worked. West and Carmen were, however, still friends. Indeed, despite their separation, they planned to buy a property together and convert it into a restaurant. West was apparently explaining his plans to Todd when DiCicco walked into the restaurant, accompanied by a man Todd did not recognise. This was Lucky Luciano, whom DiCicco was squiring around Hollywood. Todd joined both men for drinks.

Luciano had started visiting Hollywood in 1931, seeing DiCicco. One night, Luciano became enraged at the Brown Derby when he thought he saw Al Capone sitting at a table. DiCicco had to calm him down, explaining it was Ralph, Capone's brother. By 1933, when Capone was in jail, Capone's successor, Nitti, was attempting to hijack Luciano's Hollywood drug business. Luciano started visiting Los Angeles regularly, often when DiCicco was in New York. Todd told comedienne Patsy Kelly – who replaced ZaSu Pitts as her onscreen partner – that she was sleeping with Luciano. Kelly warned Todd to end the affair, which Roach and West also knew about. Kelly suspected that Luciano was feeding Todd drugs. Some days Todd was so hung-over she was unfit for work.

In March 1934 Todd divorced DiCicco on grounds of mental cruelty. She told the divorce court that DiCicco beat her. Following the divorce, Todd decided to join West in opening a restaurant. She did not have to invest any money; she simply had to lend her name to the venture and encourage film star friends to eat there. Jewel Carmen, West's estranged wife, was the financier. 'Thelma Todd's Roadside Café', a three-storey building on Roosevelt Highway (today, Pacific Coast Highway) in Pacific Palisades, opened for business in August 1934. The restaurant and drugstore were on the ground floor. A bar and offices occupied the first floor. The second floor was supposed to be empty, but West hosted after-hours gambling sessions there. Before long, Clark Gable and Spencer Tracy were regulars.

Despite its popularity, however, Todd was supporting the loss-making business by 1935. Her first thought was that the accountant, Charles Smith, was crooked. Then, one afternoon, two men confronted West in the restaurant. They told him that from now on he could only buy alcohol and meat through them. Not only that, but West was told to order more than was needed. When he protested that he had no need to increase his order, the men said the amount could remain the same, but he would still have to pay more. West realised he was being extorted. Not only that but the extortion had been going on for some time. The accountant had been party to it and had tried to cover it in the books. This explained why the restaurant was making a loss. Now the mob was turning the screw.

Returning to New York, Luciano instructed his men to pressure West into renting out the second floor of the Roadside Café as a casino. When West stood his ground, Luciano himself invited West for a drive in the back of his car. Later, West confronted Todd about the mess they were now in; he blamed her infatuation with gangsters for getting them into the situation in the first place. Now she would have to buy him out of the business. Todd protested that everything she earned went into keeping the restaurant afloat. Instead, she would reason with Luciano.

Luciano had dinner with Todd on 25 November. She told friends later that Luciano had spent the evening pressuring her about the casino. Other diners overheard Todd tell Luciano that he would open a casino over her dead body. 'That can be arranged,' Luciano is supposed to have said.

Todd told her mother that Luciano wanted to use the second floor as a front for drugs and prostitution – at best, gambling would be crooked. Alice Todd advised her daughter to go to the police. Todd telephoned Buron Fitts's office on 11 December. She made an appointment to see the district attorney on 17 December. Some Mafia historians say that Luciano had spies in Fitts's office, reporting activity back to him. Fitts himself may have been on the Syndicate's payroll, just as he took bribes from the studios.

Presumably aware that Todd was about to turn whistleblower, Luciano flew into Los Angeles on the night of Friday 13 December.

On Saturday 14 December British comedian Stanley Lupino, father of actress Ida Lupino, gave a party in Todd's honour at the Café Trocadero on Sunset Boulevard. DiCicco, who had invited himself to the party, left with actress Margaret Lindsay at about 1.15 a.m. Later, Todd's chauffeur, Ernie Peters, arrived to take the actress home. According to Peters, Todd told him to drive as fast as possible. She was frightened of either being kidnapped, or, worse, murdered by gangsters. Peters dropped Todd off at the Roadside Café at 3.30 a.m., leaving her standing by the road.

However, one eyewitness, Robert Fisher, said he saw Todd in evening clothes in a cigar store on 8th and Figueroa at nine o'clock that morning. According to Fisher, Todd was hysterical. She ran back out of the store and met a dark man holding a woman's fur coat. Todd and the dark man walked across the street and sat down on the steps of the First Methodist Church. Todd calmed down and then got into a car with the man. Fisher noticed the time was 9.10 a.m.

Another eyewitness, Sarah Kane Carter, saw Todd making a telephone call from a drugstore in Beverly Hills at 4.04 the following Sunday afternoon.

At 11.45 on Sunday night, Todd pulled in to a Christmas tree lot in Santa Monica on the coast. S.J. Cummings, the tree seller, said that Todd appeared drunk and could not walk properly. She was with a dark-haired man in dark clothes. The couple drove off again, heading west on Wilshire Boulevard towards the beach.

The next morning, 16 December, Luciano flew out of Los Angeles to New York on the 7.45 flight. Mae Whitehead, Todd's maid, discovered her employer's body just over two hours later. Todd was slumped over the wheel of her brown 1934 Lincoln Phaeton convertible, wearing evening clothes and $25,000 worth of jewellery. The car was in Roland West's garage on Positano Road. The engine was still running and the garage was full of carbon monoxide.

Alice Todd, the actress's mother, confronted Fitts in his office that afternoon. She demanded the district attorney find her daughter's murderer.

A grand jury investigation into Todd's death began three days after the discovery of her body. On the first day of evidence, Whitehead said tough-looking men had been watching Todd at the Roach studio. Not only that, but a 'couple of mean-looking men' had approached the maid the day before, warning her not to mention the mob when giving evidence. Fitts's office was already aware of Bioff, Browne and the IATSE takeover. Presumably there were also mutterings about mob involvement there. Deputy district attorney George Johnson thought the Todd grand jury investigation would be the perfect moment to expose gangsterism in Hollywood. Instead, Fitts told Johnson to concentrate on proving West was the killer.

The official verdict was that Todd, coming home late, found herself locked out of her apartment above the restaurant (West had warned her to be home by 2 a.m., otherwise he would lock her out. He disapproved of her lifestyle, which earned her the nickname 'Hot Toddy'.) Extremely drunk, Todd had decided to sleep in her car. (The coroner discovered .13 milligrams of alcohol in her bloodstream. About .10 milligrams would be enough to intoxicate.) She had left the engine running to keep warm. The inquest concluded that Todd died of carbon monoxide poisoning.

However, the inquest ignored the fact that Todd's face and clothes were covered in blood, two of her ribs were fractured, a tooth was missing and her nose was broken.

Roland Button, Todd's lawyer, thought he could prove that Luciano had had Todd murdered. He demanded that Fitts reopen the case. However, studio boss Hal Roach leaned on Fitts to drop the matter.

DiCicco, for a while a suspect in Todd's death, went on to marry seventeen-year-old Gloria Vanderbilt four years later, in 1939. Vanderbilt was due to inherit $4 million on her eighteenth birthday. They divorced in 1944. DiCicco had apparently beaten up Vanderbilt on a regular basis. Her family paid him a reported $500,000 to stay away. DiCicco went on to become vice-president of United Artists Theatres.

In the end, Luciano's plan to control narcotics and prostitution in Los Angeles was wrecked not by the Outfit but by his own hubris. Luciano had attempted to put a stranglehold on brothels in New York. Although the prosecution claimed at Luciano's trial that he was earning $1 million a year through two hundred brothels, the business attempt was in fact commercially unsuccessful. The mob charged brothel-keepers $15 a week to stay in business plus another $10 weekly for each prostitute employed. Luciano's soldiers were unmoved when madams complained about the Syndicate's greed. Brothel-keepers resented Luciano eating into their profits. Whereas before they had been happy to pay something to the mob, now they withheld payments, despite isolated acts of intimidation. Instead of achieving a monopoly, the Syndicate's income began to fall.

In 1935, New York governor Herbert Lehman appointed Thomas Dewey as special prosecutor investigating organised crime.

Dewey heard about Luciano's attempt to take over New York's brothels. Luciano was arrested in February 1936, one of seventy-three prosecutions Dewey brought against racketeers. He was charged with forcing women into prostitution. His trial began on 13 May 1936. Testimonies of a number of prostitutes were crucial in convicting him. Justice Philip J. McCook sentenced Luciano to up to fifty years in prison. He was sent to New York State's maximum-security penitentiary at Dannemora. It was the harshest ever prison sentence for compulsory prostitution. (Years later, it was alleged that Dewey fabricated evidence against Luciano to further his campaign to become New York's governor. Polly Adler, a madam who ran New York's most expensive brothel in the 1930s, knew some of the girls on the witness stand. Dewey and his staff had coached each one, Adler said, to make a convincing yarn. The prosecutor threatened the girls unless they cooperated. Adler said she had never heard of Luciano earning any money through prostitution – and she was in a position to know.) Prostitutes who testified against Luciano found themselves invited out to Hollywood, where they played themselves in several quickies rushed out after the trial, including *Missing Witnesses* (1937) and *Smashing the Rackets* (1938). Bette Davis played Cokey Flo, chief witness against Luciano, in Warner Bros's *Marked Woman* (1937), with Humphrey Bogart somewhat improbably cast as Dewey.

Ten months before his conviction, Luciano had agreed a peace treaty with Nitti about Los Angeles. Even before he started seeing Todd, Luciano realised that huge opportunities were to be had in the city. Thelma Todd's ex-husband, Pat DiCicco, had moved to New York, inveigling his way into the theatre crowd. Luciano could not rely on him any longer. Now, to realise these opportunities, Luciano needed senior men on the ground in California to expand business. Hollywood may have been shrugging off the virus of a Chicago-controlled technicians' union. However, New York gangsterism was soon to attack another part of the studio system, the extras' union. The man who would take control of the extras' union was Bugsy Siegel, a gangster who so badly wanted to become a movie star that he paid for his own screen test.

CHAPTER FOUR

Mickey Mouse Mob

Bugsy Siegel, the man who invented Las Vegas, has been compared to Cézanne by the author Tom Wolfe. Siegel, Wolfe has argued, was an artist whose view of the world changed the way we see things. If Cézanne taught us to see the world as flat and solid then the signage of Las Vegas – the boomerangs, rhomboids and trapezoids pioneered by Siegel – has gone on to fill up the rest of America. Every main street in America now has the neon palettes and Day-Glo rings sported by Siegel's Flamingo Hotel, the first modern casino in Las Vegas. The city has been called the Versailles of America and Siegel its Sun King, Louis XIV. Siegel built a monument to himself and the gangster way of life – broads, booze and gambling.

Crime writer James Ellroy, author of *LA Confidential*, dismisses this view of Siegel as capitalist visionary. In reality, says Ellroy, he was a bloodthirsty thug. 'The hard truth is that these guys were pieces of garbage. If you did the real story of gangsters, it would be a stupid, fatuous tale of greed and corruption. But Hollywood only shows the sensuality of seeking more power. It doesn't show the scum that comes with it.'

Siegel was arrested for the first time when he was twenty. He was charged with rape on 26 January 1926, but his accuser disappeared. Siegel said later that the girl changed her mind about the rape accusation after deciding it was the best sex she had ever had.

The world of gangsterdom was close-knit in those early years. In

1927, Siegel married Estelle Krakower, younger sister of Capone gang member Whitey Krakower, alias Puggy White, the gangster who had advised Howard Hawks on *Scarface*. Mr and Mrs Siegel moved to the village of Scarsdale in Westchester County, north of Manhattan. Home was a substantial Tudor-style house in the suburbs. The Siegels had their first daughter, Millicent, in 1930. Barbara, her younger sister, was born two years later. Estelle told neighbours her husband was a company executive who was often away on business.

The police arrested Siegel for a third time on 12 November 1931. Siegel and nine other men, including Lepke Buchalter, Harry 'Big Greenie' Greenberg and the man who first described Jean Harlow to Longy Zwillman, Joseph 'Doc' Stacher, were arrested for convening with criminal intent. Siegel's lawyer ensured his client's photograph and fingerprints were deleted.

In September 1931, Salvatore Maranzano, self-appointed head of the New York Mafia, hired Vincent 'Mad Dog' Coll to kill Luciano. Luciano had inherited the Masseria gang after arranging the murder of his mentor, Giuseppe Masseria, the previous April. But Maranzano drew up a list of Mafiosi who posed a threat to him, among them Luciano, Siegel and Lansky. Maranzano asked Luciano to come and see him at 2 p.m. on 10 September 1931. Ten minutes later Coll was due to arrive to murder the gangster. Luciano heard about Maranzano's plan (a Maranzano soldier named Angie Caruso had got drunk in a bar one night and talked about the murder list), so he sent Siegel, Tony Fabrizzo and a couple of others to kill Maranzano first. Posing as tax officials, they called on Maranzano at his 230 Park Avenue office. The gang boss was stabbed and shot to death. Hurrying downstairs, the four men passed Coll on the stairs making his way up.

By the autumn of 1932 Fabrizzo was talking about selling his story about the Maranzano killing to the newspapers for $10,000. At this point Siegel was recuperating in hospital. A bomb had exploded in the chimney of his Grand Street headquarters but he had escaped with only a head wound. Siegel was convinced Fabrizzo had planted the bomb, so when Luciano offered him the contract on Fabrizzo he was pleased to accept. Slipping out of hospital unseen, Siegel and some of the gang members drove to Fabrizzo's parents' house on Fort Hamilton Parkway, Brooklyn. Fabrizzo answered the door himself and was machine-gunned to death.

Luciano called on Siegel's services again on 23 October 1935. Siegel was waiting in a car with Harry Greenberg and Harry Teitelbaum near the Palace Chop House in Newark, New Jersey. They were a second line of defence in case Dutch Schultz escaped from his assassins. Luciano wanted Schultz killed before he carried out his threat to murder special prosecutor Thomas Dewey. Luciano decided it was better to kill Schultz than feel the heat of a police investigation into a state prosecutor's murder. Schultz was blasted to death that night, but before he died he lingered on for hours in hospital raving incoherently to a police stenographer.

Frank Nitti had offered Luciano a clear run at drugs, gambling and prostitution in Los Angeles providing he stayed away from the technicians' union racket. At the time, the organised crime network in Los Angeles barely existed, so much so that it was known as the Mickey Mouse Mob. Historically, organised crime in Los Angeles differed from that in New York, Philadelphia and Chicago. It was an 'open city', where for the most part anybody could operate as long as he did not step on somebody else's toes. The Combination had been broken up a couple of years earlier. It depended on the support of former mayor Frank Shaw, but Shaw had not been re-elected after a police commissioner disclosed that the mayor tried to bribe him. Fletcher Bowron, the new mayor, attempted a clean up by forcing a number of early retirements in the Los Angeles Police Department and district attorney's office. Jack Dragna ran what gambling and prostitution there was in the city. Luciano sent Siegel and Lansky to Los Angeles on a reconnaissance mission. Dragna warned Siegel and Lansky to stay away from his racket. Siegel wanted to kill Dragna immediately but Lansky argued it would be better to make him an employee.

Returning to New York, Siegel and Lansky reported that prostitution and betting were low-hanging fruit ready for plucking. Not only that, but the extras' union was not part of IATSE and therefore open to takeover. Having extras go on strike could be just as damaging to the studios as a technicians' strike. Hollywood would again have to pay up or face the consequences. Of course, such a move would encroach on the deal Luciano had made with Nitti. Nevertheless, Buchalter suggested sending Siegel to Hollywood indefinitely.

Siegel was keen to go partly because he was having an affair with Ketti Gallian, a French starlet under contract to 20th Century Fox. On arrival, he rented the home of opera singer Lawrence Tibbett at 326 McCarthy Drive, Beverly Hills. Siegel negotiated the lease with Tibbett's ex-wife, Grace, who had been given the $250,000 mansion ($3.3 million in today's money) as part of her divorce settlement.

The gangster also looked up his old friend George Raft, whom he had first met in New York back in the 1920s. He borrowed $20,000 from Raft to invest in a gambling ship moored off Santa Monica. It was fashionable at the time for Hollywood stars to gamble on ships moored at sea just outside territorial waters. Gambling was legal, provided the ships did not stray within the city boundary. Raft in turn borrowed the money from agent Myron Selznick, brother of producer David O. Selznick. Siegel acquired a 15 per cent share of the gambling ship SS *Rex*. Eventually, the law changed so that gambling ships had to move further and further out to sea. Heavy swells, seasick customers and police intimidation would ultimately put such gambling ships out of business.

By now Dragna and another gangster, Mickey Cohen, were working for the Syndicate. Siegel increased the number of illegal gambling dens in the Los Angeles area from three to about twenty, opening casinos in coastal towns such as Redondo Beach as well as at Culver City dog-racing track and the Agua Caliente racecourse in Mexico. Hollywood gamblers who used to place racing bets through the mob included Al Jolson and producer Mike Todd.

Siegel's most successful venture was setting up a horseracing wire service covering the far west of California and the states of

Arizona and Nevada. In the 1930s, bookmakers had to subscribe to a wire service that supplied the names of winners, betting odds and details of jockeys. Legally, race results were delayed until declared official. In the case of photo finishes or fouls, this delay could last up to several minutes. Gamblers could take advantage of the delay, knowing the outcome of races ahead of the bookies. The most successful wire service was the Continental, covering the Los Angeles area, which the Outfit controlled. But Siegel's own wire service, Trans-America, earned him $25,000 a month.

The movie business, meanwhile, had become America's eleventh largest industry by 1939. There were more movie theatres (15,115) than banks in the USA (14,952). The studios were releasing four hundred movies each year, watched by more than 50 million Americans each week. Hollywood was grossing nearly $700 million through ticket sales alone.

Siegel took control of the extras' union. Al Smiley, a childhood friend of Siegel's, helped him organise the extras' racket. Smiley, whose real name was Allen Smehoff, was a Russian immigrant who joined the Bugs and Meyer gang as a teenager. He got his first job in Hollywood as a carpenter at Paramount. Later, he pretended to be a movie producer and director. The truth was that he had sold a few story ideas to the studios and took racing bets on the side. He was also reputed to be a pimp. He was arrested for slicing open somebody's nose during a party given by bandleader Tommy Dorsey. Siegel and Smiley decided to replicate Bioff's takeover of IATSE. First, everybody who wanted to be an extra had to join the union. Then all the studios would have to agree to hire only union members. Siegel could line his pockets with a percentage of union dues and extras' salaries. He also threatened strike action to extort thousands of dollars in 'loans' from producers. The studios were cowed by the thought of wildcat strike action. In addition, the studios would have to pay for non-existent extras. Each day's call sheet would be padded with 'no shows' – Mafia parlance for phantom names still collecting wages. Before long, Siegel's shake-down of extras was earning him $400,000 a year.

Siegel's legal problems began in 1937 when district attorney

Buron Fitts wanted to question the gangster about two mob-related murders, one of them involving Hymie Miller, a gangster linked to the extras' racket. Fitts also wanted to interview another Siegel associate involved in the extras' union, Louis Schaumberg, alias Henry 'Dutch' Goldberg. But Siegel heard about Fitts's interest and fled beyond the district attorney's jurisdiction across the state line to Nevada. Shortly afterwards, Fitts lost his job to John Dockweiler – who undermined Fitts's supposed impartiality when he revealed that MGM had been the biggest contributor to the district attorney's re-election campaign. The Siegel investigation petered out.

It is questionable whether Siegel was still involved in the drugs business. The FBI clearly thought so, repeatedly interrogating him about heroin trafficking. Siegel already had one 1929 conviction for drug dealing. But according to Warner Bros head Jack Warner's assistant Richard Gully – who later went on a Caribbean treasure hunt with Siegel – Luciano was angry with Siegel for his refusing to have anything more to do with drugs.

The Syndicate was still pushing narcotics in Hollywood. Hearst columnist Adela Rogers St Johns said that a female employee of Luciano's was feeding drugs to the teenage Judy Garland. The same woman also supplied drugs to other Hollywood actors. When MGM executive Eddie Mannix heard about this, he arranged for the woman to meet a gangster friend of his – presumably golfing partner Eddie Nealis, the man who told him about Longy Zwillman and Jean Harlow – at a fairground. The gangster and the drugs dealer went for a ride on the Ferris wheel. When they reached the top, the gangster threatened to throw the woman over the side unless she stopped selling drugs to Garland.

By 1939 Siegel had fully immersed himself in Los Angeles society life. He regularly appeared in gossip columns. He joined the Hillcrest Country Club and became a regular at movie colony restaurants including the Brown Derby, Ciro's and Romanoff's. He dated starlets such as Lana Turner and Ava Gardner. Johnny Rosselli, the mob's original man on the West Coast, introduced him to Hollywood's inner circle. Siegel began organising private craps games in the homes of moguls including Jack Warner and

Louis B. Mayer, both of whom were addicted gamblers. Jean Harlow became a friend and godmother to his daughter Millicent. Siegel also became pals with comedian Milton Berle and gave him an eight-carat diamond ring as a present. Hollywood gossip columnist Hedda Hopper remembered that Siegel would arrive at people's houses beautifully dressed, ready to play poker with actors such as Cary Grant, Clark Gable and Gary Cooper. Hopper told Siegel's biographer, 'Crooks as well as shady ladies like to mingle with celebrity.'

Society pages referred to Siegel as a 'sportsman', a euphemism for professional gambler. Siegel certainly enjoyed gambling. Often he would bet as much as $15,000 a day at the racecourse. This, he claimed to tax officials, was his only source of income.

It was at Santa Anita racecourse in Arcadia, California – where Louis B. Mayer stabled his racehorses – that Siegel first met Countess Dorothy Taylor Di Frasso. Her husband, Count Di Frasso, stayed behind in Italy while his wife gave parties in Beverly Hills. When she met Siegel, she had just ended an affair with Gary Cooper. The gangster and the countess became lovers, accelerating his introduction to Hollywood society. One night Jack Warner invited Siegel and Di Frasso over to his mansion at 1801 Angelo Drive, Beverly Hills, for dinner and a movie. But the evening was spoiled when police knocked on Warner's door and hauled the gangster off for questioning. 'I didn't want Bugsy Siegel in my house. I wasn't going to wake up one morning and see the front page saying, "Movie Tycoon Machine-gunned by Opposition Mob,"' Warner said, before adding, 'but then I wouldn't be able to read the paper anyway.'

Siegel began building a mansion of his own on Delfern Drive, in the Holmby Hills district of Bel Air. His neighbours included Humphrey Bogart, Bing Crosby and Vincent Price. Later, Bogart's pals would call themselves the 'Holmby Hills Rat Pack', pretending they too were a gangsterish mob. Their new neighbour, however, was the real thing. Siegel had his bathroom walls lined with red marble, a row of slot machines installed in the sitting room and a secret passage built behind a sliding bookshelf in his library that led up to the attic.

Siegel swam every day either in his own pool or in George Raft's. Most afternoons he spent at the Hollywood YMCA gym. Business was conducted in the steam room. When he wasn't gambling or partying, Siegel would go to bed early, applying cold cream and wearing an elastic strap around his chin to stop his profile sagging. Most nights he was asleep by ten wearing an eye mask.

One day in 1940 Siegel appeared on set at Warner Bros while Raft was shooting *Manpower* with Marlene Dietrich and Edward G. Robinson. After watching a couple of takes, Siegel told Raft that he himself would make a better movie star. Raft said later,

> Benny took a personal interest in motion pictures. He bought cameras, projectors and other equipment and often came to the studios to watch the technical processes. He asked me to photograph him one day and I took some footage of him with his camera in my dressing room, and he later showed the film at home. I had a hunch that, like a lot of people, he was a frustrated actor and secretly wanted a movie career.

Siegel also paid for his own screen test on 16mm film. He put the word out that directors were welcome to view these personal rushes but nobody took the gangster up on his offer.

The following year, Siegel met the passion of his life, Virginia Hill, a starlet who was nicknamed 'the Flamingo'. Although he was still seeing Di Frasso, he treated her with contempt. Universal Pictures had Hill under contract. Her previous boyfriends included Al Capone's cousin Charlie Fischetti and New York gangster Joey Adonis, the model for dockworker union boss Joe Friendly in *On the Waterfront*. Siegel met Hill at a party she was giving at the Mocambo restaurant. Hedda Hopper remembered Hill as having 'the swingiest parties in town'.

Virginia Hill was born on 26 August 1916 in Lipscomb, Alabama. Her real name was Onie Hill. Her father, Mack Hill, was an alcoholic mule trader and stonecutter. Presumably unable to cope with his ten children, Mack Hill sent Virginia to live with her grandmother. Virginia dropped out of school when she was fourteen. By the time she arrived in Hollywood, she had already been married three times, first to a Latin dancer, then to a college football star and finally to the scion of a wealthy Southern family. She also had affairs with a bullfighter and jazz drummer Gene Krupa.

It is likely that Hill was a courier for the mob, transporting cash for Chicago. She was still on the Outfit's payroll during the 1960s when Murray Humphreys would send her money. The FBI had evidence of her using at least twenty aliases, including Virginia Norma Hall, Virginia Herman, Virginia Gonzalez and, improbably, Virginia Oney d'Algy.

Having first moved to Los Angeles with her brother Chick, Hill rented Falcon's Lair, a house which Rudolph Valentino once owned. Hill said that Valentino's bedroom was huge; the bed alone measured twelve feet in length and had a velvet canopy over it. 'Ben and me had some great parties in that bed,' she said. 'We used to lay in bed and daydream together.'

Hill enrolled at Columbia Pictures' drama school where she took acting and elocution lessons. After she had posed for some lubricious photographs, Universal offered her a seven-year contract. Shortly afterwards, she got her first movie part, playing an heiress in *Ball of Fire* (1942), starring Gary Cooper and Barbara Stanwyck.

Siegel and Hill began having an affair. Their circle of friends included Cary Grant, his Woolworth heiress wife Barbara Hutton, and Lana Turner. The actress remembered Siegel as 'a great dancer' and Hill as 'a fun gal'.

Under such circumstances, it was impossible for Siegel to keep the affair secret. When Estelle Siegel saw a newspaper photograph of her husband and Hill together at *Ball of Fire's* premiere she initiated divorce proceedings. The couple were divorced shortly afterwards.

Meanwhile, Elmer Irey, the IRS official who had helped send Al Capone to prison, now turned his attention to tax avoidance in Hollywood. In particular, Willie Bioff piqued his interest. In 1939, the union boss had gone on a cruise to Rio de Janeiro with his wife, paid for by Joe Schenck. Flowers filled Bioff's stateroom on the SS *Normandie*. All the studio heads came to see him off, presumably hoping the boat would sink somewhere off Guyana. Mr and Mrs Bioff then spent November and December on a luxurious tour of London, Paris and the Netherlands. In London, for example, they stayed at the Dorchester Hotel. On his return, the IRS indicted Bioff for income tax evasion. He was charged with evading nearly $85,000 of tax in 1936 and 1937. At the same time, the Chicago authorities extradited Bioff back to Illinois to serve the rest of his 1922 prison sentence for pimping.

His partner in crime, George Browne, for one, protested Bioff's innocence. Browne eulogised Bioff when IATSE returned to Louisville, Kentucky for its 1940 convention. 'William Bioff has done the most remarkable job any man has ever done for labor against terrific odds, but what a price he and his family have had to pay that our members and their families might enjoy a better livelihood in their own pursuit of happiness,' said Browne, working himself up. (*International Projectionist* magazine noted that a record number of delegates' wives attended the 1940 meeting, possibly influenced by the number of prostitutes reportedly milling around the infamous 1934 convention.) Despite Browne's praise, Bioff was convicted and sent to Bridwell Prison on 15 April 1940. On his release five months later, he handed reporters a typewritten note: 'I have paid my pound of flesh to society.' He then got into his car and drove back to Hollywood.

The IRS had dropped its income tax case against Bioff when told any prison sentence would have to run concurrently with the rest of the pimping sentence. Instead, income tax officials tipped off the FBI about the $100,000 cheque Joe Schenck had given to Bioff to build Rancho Laurie. Longy Zwillman's biographer has suggested Schenck was set up in retaliation for double-crossing the New Jersey gangster over Jean Harlow back in the 1930s. Schenck swore under oath that the cheque was a loan to Bioff and not money laundering. The authorities did not believe him. In June 1940, the chairman of 20th Century Fox was indicted for perjury and tax fraud of more than $400,000.

Bugsy Siegel was having his own legal problems, having been indicted for the murder of Hank 'Big Greenie' Greenberg in Hollywood back in November 1939. When police raided Siegel's home in Bel Air they found him hiding in the attic armed with a .38 revolver and a .38 automatic.

Despite incarceration in Los Angeles County Jail, Siegel still had special food brought in. On 8 November 1940 he was seen having lunch with British actress Wendy Barrie at Lindy's, a fashionable restaurant. He was supposed to be visiting his dentist.

Jerry Giesler, Siegel's lawyer, had acted for Charlie Chaplin and Errol Flynn in the past. On 11 December 1940, assistant district attorney Vernon Ferguson asked for the murder charge to be dropped due to lack of witnesses. District attorney Dockweiler supported the motion and the case was dropped. Shortly afterwards, it was disclosed that Siegel had contributed $30,000 to Dockweiler's election campaign.

Joe Schenck's trial for fraud began in March 1941. For the first time, the public glimpsed the lifestyle of a Hollywood potentate. Schenck's secretary disclosed that her boss kept $50,000 in cash at all times in his office. His accountant testified that Schenck spent $5000 on meat and $3000 on petrol in a single year. One $63,000 bookkeeping item described as 'exchange' was a euphemism for gambling debts. Schenck even spent $500 a year on haircuts, odd considering he was nearly bald. Charlie Chaplin and two of the Marx Brothers spoke up for Schenck as character witnesses, but the jury found the 20th Century Fox chairman guilty and sentenced him to three years in prison. One suggestion is that Schenck volunteered to sacrifice himself for the rest of the industry because he was the only mogul not to have children.

But Schenck was horrified when he learned that as part of his punishment he would be stripped of his American citizenship, the implication being that he would be deported once he got out of jail. Not having spoken during his trial, Schenck now offered to tell the authorities what he knew in exchange for a reduced sentence. He agreed to disclose everything about the Hollywood extortion racket and testify against Bioff, Browne and Circella. The authorities agreed not to prosecute Schenck for what he was about to disclose. But the Hollywood producer obviously had to be careful. What he could not say was the extent of Hollywood's collusion with the Mafia – or his own stealing of hundreds of thousands of dollars from shareholders. Schenck's sentence was duly reduced from three years to eighteen months. In May 1942 he was transferred to a minimum-security prison at Danbury, Connecticut. He was released in September the same year. Another factor behind Schenck's release, according to future Outfit boss Sam Giancana, was that he had funnelled more than $500,000 from the underworld to the Democratic Party. President Truman granted Schenck a full pardon on 26 October 1945.

The New York grand jury indicted Bioff and Browne for extorting money from Fox, MGM, Paramount and Warner Bros on 23 May 1941. Two days after the indictment, Johnny Rosselli introduced Bioff to lawyer Sidney Korshak at the Ambassador Hotel in Los Angeles. By now, Rosselli was married to Hollywood actress June Lang. His neighbours included Judy Garland, her husband Vincente Minnelli and Zsa Zsa Gabor. Korshak was an ambiguous figure, the interlocutor between the mob and Hollywood, the interface between Mafia-controlled unions and the studios. Former FBI agent Bill Roemer considered Korshak the most important contact the mob had in Hollywood. Paramount Pictures' former president Frank Yablans said: 'Sidney was in the mob but the way a Jew is in the mob. They wanted him to handle Hollywood but not to kill people in Hollywood.' Korshak was so smooth that back in Chicago his nickname was 'Mr Silk Stockings'. President John F. Kennedy's mistress Judith Campbell said that everything about Korshak was 'slow, deliberate, relentless . . . Sid frightened me. I could feel the power he wielded.'

It was rumoured that Korshak had earned money when younger by working as a driver for Al Capone. The gang boss supposedly paid Korshak's law school fees because he thought it would be useful for the Outfit to have its own lawyer. On leaving law school, Korshak began defending Outfit soldiers before migrating to senior figures being harassed by the police. Korshak developed a reputation as the man to hire to solve union disputes in Chicago. In 1935, Korshak began making frequent trips to Los Angeles to see Dorothy Appleby, an actress friend of Jean Harlow's. Appleby had worked with Harlow on *Riffraff* (1936). About this time, Tony Accardo asked Korshak to move to Los Angeles permanently. Korshak's protégé, Robert Evans, production head at Paramount Pictures, said that his mentor's greatest insurance policy for staying alive was keeping silent. Korshak talked to Outfit board members in code. He gave board members codenames of American presidents. Murray Humphreys, for example, was codenamed Mr Lincoln. When Korshak and his wife Bernice got back from their honeymoon, they found a list of people who had called while they were away. George Washington, Thomas Jefferson and Theodore Roosevelt had all left messages. Bernice remarked that Sidney's friends sure had a strange sense of humour – who were they really? 'Exactly who they say they are,' Korshak replied. 'Any other questions?'

Rosselli informed Bioff that Korshak spoke on the Outfit's behalf. Korshak told the union boss that he must plead guilty. He then coached Bioff on what to say – in particular, that he had only met Rosselli once before in 1936. The Outfit was circling the wagons to protect itself. Korshak then gave Bioff $15,000 to help pay for his legal costs. Later, Korshak would deny to the FBI ever having known Rosselli.

On 6 October 1941, Bioff and Browne went on trial for extorting the studios. The two men defied Korshak and pleaded not guilty. Even worse, Bioff allowed himself to be cross-examined, walking a tightrope between maintaining his innocence and trying not to implicate anybody. Bioff's argument was that Hollywood had sought him out to take control of the bothersome technicians' union. But Mafia involvement became apparent when Warner Bros mogul Harry Warner let slip that Bioff had told him, 'the boys in Chicago insist on more money'. After three weeks of testimony and only two hours of deliberation, the jury found both men guilty. Bioff was sentenced to ten years in jail and Browne to eight.

The Outfit was unhappy that Bioff and Browne had defied it and pleaded not guilty. It wanted to send the men a warning not to talk to the authorities while in jail. Nick Circella, the gangster who first overheard Browne and Bioff boasting about their movie extortion racket back in 1933, went on the run after being indicted. Circella had gone into hiding with his girlfriend, Estelle Carey, a hostess at the Colony Club. Circella was caught on 1 December 1941 and pleaded guilty on 8 March 1942. He joined Bioff and Browne in prison. On 2 February 1943, Carey was found murdered in her apartment. Police found the weapons used to torture her in the kitchen, including an electric iron. Blood and hair covered the walls and floor of the kitchen and dining room. She had been beaten, stabbed with an ice pick and set on fire. Her flesh was charred up to her knees. One month later, Browne's wife started receiving threatening phone calls. The authorities moved Mrs Browne and her children into hiding in a New York hotel room. But if Carey's murder and threats to the Browne family were meant to intimidate Bioff into silence, it had the opposite effect. 'While we do time for them, they are murdering our families,' Bioff said. He offered to tell the authorities everything.

In early 1943 Siegel convinced the Syndicate to lend him money to build a casino in Las Vegas. What would later be known as the Strip was then a dusty line of hotels on the Los Angeles Highway. Although Hollywood has portrayed Siegel as a visionary, building a monument to gangsterism in the desert, two casino hotels – the Last Frontier and El Rancho Vegas – were already open. Indeed, the building that Siegel would christen the Flamingo after Virginia Hill was under construction before Siegel muscled his way in. The casino would cost, he told Luciano, Lansky and the others, $1 million to build.

Based on Bioff's testimony, Outfit board members Frank Nitti and Paul Ricca, along with Johnny Rosselli and five others, were indicted for conspiracy and fraud on 18 March 1943. The authorities promised Bioff a reduced jail sentence, federal protection and a new identity on release if he cooperated. At a meeting held that night at Nitti's house, everybody blamed the Outfit boss for getting them involved in the studio extortion. Nitti himself could not face going back to jail. The next afternoon he was seen staggering drunk along a railway track before shooting himself in the head.

The trial against the Outfit racketeers opened in Chicago but was quickly moved to New York in order to protect witnesses. Instead, the trial reopened on 5 October 1943. Bioff began by admitting he had lied throughout his 1941 trial. He then disclosed how the Schencks had stolen from shareholders, how the MGM chairman had bribed a private investigator with $200,000 to bury an investigation into the studio and how Korshak was Chicago's representative in Hollywood. Studio bosses then testified to the extent of the corruption. Bioff laughed out loud when a Warner Bros accountant testified that one payoff was billed to the production costs of *Gold Diggers of 1937*. In a moment of self-reflection, Bioff admitted, 'I am a low-type sort of man. People of my calibre don't do nice things. Oh yes, I am a very despicable man.' At one point, the prosecution asked about IATSE's five-year plan to take 20 per cent of Hollywood's profits. Was it true that Chicago's long-term goal was to own half of the studios themselves? Bioff replied, 'If we'd lasted that long we would have.'

During the trial, members of the Chicago projectionists' Local 110 tried to sue union officials and cinema owners. They wanted to recover wages lost through the sweetheart deals agreed between the Outfit and the studios, but the dissident IATSE members backed down when their families too started receiving threatening phone calls.

After listening to seventy-three days of testimony, the jury found all seven men guilty on 31 January 1944. Two weeks later, the judge sentenced Phil D'Andrea, Louis Campagna – a gangster who implied to Bioff he was prepared to murder him, saying, 'Anybody resigns from us resigns feet first, understand?' – Charles 'Cherry Nose' Gioe, Frankie Diamond Maritote, Ricca and Rosselli to ten years in jail each – and all of them received an individual $10,000 fine. All seven were sent to the notoriously overcrowded federal penitentiary in Atlanta, Georgia. Another conspirator, New Jersey union boss Louis Kaufman, was jailed for seven years. Kaufman ran Local 244, the New Jersey branch of the Motion Picture Machine Operators' Union whose members included Longy Zwillman's brothers Barney and Irving. But the name of the man who had first dreamed up the Hollywood extortion racket, Murray Humphreys, was never even mentioned in court.

Bioff and Browne were released after serving three years of their combined eighteen-year prison sentences. On his release, Browne withdrew from public life to live quietly with his family in Chicago. Bioff adopted his wife's maiden name and moved to the outskirts of Phoenix, Arizona. As Bill Nelson, he told neighbours he was a retired businessman. One day, however, Bioff was recognised in one of the mob-controlled casinos in Las Vegas, where, oddly, he had taken a job. On 4 November 1955, Bioff waved goodbye to his wife, climbed into his Ford pickup truck and switched on the ignition. The ensuing explosion hurled his body about 25 feet away from the vehicle. Laurie Bioff said later that her husband was a good, kind man who did not have an enemy in the world.

Like a Hollywood producer creating a blockbuster regardless of cost, by 1944 Siegel's obsession with building the Flamingo meant the budget had spiralled to $4 million and rising. The war effort meant building materials were scarce and wartime building regulations were in force. Siegel asked studio moguls to raid their props departments for timber, piping and cement. But everything kept going wrong. The casino curtains turned out to be highly flammable and had to be chemically treated; the boiler room was too small and had to be enlarged at a cost of $115,000. Siegel even spent $22,000 moving a ceiling girder in his penthouse. Fast running out of money and credit, he began selling shares in the Flamingo to friends, oversubscribing his shareholding many times over. Actress Loretta Young tried to buy Siegel's home for $85,000, a bargain considering he had spent $150,000 buying and renovating it, but they could not come to a deal. Eventually, Siegel did sell his house and its entire contents – anything to maintain the cash flow.

Siegel and Hill had now begun fighting regularly. Siegel was under pressure trying to keep Mafia investors on side. Dragna, who ran the wire service for Bugsy, was warned Bugsy had displeased the Syndicate. Hill, fed up with the Nevada desert and Siegel's pipedream, moved back to Beverly Hills, renting a house on North Linden Drive. She began having an affair with Carl Laemmle Jr, son of the founder of Universal Pictures and a movie producer in his own right. Hill and Laemmle saw each other during the summer of 1944. His presents to her included a diamond bracelet. Laemmle later calculated that his affair with Hill had cost him $5000 over a five-month period. In the middle of an argument one night, Hill ripped off a pair of earrings Laemmle had given her – while still in her pierced ears. George Raft came across Laemmle on his hands and knees scrabbling in the undergrowth for the bloody earrings.

The incident was typical of Hill's overheated personality. For Siegel, her dramatics must have been exciting at first but the histrionics must, equally, have been tiresome by the end. Virginia Hill liked to create drama by taking overdoses. Once she dislocated the vertebrae of a Flamingo cloakroom attendant she thought was flirting with Siegel. Los Angeles private eye Barney Ruditsky later told a Senate investigation that, in his opinion, Hill was psychopathic – somebody unable to feel empathy for others or remorse for her behaviour.

During the Second World War Luciano cut a deal with the American government. In February 1942 the French cruise ship *Normandie* had sunk in New York harbour while being refitted as a troop carrier. Naval intelligence suspected German and Italian agents of scuttling the liner. The Mafia agreed to spy for the government, patrolling the docks for saboteurs. In fact, as Luciano well knew, there were no Axis agents in the dockyards. The biggest threat to US cargo ships was looting by the Mafia itself. A government investigation into the sinking of the *Normandie* later concluded that the ship caught fire and capsized due to carelessness. Nevertheless, the government released Luciano from prison early as a reward for his contribution to the war effort. However, on 9 February 1946 Luciano was deported back to Sicily.

Siegel, meanwhile, decided to open the Flamingo early to try to recoup some of his investors' cash. He invited every Hollywood star he could think of to the 26 December 1946 gala opening, but newspaper publisher William Randolph Hearst made clear to studio bosses that he would name and shame actors who frequented the casino. Studio bosses including Louis B. Mayer ordered their stars to stay away from the Flamingo. Not only that but bad weather grounded the plane Siegel had chartered to ferry stars to Las Vegas. In the end, a handful of second-rate celebrities, led by Raft, struggled through the storm. Inexperienced dealers suffered big losses on the gaming tables. Because the casino was only half-finished, none of the bedrooms was open. Gamblers went home with their winnings; had there been somewhere for them to stay overnight, at least the casino would have had a chance of making some money back. Half a million dollars in the red by the end of the first fortnight, Siegel decided to close the Flamingo down until it was properly ready.

Siegel may have been strangled by debt but he still cut a dash in Hollywood. One person whom Siegel impressed was thirty-one-year-old singer Frank Sinatra. According to Sinatra's biographer Kitty Kelley, comedian Phil Silvers's wife Jo-Carroll was having dinner with her husband and Sinatra one night in 1946 at Chasen's restaurant. Sinatra stood up as Siegel walked past their table, hoping the gangster would acknowledge him. Jo-Carroll Silvers remembered the reverence with which Sinatra talked about Siegel. He began dressing like Bugsy in flashy, vulgar clothes and giving extravagant, showy presents.

More than any other Hollywood star, Sinatra is synonymous with gangsterism. *Time* magazine said of him, 'The man looks, in fact, like the popular conception of a gangster, model 1929. He has bright, wild eyes and his movements suggest spring steel; he talks out of the corner of his mouth. He dresses with a daring, George Raft kind of sassiness – rich, dark shirts and white-figured ties.'

The Mafia helped Sinatra in his career from the 1930s, when he was starting out as a big-band singer, right up to the 1960s when he was at the top of his form. As late as the 1970s, when Sinatra's friendship with President Nixon influenced the Justice Department to stop using the words 'Mafia' and 'La Cosa Nostra', Sinatra was giving benefit concerts for the families of imprisoned Mafiosi.

For some, what was so objectionable about Sinatra was that he bestowed a kind of legitimacy on gangsters. Here was this talented singer, who would become a friend of presidents and royalty, associating with hoodlums and thugs. The implication was that if Sinatra was mixing with goombahs then the Mafia was not so bad after all – a kind of absolution by association.

Jimmy 'Blue Eyes' Alo said that Sinatra always wanted to be a gangster. Bing Crosby thought that, secretly, Sinatra had always nurtured a childhood desire to be a Mafioso. Singer Eddie Fisher remembered Sinatra telling him that he would rather be a Mafia don than president of the United States. The line between right and wrong was blurred for Sinatra when he was a child. Dolly Sinatra and her husband Marty ran a bar in Hoboken, New Jersey, frequented by bootlegger Waxey Gordon. Marty Sinatra also ran with the mob, once being bludgeoned while unloading an alcohol shipment. Sinatra empathised with the powerless, which is why he turned to the Democratic Party. Perhaps he saw the mob in the same way – an organisation that stood up for the little guy, for the disenfranchised who could not turn to the law. Sinatra also had an innate dislike of authority. The Mafia was an organisation that stuck up its middle finger at convention. According to long-time Sinatra accompanist Gene DiNovi, Italians tend to break down into two kinds of people – Lucky Luciano or Michelangelo. 'Sinatra was an exception,' said DiNovi, 'he was both.'

Longy Zwillman's friend Joseph 'Doc' Stacher, who later became a silent partner in Columbia Pictures, said the mob spent a lot of money helping Sinatra. Back in the 1930s, Sinatra was desperate to get out of his contract with bandleader Tommy Dorsey. The official version was that talent agency MCA secured Sinatra's release for $60,000 – of which Sinatra contributed $25,000 (the equivalent of $625,000 today). But according to Dorsey, gangster Willie Moretti – cousin of Sinatra's first wife – threatened the bandleader at gunpoint to relinquish the singer. Not only did Willie

Moretti – who, according to the Federal Bureau of Narcotics, was one of Luciano's minions – threaten Dorsey with a gun but also the mob then invested in Sinatra's career. Luciano assigned Joe Fischetti, youngest and least powerful of the Fischetti brothers, to handle Sinatra. Sam Giancana was there to back up Fischetti should strong-arm work be needed. Luciano said before his death that the Mafia invested about $60,000 in Sinatra through a common fund with 'some guys' putting in a little more personally. It may be that this was the cash used to pay Dorsey off. In any case, Sinatra was now indebted to the mob, a debt they would never let him forget.

Chicago mob boss Sam Giancana later told his brother Chuck that, in addition to Sinatra, other stars the Outfit helped with their careers included the Marx Brothers, Cary Grant, Clark Gable and Gary Cooper. If Rosselli spotted somebody with talent, he would phone Giancana. One of the studios would then be told to offer that person a movie contract. But it was made clear that when the Outfit wanted a favour, the star would reciprocate. As Chuck Giancana put it, 'The bigger the star became, the bigger the debt to Chicago.'

Early in 1947, Fischetti telephoned Sinatra. They had known each other since 1938. Fischetti ran some Mafia-connected nightclubs and restaurants. Later he was described as 'entertainment manager' – a euphemism for somebody with mob connections – at the Fontainebleu Hotel in Miami, guarding the mob's investment. Fischetti invited Sinatra to join him and his brother Rocco on a trip to Cuba. What Fischetti may or may not have told Sinatra was that all the Mafia bosses were also flying to Havana, to pay tribute to Luciano – literally to hand over cash to the exiled *capo di tutti capi* who was visiting the island. Sinatra told the Nevada gaming commission in 1981 that all he went to Cuba for was 'to find some sunshine'.

Before flying to Cuba, Sinatra played at the Colonial Inn in Hallandale, Florida, a casino owned by Lansky and Virginia Hill's ex-boyfriend, Joe Adonis. Sinatra and the Fischetti brothers stayed at Luciano's mansion on Allison Island just off Miami Beach the night before they flew to Havana on 11 February 1947. What none of them knew was that federal agents were watching them.

Federal Bureau of Narcotics agents monitoring Sinatra and Fischetti saw each man carrying attaché cases, which they suspected contained $2 million in cash. Sinatra later said his attaché case held oil paints and artist's materials. (His wife Nancy later unwittingly contradicted him, saying his interest in painting only began at the end of 1947.) In any case, he said, a briefcase containing $2 million in cash would weigh nearly 600 pounds – assuming, of course, the money was in dollar bills.

Sinatra's friend Giancana once remarked that the only thing Hollywood stars were good for was acting as bagmen, ferrying money around the country. 'Everybody's too busy bein' dazzled by the star and askin' for their autograph to ask what's in a briefcase,' he told his brother.

In 2003, Jerry Lewis said that Sinatra acted as a courier on other occasions as well. Sinatra nearly got caught once carrying $3.5 million in fifty-dollar bills through customs in New York, said Lewis.

Luciano had registered at the Hotel Nacional in Havana. The visiting gangsters had reserved thirty-six other hotel suites. Among those paying obeisance to Luciano were Tony Accardo, Albert Anastasia, Frank Costello, Vito Genovese, Meyer Lansky, Tommy Lucchese, Carlos Marcello, Joe Profaci and Santo Trafficante. Actor Bruce Cabot (*King Kong*) was on the same flight as Sinatra, coming to pay his respects to the mob boss.

The purpose of the meeting – which inspired the sequence in *The Godfather Part II* where Michael Corleone visits exiled gangster Hyman Roth in Havana – was to decide what to do about Siegel. The gangsters were becoming agitated about their $4 million investment in the Flamingo. Lansky discovered Siegel had skimmed $600,000 from his partners and was planning to abscond to Paris with Hill. Luciano smoothed the Flamingo investors' feathers. Costello would make sure everybody got their money back, Luciano said emolliently. Indeed, Costello would step down as acting head of the New York Mafia until they did so. It was decided that Siegel had transgressed the rules of gangsterism. He would have to be punished. In effect, Luciano was signing Siegel's death warrant.

The Federal Bureau of Narcotics, meanwhile, had two informants working at the Hotel Nacional, a lift operator and a telephone operator. Both reported on comings and goings from Luciano's suite on the eighth floor and Sinatra's on the floor below. The idea was not so much to shame Sinatra as to draw attention to the problem of organised crime. At the time, the FBI did not believe organised crime existed. This was because the Mafia was blackmailing FBI director J. Edgar Hoover in order to keep his homosexuality secret. It took the mass arrest of fifty-eight Mafiosi at a summit in upstate New York ten years later for Hoover to admit he had been wrong.

New York World-Telegram society writer Charles Ventura tipped off *Washington Daily News* columnist Robert Ruark – whose column was syndicated across America – that he had seen Sinatra at the casino with Luciano on two consecutive nights. Singer and gangster had also been spotted together at the racetrack, said Ventura. The society reporter later wrote to Ruark telling him that Sinatra had attended a party at which Ralph Capone was another guest. An FBI informant said that the Fischetti brothers paid for prostitutes to be flown into Havana for a party attended by Sinatra.

Ruark castigated Sinatra for consorting with gangsters. 'If Mr Sinatra wants to mob up with the likes of Lucky Luciano, the chastened panderer and permanent deportee from the United States, that seems to be a matter for Mr Sinatra to thrash out with the millions of kids who live by his every bleat,' Ruark fulminated.

In a swipe at Sinatra's work combating racism, Ruark continued, 'This curious desire to cavort among the scum is possibly permissible among citizens who are not peddling sermons to the nation's youth and may even be allowed to a mealy-mouthed celebrity if he is smart enough to confine his social tolerance to the hotel room.'

Sinatra denied he had voluntarily mingled with gangsters, but he did admit to being on the same plane as the Fischetti brothers. And he confessed to meeting Luciano twice during his Cuba trip – although on both occasions he had only mingled with the gangster because it would have seemed rude not to. The way he had been brought up, said Sinatra, was to shake a man's hand first without investigating his past. Sinatra claimed he had only met Luciano twice at the Havana casino, despite plenty of evidence to the contrary. But in 1962 Italian police discovered a gold cigarette case at Luciano's house in Naples inscribed 'To my dear pal Lucky from his friend Frank Sinatra.'

Two months later Sinatra punched *New York Mirror* entertainment editor Lee Mortimer after he referred to him as 'Frank (Lucky) Sinatra' in a movie review. Sinatra paid Mortimer $9000 in compensation after the assault. According to the singer's actor friend Brad Dexter, Sinatra later urinated on Mortimer's grave in 1963 after the journalist died of a heart attack.

The Flamingo reopened in March 1947 but Luciano had already decided Siegel must die. Jack Warner's assistant Richard Gully said that Al Smiley was told to arrange the killing of his childhood friend or be killed himself. 'It's a heartbreaking story,' said Gully. 'Smiley loved him but he had to follow the rule of the underworld.'

But Sidney Korshak implied to screenwriter Edward Anhalt that the reason Siegel was killed had nothing to do with the Flamingo, which by now had begun to show a profit, the only thing which concerned the Mafia. Virginia Hill was also sleeping with Moe Dalitz, head of the Purple Gang in Detroit. She had shown Dalitz scars and bruises from where Siegel had beaten her up. Dalitz sent Siegel a warning but the domestic violence continued. Eventually Dalitz lost patience and arranged for Siegel to be murdered, said Korshak.

Siegel flew to Los Angeles just after midnight on Friday 20 June. He let himself in to Hill's house on 810 North Linden Drive with a key that Hill had given him. Hill herself was in Paris but her brother Chick was staying in the house with his girlfriend Jerri Mason.

The following night, Siegel drove to Jack's, a seafood restaurant in Ocean Park. Siegel had wanted to have dinner with George Raft that night but the actor had a prior meeting with a producer. Hill, Mason and Al Smiley joined him instead. They left the restaurant shortly after 9 p.m. and Siegel bought a newspaper on the way home. When they got back into the house, Siegel started sniffing the air. There was a strong smell of flowers, he said. Could any of the others smell it? Hill and Mason could not. The couple went upstairs to bed, leaving Siegel and Smiley in the sitting room. According to Gully, Smiley had been told to leave the curtains open so that the would-be assassin would have a clear aim. Smiley was also to sit next to Siegel so as not to attract suspicion. Smiley is supposed to have wondered aloud whether the gunman was a good enough marksman. Meanwhile, Hill and Mason were preparing for bed. Hill remembered his grandmother telling him that anybody who smelled flowers when there weren't any was about to die. Mason called that a silly superstition.

Suddenly it seemed to Smiley as if the room was exploding. A bullet smashed the back of Siegel's skull, blowing out his right eye and sending it flying 15 feet on to the tiled floor of the dining room. A second bullet tore through Siegel's neck, burning into Smiley's sleeve as he dived to the floor. The third bullet hit Siegel again in the neck and on exit tore a painting of an English duchess. Siegel's body jerked on the sofa as glass flew everywhere. Another bullet shattered a marble statue of Bacchus standing on the piano. Other bullets blasted the walls, tearing another hole in a painting of a nude holding a wine glass. In total, the assassin fired his .30 M1 Carbine rifle nine times. Hill and Mason ran naked into the sitting room. Seeing the blood and carnage, the girl began to scream hysterically. Smiley cowered by the fireplace, shaking uncontrollably. He was still shaking when the police arrived an hour later.

Sinatra's girlfriend Shirley Ballard remembered Sinatra taking her and some friends of his to 810 North Linden Drive shortly after Siegel's murder. There the singer sat in the bullet-riddled living room drinking a toast to Siegel's memory.

Siegel was buried next to RKO Studios in the Jewish section of the Hollywood Memorial Park Cemetery (now called Hollywood Forever Cemetery), the future resting place of Tyrone Power and

Cecil B. De Mille. None of the Hollywood pals he had made over the last ten years – Cary Grant, Lana Turner or George Raft – bothered to attend his funeral. Raft tried to buy a 2 per cent share of the Flamingo after Siegel's death but was blocked by the authorities because of police reports linking him to other underworld figures, including Mickey Cohen and Al Capone's brother John. Raft was 'very, very hurt' by the authorities' response. 'People pop off these names,' he said, 'but they never mention that I know the President and half a dozen governors.' The police never ascertained who killed Siegel or why. But in 1987, Eddie Cannizzaro, a former driver for Jack Dragna, told the *Los Angeles Herald Examiner* that he was the assassin. Cannizzaro said he was chosen because he knew Siegel and because of his accuracy with a gun.

More than forty years later, Columbia TriStar released *Bugsy* (1991), Warren Beatty's biopic of Bugsy Siegel. Siegel's story had interested Beatty for a long time. He described Siegel as a movie star who did not make movies. 'Bugsy himself is a terrific metaphor for Hollywood,' said Beatty. 'The man made himself over, got rid of his Brooklyn accent. He dressed well, he cavorted around with movie actresses . . . he developed a well-mannered, happy-go-lucky personality that concealed a real killer.'

Beatty first commissioned his friend director James Toback to write a screenplay about Siegel back in 1984. Toback, who was deeply in debt, said he could write *Bugsy* in ten days. In the end, it took him six years. Toback ploughed through some five thousand pages of screenplay before boiling down what he had to a final draft – which he then lost. He eventually delivered the script in 1990, hoping to direct it himself. But as none of Toback's films had ever found a wide audience, Beatty instead hired Barry Levinson (*Diner*). Beatty's theory was that three minds would be better than two when making the movie. 'America has always been fascinated by gangsters, no matter what period or administration,' said Levinson. 'It's part of our need as a young country, to create our own mythology.'

Bugsy won Best Picture at the Golden Globe Awards and the Los

Angeles Film Critics' Association. Nominated for ten Academy Awards, in the end it won only two – for best art direction and best costume design.

Lucky Luciano settled in Naples after the 1947 Cuba meeting that sealed Siegel's fate. He had always loved the movies. In his ghosted autobiography, he compared his childhood to 'a movie called *Oliver Twist*. It was written by some English guy by the name of Charles Dickens.' He tried to set up his life story as a film. He wrote a screenplay portraying himself as a hapless gambler wrongfully imprisoned by the authorities. Luciano approached Academy Award-winning Italian producer Paul Tamburella to see whether he was interested. Luciano said he would provide everything: the screenplay and the finance. He even nominated his girlfriend to play the love interest. Tamburella turned him down. Luciano then signed a contract with Hollywood producer Barnett Glassman for $100,000 plus 10 per cent of net profits. It says a lot about Hollywood that Lucky Luciano, possibly the most feared gangster after Al Capone, complained to an undercover narcotics agent about how he had been ripped off on the movie deal. 'Pity Humphrey Bogart is dead,' Luciano told journalists. 'Boy, that would have been the man to play Luciano. Now maybe George Raft, he's about the only tough type left.'

Despite the disaster of the Hollywood extortion trial, it would be wrong to think that by the late 1940s gangsterism was finished with Hollywood. On the contrary; the Outfit continued to be just as embedded in the studio system. Sam Giancana's wife Ange remembered going on a tour of Hollywood where they were treated better than stars by studio heads. Mrs Giancana said that famous actors behaved as if her husband was their best friend. As Sam Giancana put it, 'We're not about to turn our back on so much money, and power. Besides, those guys (Cohn, Mayer and Warner) are more than business contacts. They're our friends now.'

Gangsters' children also benefited from their parents' close ties to Warner Bros, MGM and Paramount. Children of Outfit members also went on private tours of the studios conducted by the moguls themselves. MGM executive Boris Pasternak gave Giancana's fourteen-year-old daughter Antoinette a tour of the studio, ensuring the teenager met leading actors such as James Stewart and Spencer Tracy. Murray Humphreys's daughter Llewella remembered being taken on to the set of a Joan Crawford movie in 1941. Humphreys's wife Mary had wanted to meet the actress. Crawford, who was at the peak of her fame, was filming *A Woman's Face*, playing a disfigured woman. She would only work on a closed set, barring visitors. Nevertheless, Louis B. Mayer took Mary Humphreys and her daughter on to the soundstage. Crawford stopped right in the middle of her scene and said, 'Get those two out of there. I will not have it on my set. It's closed.' Mayer went over to her and told her, 'Either they stay, or you go and you are through in pictures.'

With Rosselli being sent to prison in February 1944, Giancana took control of the Outfit's interests in Hollywood. Giancana had nothing but contempt for the movie business. 'Don't ever be starstruck by this movie baloney,' he told his half-brother Charley. According to Giancana, Hollywood was a place where everybody was waiting to be used. All anybody cared about was whether they were going to be a star or not. 'We help 'em along and own 'em,' said Giancana. Celebrities Giancana said the mob had given a career push to included Ronald Reagan, who used to share women in the same hotel room with Sidney Korshak, and talk show host Ed Sullivan. Giancana was especially contemptuous of actresses, whom he described as beautiful and dumb. As far as he was concerned, movie stars were 'worthless bums and whores'.

In February 1947, Rosselli, Ricca and the others were released on parole. All of the Chicago Seven apart from Rosselli had been transferred to Leavenworth Penitentiary, Kansas, back in 1945. It is thought the Outfit leaned on the Truman administration to release the prisoners early. Joseph Kennedy had forwarded millions of Mafia cash to the Democratic Party's election campaign.

Moving back to Hollywood, Rosselli picked up the phone and made an appointment to see his old friend Harry Cohn. Surely a sinecure could be found for his old pal Johnny? Cohn and Rosselli met at the studio boss's office. After chitchat about Cohn's family and Columbia's recent releases, Rosselli got down to business. Having been turned down once before, Rosselli asked again if he could now have a job at the studio. Rosselli later told Cohn's biographer that 'Cohn looked pained. "Johnny, how could I give you a job? The stockholders would scalp me."' Rosselli tore into Cohn, calling him 'a rotten shit'. 'Did the stockholders complain when I got ten years of prison because of you?' he asked.

Instead, Rosselli found a job at Eagle Lion Studios through his friend Bryan Foy. The Eagle Lion Studios unit churned out B-movie gangster dramas that played as the bottom half of double features. Foy had made a name for himself producing low-budget features, sometimes more than thirty a year. Like Roger Corman later, he would cut costs by shooting on sets left over from major productions. Foy specialised in gritty film noir but could turn his hand to most things – from *Rembrandt* to *I Was a Communist for the FBI*. Foy was friendly with Siegel's pal Al Smiley and, according to one FBI informant, had a reputation for hiring any gangsters or ex-convicts who came out to Hollywood looking for work.

Eagle Lion began cranking out a series of fast-paced semi-documentary thrillers based on stories ripped off from the tabloids. Rosselli was hired as an assistant purchasing agent for $50 a month before being promoted to associate producer. Eagle Lion publicist Eddie Jaffe remembered Rosselli as 'a gentleman as far as women were concerned and he actually protected some of the stars from being bothered by some of our producers'. Critics praised crime dramas *T-Men* and *Canon City* for their realism, little realising they were being made by a real honest-to-God gangster. In particular, *He Walked by Night* (1948) was based on a real 1946 Hollywood police case and inspired the television cop show *Dragnet*. 'It was very important to Johnny to prove to the Hollywood community that he was back,' remembered Betsy Duncan, a girlfriend of Rosselli's who met him in the late 1950s.

Rosselli later called his time with Foy the best years of his life. He told fellow hood Jimmy 'the Weasel' Fratiano that he wished he had stayed a movie producer rather than a gangster.

But Eagle Lion production head Max Youngstein said that Rosselli knew nothing about film production. He could not even read; all he wanted to do was chase women. Once, Rosselli and Foy chartered a plane to fly in eighteen actresses from Mexico City auditioning for a part. The story goes that they had sex with every single one, put them back on the plane and sent them back to Mexico. The movie was never made.

Despite the success of his movies, Foy did not get on with his employers and Eagle Lion did not renew his contract at the end of three years. Warner Bros offered Foy another deal but there was no room for any of his jailbird friends. Rosselli found himself out in the cold.

But he still had his loan-sharking business, lending money to stars to pay off gambling debts or for other addictions. Cohn was still using 'shylocks' – high-interest, short-term Mafia street lenders – in the 1940s if he was short of cash to meet the payroll. Other producers also borrowed from the mob. Actor Nelson Eddy was horrified when making a movie during the war years to be given his weekly salary of several thousand dollars in cash. Eddy demanded an IRS-traceable cheque. The hoodlum loan sharks supposedly shook their heads, wondering how anybody could be so honest.

Rosselli's taking charge of the Outfit's dealings with actors and studio executives was fine by Giancana. Rosselli was perfect for Hollywood, he said. 'Out there you gotta have class and Rosselli's smooth as fuckin' silk.'

Even though Rosselli was again the Outfit's capo in Hollywood, Giancana still had favours to call in. Giancana's daughter Antoinette told her father in 1949 that she wanted to become an actress. Giancana got her a foot in the door at MGM. 'If Sam wanted to send his little girl to Hollywood, or if he wanted a friend to play a movie role, or if he wanted to see the studio sights and meet some stars, he got what he wanted, and he got it with red-carpet treatment,' Antoinette Giancana recalled.

Antoinette Giancana said that in 1949 Hollywood was very much aware of the power of the Chicago underworld. 'They still,' she said, danced to the tune my father and his friends Ricca, Campagna, Fischetti, or Accardo wanted to play. One would never have found Sam at the studio in those years nor would anyone have dared talk about his influence in Hollywood. There are many who would never have known or believed it. His power was unseen, unspoken but very real – and it was awesome. Its long reach extended not just to MGM, but to Paramount, to 20th Century Fox, to Warner Bros.

But perhaps the most notorious example of the mob's influence in Hollywood still lay in the future. Rosselli would take revenge on Cohn for refusing to help him. And the incident would inspire the scene in *The Godfather* where a Hollywood producer wakes up in bed next to a horse's bloody head.

CHAPTER FIVE

'It's not a Business, It's a Racket'

'Severed from its body, the black silky head of the great horse Khartoum was stuck fast in a thick cake of blood.' So Mario Puzo, author of *The Godfather*, describes the moment when a Hollywood mogul discovers the head of his prize racehorse in bed with him. It is perhaps the most notorious incident in Puzo's 1969 novel. Johnny Fontane, an Italian singer whose career is on the turn, asks Mafia boss Don Corleone to help him get a role he wants in a new movie. Corleone sends lawyer Tom Hayden out to Los Angeles to intercede with studio boss Jack Woltz. Hayden assures Woltz that if he gives Fontane the part the studio will have no more union problems. But Woltz brushes Hayden aside. In retaliation, the Mafia destroys his $600,000 racehorse Khartoum.

Fontane is clearly based on Frank Sinatra and how the singer supposedly won his role in *From Here to Eternity*. Parallels between Sinatra and Fontane are much stronger in the book than in the 1971 film. Fontane is married to actress Margot Ashton; their marriage is based on Sinatra's unhappy relationship with Ava Gardner. Fontane's best friend is another singer, Nino Valenti. Supposedly like Dean Martin, Valenti is an alcoholic killing himself with drink. (In reality, Martin's image as a stumbling drunk was just an act – he was a light drinker.) Studio boss Jack Woltz is a mixture of Harry Cohn and Louis B. Mayer. Like Cohn, Woltz was a street hawker on New York's Lower East Side before running a sweatshop in the garment district. Like

Mayer, he has become fascinated by horses and now owns his own racing stud farm.

Clearly, Sinatra also thought Fontane was based on himself. One night after the book was published in 1969 Puzo was having dinner at Chasen's restaurant in Los Angeles. A mutual acquaintance suggested Puzo introduce himself to Sinatra, who was sitting nearby. Sinatra began swearing at the author, threatened to break his legs and called him 'a stool pigeon and a fink for the FBI'.

It is important to understand the tight corner Sinatra found himself in at the beginning of the 1950s. Louis B. Mayer had fired Sinatra in April 1950 after word got back to the MGM boss of Sinatra badmouthing him. By 1951, Sinatra's career appeared to be in freefall. His relationship with Ava Gardner was tempestuous and making him suicidal. His record company had dropped him, his television show was cancelled and he had even been let go by his agent. Now a Senate committee investigating organised crime had photographs of him with his arm around Lucky Luciano during the 1947 Cuba trip. It was about to pour the last shovelful of earth on what had been his career. Nevertheless, a few friends still rallied around – one of whom was Mickey Cohen.

When Bugsy Siegel died in 1947, Mickey Cohen proclaimed himself king of the Los Angeles underworld. Like Siegel, Cohen loved publicity. Owney Madden, the gangster who had brought George Raft into the Mafia, also brought the teenage Cohen into the fold. Cohen had fled to Los Angeles from Chicago after killing a man in public. He agreed to work for Siegel as an enforcer, robbing and beating up people. One of his first robberies was at a nightclub on Sunset Strip, where he robbed actress Betty Grable of her jewellery. On another occasion Cohen and his gang robbed a brothel, one of whose clients was a Hollywood producer with $45,000 of studio cash on him. The money was meant to finance a production. In time, Cohen would invest in movies himself.

After Siegel's murder Cohen opened a gambling den in Burbank, near Warner Bros and the other studios. Warner Bros's chief of police, Blaney Matthews, was on Cohen's payroll. Matthews was the former district attorney's office investigations chief who acted

as go-between when MGM wanted to bribe district attorney Buron
Fitts after Paul Bern's murder. Every afternoon, Cohen's Burbank
casino would be full of extras gambling their wages away, Red
Indians rolling dice next to showgirls and medieval knights.

Cohen put up the money for Dean Martin and Jerry Lewis to
bring their act to California early on in their careers. Errol Flynn,
Robert Mitchum and Ben Hecht were all friendly with Cohen, as
was Judy Garland. Cohen leaned on scandal magazine *Hollywood
Night Life* to drop a story about Garland's drug addiction. Jimmy
Durante once paid a $20,000 fine to get Cohen out of jail. Another
friend of Cohen's in the 1950s was comedian Red Skelton. Sam
Giancana was later recorded by the FBI telling an associate that
Red Skelton had been taken over by a mob associate who in turn
was refusing to share his profits with the Outfit. It was common
knowledge around Hollywood that Skelton's manager was sleeping with his client's wife. Coming across the manager one night in a
Beverly Hills restaurant, Cohen clambered on to his table and
kicked him in the face until he was unconscious.

Sinatra was also Cohen's pal. The gangster arranged a testimonial dinner for Sinatra at the Beverly Hills Hotel in 1951 but it
was poorly attended.

Meanwhile, the Senate committee investigating organised crime
across America confronted Sinatra. The Senate Special Committee
to Investigate Organised Crime in Interstate Gambling, chaired by
Senator Estes Kefauver, had obtained Federal Bureau of Narcotics
photographs showing Sinatra with Luciano. Presumably, Kefauver
saw the chance to bask in the publicity glow of a Hollywood star. If
Sinatra had to give televised evidence before the Kefauver committee, it would destroy what was left of his career.

The first Kefauver committee hearings in Miami were held in
private in May 1950, but Kefauver was aware of the publicity
Senator Eugene McCarthy's hearings into supposed Communist
subversion of Hollywood had generated in 1947–8. He calculated
that televising his own hearings would help his presidential aspir-
ations. He therefore invited television networks to cover his
committee as it criss-crossed America, from Cleveland to Tampa

and Detroit. Snippets of the hearings began appearing on the evening news. Then in January 1951, local television station WNOE-TV began televising the New Orleans session in full. Ratings were impressive and other stations followed suit. By the time the committee convened in New York, *Time* magazine was sponsoring this new kind of 'infotainment' that we are so familiar with today. In many ways, the Kefauver committee was the precursor of the televised trial of the Menendez brothers or the O.J. Simpson murder case of the 1990s; it was the forerunner of cable television station Court TV. Americans sat mesmerised in front of their big new television sets as Frank Costello, Meyer Lansky, Albert Anastasia and others gave evidence. Witness Virginia Hill was supposedly asked before her appearance why it was that men gave her money, jewellery and furs. 'Because I'm the world's best lay,' was her reported reply. In court Hill claimed never to have been very friendly with Bugsy Siegel – and then punched a woman reporter outside the courtroom. Soon Kefauver, with his Davy Crockett-style coonskin cap and toothy grin, was as popular a television star as Lucille Ball. Twenty million Americans watched Kefauver's exposé of organised crime.

One footnote that attached itself to the Kefauver committee was the mob's attempt to move in on the early television business. Based on their experiences with jukeboxes, Lansky, Costello and others decided the future of television lay in men sitting around in bars watching vaguely pornographic film clips. They set up a company, Consolidated Television, to produce these video jukebox reels. But the idea foundered when it became clear that people preferred to watch television at home. As Lansky admitted to the committee, 'We should have gone in at the home-set end, and maybe I would have been a very rich man today.'

The name of one Jewish-Canadian family, the Bronfmans, came up repeatedly during the hearings but no family member ever testified. During the New York session, one witness implied that the four Bronfman brothers ran hotels used for prostitution. By Prohibition, the Bronfmans had moved into the alcohol business. Costello and Longy Zwillman admitted smuggling Bronfman alcohol in speedboats across Lake Erie in Illinois. Booze even flowed through a pipeline from Canada into America, running from Emerson, Manitoba, to a barn a few miles south in Pembina, North Dakota. In 1926, Samuel and Harry Bronfman became Canadian licensees and distributors for the Distillers Company of London and Edinburgh, which supplied half the world's whisky. The following year the Bronfmans bought Canada's largest rye whiskey manufacturer, Joseph E. Seagram and Sons. The Bronfmans made millions selling booze to gangsters, which was then resold in America at inflated prices. 'Of course we knew where it went,' Sam Bronfman told *Fortune* magazine in 1966, 'but we had no legal proof. And I never went to the other side of the border to count Seagram bottles.' By the repeal of Prohibition in 1933, Seagram was the second-largest distributor of spirits in North America. As is often the case, the son of the man who founded the family fortune decided the alcohol business was boring. Sam Bronfman's son Edgar tried to gain control of Paramount Pictures in the 1960s. He managed to buy a 15 per cent share in MGM. Sam Bronfman asked his son whether he was buying all this movie stock just to meet actresses. 'Oh no, Pop,' Edgar replied. 'It doesn't cost $40 million to get laid.' In 1995 Sam Bronfman's grandson, Edgar Jr, moved Seagram into the entertainment business. Seagram acquired entertainment conglomerate MCA – owner of Universal Studios – for $5.7 billion.

Another name that came up in the committee hearings was that of Sidney Korshak. Witnesses including Charles 'Cherry Nose' Gioe – jailed for his role in the 1930s Hollywood shakedown – and mob tax lawyer Eugene Bernstein referred to Korshak and his part in the scandal. Kefauver decided to go after Korshak, who, by 1951, was established as organised crime's legal representative in Hollywood. (Puzo later denied basing Corleone family lawyer Tom Hayden on Korshak.) Ironically, the Kefauver committee gave Korshak the opportunity to further enhance his reputation. After much advance publicity, the committee moved its investigation to Chicago. There Kefauver met Korshak for forty-five minutes, during the course of which Korshak produced some photographs.

They showed the forty-seven-year-old senator in bed with two showgirls. The mob had rigged up an infrared camera in Kefauver's bedroom at the Drake Hotel in Chicago. Supposedly, Korshak threw the photographs on Kefauver's desk saying, 'Now, how far do you want to go with this?' Kefauver and his staff suddenly left Chicago without holding its much-publicised hearings. A friend of Korshak's who saw one of the photographs told the *New York Times*: 'Sid showed it to me. That was the end of hearings, and this also made Sid a very big man with the boys.'

In October 1952 Korshak put together a consortium that attempted to buy RKO from Howard Hughes. Its members included Ray Ryan, one of Costello's business partners, and Chicago businessman Ralph Stolkin who had made a fortune with the punchboard, a primitive gambling device. Korshak was described in the press as 'a sort of catalytic agent excluded from the group which purchased Hughes's stock'. Hughes changed his mind about selling after news of the deal broke in the *Wall Street Journal*. Nevertheless, Korshak remained connected to the studio. According to an FBI report dated 7 May 1962, Korshak had considerable stock in RKO and handled its union problems.

Korshak may have sashayed away from Kefauver but the senator still had Sinatra. By March 1951, after eleven months on the road interrogating eight hundred witnesses in fifteen cities, his committee was winding down. Nevertheless, Kefauver had obtained eight photographs of Sinatra snapped during his 1947 Cuba trip. As well as the one showing him on the balcony of the Hotel Nacional with his arm round Lucky Luciano, another showed Sinatra sitting with the exiled mob boss in the Havana casino. Yet another showed Sinatra with Johnny Rosselli. Kefauver told committee lawyer Joseph Nellis to arrange a meeting with Sinatra. Nellis duly met him and his lawyer Sol Gelb at four o'clock on the morning of 1 March 1951 at the Rockefeller Center in New York. Nellis thought that Sinatra came in looking 'like a lost kitten, drawn, frightened to death'. Sinatra denied being a bagman for the mob and said he knew Adonis, Costello, Lansky, Siegel and Zwillman only vaguely. He said that he first met Joe Fischetti backstage at a Chicago theatre in 1946. Occasionally, he and Fischetti would have dinner together, or go to the theatre, or go for rides on Fischetti's boat. Nellis questioned Sinatra about his friendship with Willie Moretti. Sinatra admitted that Moretti made some bookings for the band early in his career but that was the extent of their relationship. The singer complained that he was being railroaded for the crime of association. 'You go into show business, you meet a lot of people. And you don't know who they are or what they do,' Sinatra said. After two hours, Nellis had learned nothing that would justify Sinatra appearing before the committee. At 5.48 a.m. the committee's co-counsel told Sinatra and Gelb they were free to go. Sinatra had wriggled out of this Senate investigation, but in the future he would give evidence about his Mafia connections before five grand juries and the New Jersey State Crime Commission.

In the end, the Kefauver committee uncovered very little. It entertained viewers by forcing war, surly hoods into the open, where they were prodded and poked by senators like freshly captured rhinos. One resonant image was a close-up of Frank Costello's tattooed thumbs wrestling as he tried to avoid questions – the mob boss had agreed to testify only if his face was not shown. Years later, Marlon Brando would base Don Corleone's voice on Costello's after listening to his Kefauver committee evidence. A botched childhood operation to remove Costello's adenoids and tonsils had left him with a hoarse whisper lending authority to whatever he said.

Sinatra told Ava Gardner that Giancana kept his career on life support in 1950. Giancana was the secret owner of the Worldwide Actors Agency, whose clients included Jimmy Durante. The mobster ensured Sinatra got nightclub work, even when venues did not want him and audiences were cold. In January 1950, Sinatra had played the Shamrock in Houston, where Al Smiley had influence. In March that same year he sang at the Copacabana Club in New York, of which Frank Costello owned a percentage. He would go on to become a regular at Skinny D'Amato's 500 Club in Atlantic City, New Jersey. When British actor Donald Sinden expressed surprise that a star of Sinatra's magnitude was playing such poky clubs, Sinatra admitted that the mob made him do it.

Sinatra first performed in Las Vegas in 1951, playing at the

Desert Inn, controlled by Lansky's television business partner Moe Dalitz. He then took up residency at the Sands Hotel, owned by Joseph 'Doc' Stacher – although its profits were split between the mob. Sinatra was offered a 2 per cent share of the casino for $54,000.

James Jones's eight-hundred-page novel *From Here to Eternity* was published in February 1951. Columbia Pictures president Harry Cohn bought the film rights to the novel. Although a bestseller, *From Here to Eternity* was regarded as unfilmable because of its sympathy with an adulterous affair and criticism of the army. At the time, Martin Jurow was a William Morris agent in New York. Jurow, who would go on to produce *Breakfast at Tiffany's* and *Terms of Endearment*, remembered fellow agent George Wood bringing Sinatra into his office. Wood, who was friendly with Costello and Lansky, wanted to know if Jurow had any ideas as to what might revive Sinatra's career. Jurow knew that *From Here to Eternity* was being cast and there was something about Sinatra's despondency that day that reminded him of bullied, picked-upon Private Maggio. Shortly afterwards, Jurow suggested Sinatra to director Fred Zinnemann, who said he was interested. Cohn, however, was adamant on the phone to Jurow. He would not have 'that bum' Sinatra working in his studio.

Hours after Cohn's telephone tirade, Jurow went to see George Wood at his apartment on Central Park South. Wood had somebody with him, Jimmy 'Blue Eyes' Alo, a friend of Meyer Lansky's tied to the Genovese crime family. Alo was also a friend of Wood's. Journalist Lee Mortimer – the man who had sued Sinatra for assault in 1947 – said that the mob was tied in with the larger talent agencies, clawing back as much as half the earnings of some of the $10,000-a-week television and film stars whom it had helped. Indeed, investigative reporter Hank Messick said that Alo became a shareholder in William Morris in 1955. (One day Alo had dropped by the William Morris office to see Wood and found a new receptionist on duty. When he told her his name was Jimmy Blue Eyes, she buzzed Wood and said, 'Mr Eyes is here to see you.')

Jurow explained to Alo how Cohn was blocking Sinatra from

having the part. 'Harry Cohn, huh?' Jurow remembered Alo saying. The gangster asked whether the agent had Cohn's private number. Then he patted Jurow on the head. 'He owes us,' said Alo. 'Expect a call.'

Meanwhile, Ava Gardner also suggested that Sinatra would be perfect for Maggio to her friend Joan Cohn, wife of the studio boss. Gardner pitched the idea of Sinatra in the film to Cohn himself. Sinatra campaigned to get the part throughout the second half of 1952. He saw the role as reviving his career. The unmade film was by now being touted as a potential Academy Award winner. Sinatra had lunch with Cohn but the studio head was adamant the part would go to a proper actor. 'You're nothing but a fucking hoofer,' Cohn is supposed to have said. 'Who the fuck,' Cohn asked his assistant Jonie Taps as Sinatra was leaving, 'would want to see that skinny asshole in a major movie?'

It was at this point that the mob is thought to have interceded. Frank Costello supposedly told friends over dinner at the Copacabana that he received a phone call asking for his help. Although Costello was not particularly friendly with Sinatra, he telephoned Mafia associates who controlled Hollywood unions asking them to apply pressure. One version of events has Mafia associate Jack Farrell, who worked for Costello, flying to Los Angeles and meeting Johnny Rosselli.

Despite being fired from Eagle Lion, Rosselli continued to invest in its movies. In 1951, he ploughed $400,000 into the company in exchange for a 10 per cent revenue share. He also tried to become a producer himself, buying the rights to a religious story, *The End of the Santa Fe Trail*. Being a movie producer is a relentless job, involving persistence, passion and a sprinkling of luck. Presumably, Rosselli found life as an independent just too tough.

Together, Rosselli and Farrell paid a call on Cohn, pointing out how much he owed to the mob. By the early 1950s, Columbia employed 19,000 people and had an annual payroll of $18 million. Despite what he had achieved, Cohn had no illusions about Hollywood. Summing up the industry one day, he said, 'It's not a business, it's a racket.' Rosselli and Farrell told him that without

Mafia money there would be no Columbia Pictures. Joan Cohn told Ava Gardner's biographer that one day two Mafiosi turned up at Columbia and told her husband he was *going* to cast Sinatra. Louis B. Mayer's former assistant Meredith Harless said she heard Rosselli had given Cohn an ultimatum – either cast Sinatra or the mob would have the studio boss killed.

Years later television presenter Steve Allen and his wife went to a preview of *The Godfather*. A lot of New Jersey Mafiosi were also at the screening. When the lights came up, Mrs Allen turned to her husband and wondered aloud if the horse's head was the way Sinatra had won the role in *From Here to Eternity*. The next morning the Allens awoke to find a horse's leg on their front porch. Allen suspected that Jonie Taps, Harry Cohn's former assistant and a friend of Johnny Rosselli's, was behind the intimidation.

Of course Sinatra always denied Costello had intervened and he successfully sued the BBC for making the allegation. Cohn disliked Sinatra so much that he made him pay his own plane fare back from Africa to Hollywood for the screen test. Fred Zinnemann said that Sinatra was his first choice for Private Maggio, just as Montgomery Clift had been his choice for the lead – again against Cohn's wishes. And Puzo himself pointed out *The Godfather* was mostly made up, a fairy story for grown-ups – consider how one could slip a horse's head into somebody's bed without him waking up.

On the other hand, Sinatra's factotum, George Jacobs, once asked his employer if Giancana had leaned on Rosselli to lean on Cohn to give him the part. 'Hey, I got that part through my own fucking *talent*,' he said – and then gave Jacobs a wink.

Sinatra's career was still in the doldrums as he waited for *From Here to Eternity* to be released in August 1953. In terrible debt, Sinatra was desperate for work. He was, claimed one Mafioso, begging for nightclubs to sing in. In response, the Boston-based Palladino Mafia family – Joseph Palladino Sr, known as Joe Beans; Joseph Jr, known as Little Beans; and Rocco Palladino, brother of Joe Beans – said Sinatra could sing at their Copa nightclub. After his act, Sinatra asked to borrow money from Joe Beans. His comeback movie, *From Here to Eternity*, would be out in a month.

The cash would be repaid, said Sinatra, when he next came to sing at the Copa. Joe Beans lent him the money. As Sinatra predicted, *From Here to Eternity* was a hit. It was nominated for ten Academy Awards and won eight Oscars at the 1954 ceremony, including Best Supporting Actor for Sinatra's performance. It also sky-rocketed Sinatra's future potential earnings. The singer had accepted a scale $8000 fee for *From Here to Eternity*. Four years later, this ballooned to $150,000 plus 30 per cent of net profits for *Pal Joey* (1957). Sinatra repaid Joe Beans the money he owed, but he reneged on his promise to play the Copa again. The Palladinos never forgave him.

In hindsight, Gardner came to regret Sinatra reviving his career. 'When he was down and out he was so sweet,' she said. 'But now that he's gotten successful again, he's become his old arrogant self. We were happy when he was on the skids.'

Johnny Rosselli, meanwhile, was next offered freelance work as associate producer at Poverty Row studio Monogram Pictures. In the 1940s alone Monogram produced 402 movies, employing people who could not find work elsewhere. Rosselli was friendly with Monogram board director George Burrows. The gangster also found work at Mutual Pictures, a rival film company whose president, Jack Dietz, had once owned the Cotton Club in Harlem. In 1952, all three men – Rosselli, Burrows and Dietz – formed a joint company to executive produce science-fiction movie *Invasion USA*. The production company went on to make *Paris Model* (aka *Nude at Midnight*) the following year.

With his career righting itself, Rosselli moved into the Garden of Allah bungalow apartments, whose other residents included Humphrey Bogart and Edward G. Robinson. After his divorce from June Lang in 1942, Rosselli dated other actresses including Betty Hutton and the impossibly beautiful Anne Corcoran, who had written more than 250 letters to him in prison. He also became friendly with another young actress introduced to him by Joe Schenck. Later, the world would come to know her as Marilyn Monroe.

CHAPTER SIX

Chrome-Tipped, Fin-Tailed Blondes

In 1948 seventy-year-old Joe Schenck was being driven through the 20th Century Fox lot when he saw an attractive girl walking ahead. He told his chauffeur to pull over and called the girl over to his limousine. The girl told him that she was under contract to the studio for $74 a week. Schenck gave the girl his telephone number, little knowing that she had been christened Norma after his first wife, Norma Talmadge. The creation, and lover, of William Morris agent Johnny Hyde, she was now calling herself Marilyn Monroe. Like many sexually adventurous women, Monroe may have been molested as a child. She certainly claimed that she was sexually abused in an orphanage. In a sense, she continued to act out pleasing older men. Monroe told her friend Amy Greene, using an obvious allusion, that at the beginning of her career she spent a lot of time on her knees. On the other hand, she pointed out to British journalist W.J. Wetherby, 'You can't sleep your way into being a star, though. It takes much, much more.' Once asked straight out in an interview, Monroe denied having had sex with Schenck. She told friends that Schenck had trouble maintaining an erection but he loved playing with her breasts.

Schenck introduced Monroe to Johnny Rosselli, who is also thought to have received sexual favours from the starlet in exchange for help with her career. Monroe's friend and neighbour Jeanne Carmen said she met Rosselli at Monroe's apartment several times. When Monroe was let go from Fox, Schenck telephoned Harry Cohn's assistant Jonie Taps asking for Monroe to be taken on for twenty-six weeks. Columbia Pictures gave Monroe a six-month contract at $75 a week in March 1948. (Seven years later, when asked what signing the fattest movie deal in Hollywood history meant to her, Monroe told reporters, 'It means I'll never have to suck another cock again.')

Cohn, however, was unimpressed with what he saw even though, according to Sam Giancana, he too enjoyed Monroe's sexual favours. He therefore did not bother renewing Monroe's contract. Watching the rushes of a movie in which Monroe briefly appeared, Cohn turned to the producer and asked, 'Why'd you put that fat cow in the picture? You fucking her?'

During the 1950s, Monroe came under investigation for her contacts with the Mafia, although federal agents were unaware of the Rosselli connection. Towards the end of 1959 Los Angeles District Attorney's office investigators Frank Hronek and Gary Wean saw Monroe leaving a Sunset Boulevard restaurant with another woman and two men. One of the men was Mickey Cohen associate George Piscitelle. Monroe and Piscitelle were observed checking into a motel on Van Nuys Boulevard. Monroe was also later seen with another Cohen gang member, Sam LoCigno. The state prosecutor's office suspected Monroe was being blackmailed but the investigation fizzled out.

Cohn, of course, rued the day he let go of the 1950s' biggest star. Soon Hollywood had a production line of big, curvy blondes – Jayne Mansfield, Mamie Van Doren, Diana Dors – all signed to compete with Monroe and built like that decade's Chevys and Buicks. Columbia's own Monroe *manqué* was Kim Novak, the Pygmalion creation of Harry Cohn who groomed Novak to replace Rita Hayworth, who had upped and left him. Nevertheless, Cohn used to call Novak 'that fat Polack' behind her back.

Columbia reinvented Novak as a lavender blonde, a gimmick to distinguish her from all the other chrome-tipped, fin-tailed blondes. 'Miss Novak,' cooed studio publicity, 'sleeps in lavender-scented sheets and bathes in lavender bubble bath while making calls on her lavender-coloured phone.' In fact, Novak detested the colour lavender.

Cohn's reinvention worked despite Novak's own misgivings about her acting ability. The former Miss Deep Freeze said of herself that she could open a refrigerator door 'gracefully, that was it. Period.' Nevertheless by 1956 Novak was Columbia's most popular star, receiving 3500 fan letters a week. Like many stars Novak was a blank screen on to which the audience could project its emotions – something Alfred Hitchcock caught in *Vertigo* (1958) when James Stewart forces Novak to impersonate his fantasy of a dead woman.

Novak began to chafe against Cohn's I-can-make-her-I-can-break-her attitude. She was angry that Cohn pocketed $100,000 for lending her to United Artists for *The Man With the Golden Arm* (1955), starring Sinatra – and told journalists so. Cohn in turn was furious that Novak's salary grievances were mentioned in a July 1957 *Time* magazine cover story. About this time, Novak met nightclub singer Sammy Davis at a party given by Tony Curtis and his wife Janet Leigh. 'I'm awfully glad to see you,' said Novak with a smile. 'I admire your work tremendously.' The two spent the night deep in conversation. Each resented the circumscribed world they found themselves in. Davis was held back by the colour of his skin, while Novak was suffocated by Cohn's hold over her. Shared claustrophobia gave their relationship instant sympathy and earnestness.

It is difficult to imagine more of an outsider than Davis. The odds were so stacked against him. He was black and, according to one ex-lover, bisexual to boot. During the Second World War Davis was attacked by his fellow soldiers. He was ordered to repeat army basic training at the Fort Francis E. Warren base in Cheyenne, Wyoming, several times. White soldiers repeatedly beat him up, broke his nose permanently and forced him to drink beer laced with urine.

After the war, Davis toured America with his struggling nightclub act, the Will Mastin Trio. The other two members were his father and uncle. Davis did not want to break up the act for fear of upsetting his father, even though Davis Jr was the performer audiences wanted to see. His break occurred in 1951 when he opened for singer Janis Paige at Ciro's nightclub in Los Angeles. Paige was an average singer who only got the booking because she was married to Errol Flynn. Davis, who was only meant to be on stage for twenty minutes as a warm-up, performed for two hours, egged on by Hollywood celebrities in the audience, among them Clark Gable and Humphrey Bogart. For his finale, Davis brought the house down with impressions of white stars including Frank Sinatra and Jerry Lewis.

Davis's career rocketed but in November 1954 he was badly hurt in a car crash. He lost an eye after impaling it on the Cadillac ornament on his steering wheel. In March 1955, he returned to Ciro's cheered on by Hollywood pals including Bogart, Lauren Bacall and Cary Grant. He began working nightclubs again but would be devastated to hear somebody call out 'nigger' after receiving six standing ovations.

Davis also found himself in debt to the mob. Hopelessly extravagant, he would borrow cash from nightclub owners which he would then have to pay off by working another night. Soon he was working round the clock just to meet interest payments. Because the Mafia owned every nightclub he was in fear of mob retribution. As Davis's business partner, former William Morris agent Sy Marsh, explained, 'Either you hung out with the mob and became very buddy-buddy or you tried to keep a respectful distance. What you never wanted to do was to owe them.'

Cynics suggested that Davis was only interested in Novak because publicity from the affair might help his career. Novak having a relationship with a black man was seen as a way of flaunting her independence to Cohn. Davis later said that the glue of their relationship was defiance.

According to the studio publicity machine, in 1957 Columbia was at the top of its form. It had released forty-seven films that year, making a $10 million profit. Privately, however, Columbia's board was feeling mutinous. The studio had painted a bleak picture at a New York shareholders' meeting. Columbia expected to make a loss in the first financial quarter of 1958. Just two movies, the Academy Award-winning *Bridge Over the River Kwai* and *Pal Joey*, accounted for 1957's profit – and Cohn had been overruled by New York when he tried to stop *Kwai* being made. In December

1957, the studio held a dinner in New York to commemorate Cohn's brother Jack, who had died the year before. During the evening, a marketing assistant whispered something into Cohn's ear. Guests saw his hands shaking as he got up and left the room. Doctors later diagnosed that Cohn had suffered a heart attack when told about the affair. A couple of hours later Cohn telephoned his assistant and told him Novak was 'fucking that coloured Cyclops, Sammy Davis'. He had a second heart attack the next day flying back to Los Angeles.

Columbia's board members and several shareholders pressured Cohn to end the affair after it became public knowledge in January 1958. Novak was, after all, one of Columbia's biggest box office draws. Cohn threatened to have the mob 'put out Sammy's other eye'.

Frank Costello telephoned Mickey Cohen from New York and told him to meet the Columbia boss. Costello explained that Cohn had done the mob some favours in the past. Now Cohn wanted Cohen to murder Davis, or 'that fucking nigger bastard' as the mogul called him. When they met, Cohn explained to Cohen that Novak's affair was hurting her status in the film community. However, Cohen got the firm impression that Cohn lusted after Novak himself.

Cohn was also friendly with Frank Sinatra's agent at William Morris, George Wood. Sinatra had just made *Pal Joey* for Columbia. According to Jimmy 'Blue Eyes' Alo, Wood asked Alo to lean on Davis, but the gangster demurred, saying he did not do that kind of thing.

Davis's father, Sam Davis Sr, used to spend afternoons at the Hollywood Park racetrack in Inglewood, Los Angeles. One afternoon at the beginning of January 1958, Cohen approached Davis Sr and told him he was under orders to harm his son. When Davis Sr panicked, Cohen told him the only solution was for Davis to marry a black girl within the next twenty-four hours.

Meanwhile, two gangsters accosted Davis. One of them said, 'You're now a one-eyed nigger Jew. You ever see this blonde again, you're going to be a blind nigger Jew. You're getting married this weekend – go figure out who you're marrying.' Photographer Billy Woodfield heard raised voices from Sinatra's Las Vegas dressing room before Davis emerged and began pacing up and down. Wood-field heard Sinatra saying, 'Get me Fischetti.' Sinatra spoke on the telephone, presumably to Joe Fischetti, the singer's Mafia handler, and then talked to Davis again. Davis left looking 'really distraught'.

Arthur Silber Jr, whose father was Sammy Davis's agent, was staying with Davis in Las Vegas. Davis, said Silber, called his supposed friend Sam Giancana, head of the Chicago Outfit (the same Giancana who called Davis a 'nigger weasel' behind his back). Davis asked to speak to 'the doctor' – Giancana used the alias 'Dr Goldberg' when visiting Las Vegas. According to Silber, Giancana told Davis he could protect him when he was in Chicago or Las Vegas but not in Hollywood. He further warned him not to go to Los Angeles unless he made peace with Cohn.

Davis riffled through his address book for somebody to marry. He picked out a black chorus girl named Loray White. They were married on 10 January 1958. The new Mrs Davis spent the night in the presidential suite of the Sands Hotel but the marriage was never consummated. Giancana called Davis from Los Angeles, reassuring him, 'Mickey says the pressure is off. You can relax.' Davis and White divorced a couple of months later, White pocketing $25,000 in cash plus another $10,000 in clothes and shoes.

Burt Boyar, a newspaper columnist who ghosted Davis's two autobiographies, never felt that the singer's life was in danger. Davis was far more valuable to the mob than Cohn because the Mafia owned every nightclub Davis sang in. But former William Morris agent Sy Marsh insisted that 'Sammy was inches away from getting killed'. Indeed, Kim Novak remembered being called into Cohn's office 'where she found him "surrounded by all these men, including people in the mob"'.

Cohn died of a heart attack on 27 February 1958, two months after learning about the affair. His widow Joan blamed Kim Novak for killing her husband.

It is thought that Cohn held shares in Columbia on behalf of gangster investors, using his shareholding to mask their invest-ment. With Cohn dead these investors wanted to reclaim their shares without their names becoming public, as would happen during probate. Cohn left $4 million to his widow Joan, who hired Sidney Korshak as her lawyer. A union lawyer with mob connections is not an obvious choice for probate work. Indeed, Korshak's speciality was circumventing probate. He connived for Joan to marry his friend Harry Karl, head of the Karl's Shoes chain. The FBI described Karl as 'an associate of many hoodlums arriving in Los Angeles from Chicago'. His ex-wife, Marie 'the Body' Macdonald, was an old girlfriend of Bugsy Siegel's – and her first husband had been gangster-cum-agent Victor Orsatti, brother of Louis B. Mayer's pal Frank. Joan Cohn and Harry Karl were married in Korshak's apartment on 1 September 1959. They divorced three weeks later. Some considered this was all the time Korshak needed to spirit away the mob's assets.

Another of Rosselli's girlfriends during the 1950s was Lana Turner. In a sense, Turner was the bridge between Jean Harlow and Marilyn Monroe. Like Monroe, she was an abused child farmed out to various family friends during childhood. One family Turner stayed with used to abuse her physically. Looking back, Turner admitted, 'the shock I suffered then may be a valid excuse for me now. It may explain things I myself do not understand.'

After being discovered at the age of fifteen while playing truant from Hollywood High, Turner starred opposite John Garfield in *The Postman Always Rings Twice* (1946). In the early 1950s she was one of the biggest stars in the world. She was earning $5000 a week and lived in a fifteen-room mansion in Holmby Hills replete with a soda fountain, a beauty parlour and ten servants, including a young woman whose only duty was apparently to play soothing records in Miss Turner's dressing room as she prepared for her next scene.

By 1956, however, Turner's career was going sour. MGM did not bother renewing her contract, and in 1957 she divorced her fourth husband, Tarzan actor Lex Barker, after her teenage daughter Cheryl (Turner had divorced Cheryl's father, restaurant owner Stephen Crane, when their daughter was just nine months old) accused her stepfather of systematically raping her since the age of ten. Turner gave Barker twenty minutes to pack. He would maintain his innocence until his death in 1973.

Al Capone shows off the scar running down his cheek that earned him the nickname 'Scarface'. (© Library of Congress NYWTS)

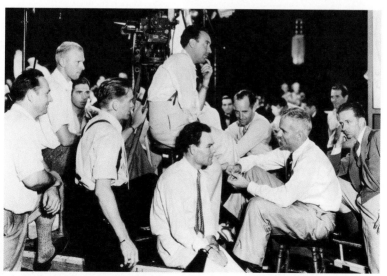

Director Howard Hawks was inspired to create the movie *Scarface* (1932) after hearing about Capone beating gangster rivals to death with a baseball bat. Hoodlums visited Hawks on the set of the movie. (Courtesy of the Academy of Motion Picture Arts and Sciences/Universal Studios Licensing LLP)

Bello is thought to have asked New Jersey gangster Longy Zwillman (above left) to arrange Bern's murder because he was frightened of losing control of the star's money. Zwillman had an affair with Harlow and gave lockets containing her pubic hair as gifts to gangster pals. (© Bettmann/Corbis)

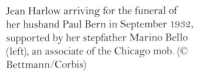

Jean Harlow arriving for the funeral of her husband Paul Bern in September 1932, supported by her stepfather Marino Bello (left), an associate of the Chicago mob. (© Bettmann/Corbis)

Harry Cohn, who borrowed half a million dollars from Zwillman in 1932 to buy Columbia Pictures. Several Chicago gangsters are thought to have owned stock in Columbia. Summing up Hollywood, Cohn said, 'It's not a business, it's a racket.' (© Ronald Grant Archive)

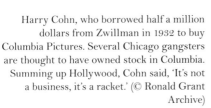

Actress Thelma Todd, who began having an affair with Lucky Luciano in 1934 as New York gangsters battled Chicago for control of drugs in Hollywood. (© Hulton Archive/Getty Images)

Luciano, who had supplied cocaine and heroin to Hollywood movie stars since the days of silent movies. (© Bettmann/Corbis)

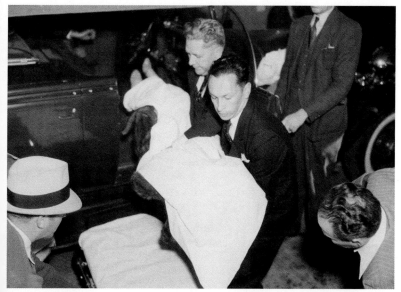

But Todd was going to blow the whistle on the mob moving in on Hollywood. She was found dead in December 1935, having been murdered supposedly on Luciano's orders. (© Bettmann/Corbis)

Eddie Mannix, Jack Warner and Herbert Preston. Warner Bros. boss Warner (centre) was one of the Hollywood moguls the Chicago mob lent on for protection money to stop strikes. Actress Ava Gardner described MGM executive Mannix (left) as 'a gangster, Irish Mafia'. (© Photofest)

The Outfit put union leader Willie Bioff in charge of milking Hollywood for millions of dollars. Asked during his trial whether the mob planned to own the studios themselves, Bioff said, 'If we'd lasted that long, we would have.' (© Bettmann/Corbis)

Actress June Lang with her husband Johnny Rosselli, the Chicago mob's man in Hollywood. Rosselli, who became pals with Harry Cohn, produced several crime movies praised for their realism. He later regretted ever having left the movie world. (© Bettmann/Corbis)

Bugsy Siegel (left) photographed with movie star pal George Raft. Siegel copied the Chicago Outfit's control of Hollywood technicians by taking over the extras' union. He was so infatuated with Hollywood that he paid for his own screen test. (© Bettmann/Corbis)

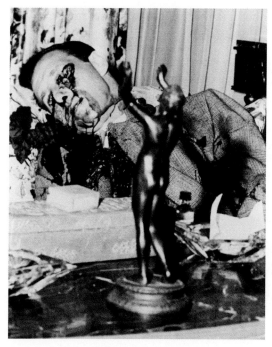

Siegel was shot to death in 1947. None of the friends he made in Hollywood, including Louis B. Mayer, Jack Warner and Cary Grant, attended his funeral. (© Bettmann/Corbis)

Marilyn Monroe seen with lawyer Jerry Giesler, whose other clients included Bugsy Siegel and Charlie Chaplin. The FBI kept Monroe under surveillance for associating with gangsters. One theory is that the Mafia murdered Monroe in a plot to embarrass Robert Kennedy, who was waging war on organised crime at the same time as he was having an affair with the star. (© Time Life Pictures/Getty Images)

Lana Turner with gangster boyfriend Johnny Stompanato, who worked for the Los Angeles mob. Turner supposedly confessed to murdering Stompanato shortly before her death. (© Bettmann/Corbis)

Kim Novak, Columbia's number one star. Harry Cohn threatened to have the mob kill Sammy Davis Jr. when he found out the singer was having an affair with her. Cohn warned that the mob would 'put out Sammy's other eye'. (© Time Life Pictures/ Getty Images)

Sammy Davis Jr. (centre) was hopelessly in debt to the mob. (© Getty Images)

Sinatra (centre): the man who triangulated Hollywood, the mob and politics, pictured here in Havana. His friend Jerry Lewis claimed that Sinatra acted as a bagman for Chicago, ferrying mob cash around the country. (© Anthony Summers)

Sinatra's underworld mentor Sam Giancana had nothing but contempt for Hollywood, calling movie stars 'worthless bums and whores'. (© Bettmann/Corbis)

Sidney Korshak, the mob's Beverly Hills lawyer, was one of the most powerful people in Hollywood. Studios relied on him for getting stars out of trouble and for keeping unions sweet. (© Bettmann/Corbis)

Wall Street criticised Universal boss Lew Wasserman (left) for his ties to Korshak and unions he represented. Wasserman borrowed millions from the Teamsters union to buy stars for Universal. Fellow mogul Edgar Bronfman Jr. (right) also had old family ties to gangsters. (© Gamma/Camera Press London)

The Godfather's infamous horse's head scene was based on fact. MGM boss Louis B. Mayer was the mogul who kept horses. (© Harold B Lee Library/Brigham Young University)

The Mafia threatened to kill one Paramount executive's baby when the studio started filming *The Godfather*. Producer Al Ruddy (left) was forced to make a deal with gangsters. (© Ronald Grant Archive)

Warner Communications invested alongside the Mafia in a New York concert venue in the 1970s. Sinatra, pictured here backstage with Gambino crime family members, played benefit concerts for Mafiosi relatives. (© Getty Images)

Warner chairman Steve Ross, who had his own ties to New York gangsters. (© Getty Images)

Michele Sindona, who laundered Mafia heroin profits and used some of the money to buy Paramount's studio backlot. (© Gianni Giansanti/Sygma/Corbis)

Paramount chairman Charles Bludhorn took a seat on the board of Sindona's company. (Courtesy of the Academy of Motion Picture Arts and Sciences)

The Colombo crime family financed porn movie *Deep Throat* – the most profitable film ever made. (© Bettmann/Corbis)

Gangster Louis Peraino, who produced *Deep Throat*, used the profits to set up the most successful indie movie company in Hollywood. Porn star Fred Lincoln described Peraino as 'a mobster's son who wanted to be an auteur'. (© *Variety*)

A scene from *The Cotton Club*, financed by Las Vegas investors as a way to launder money. (© MGM)

Robert Evans (centre), producer of *The Cotton Club*, also borrowed underworld cash to keep filming. As costs ballooned, 'the guys from Vegas were in no mood for creative flack,' said Evans. (© Ronald Grant Archive)

Giancarlo Parretti, protégé of a Sicilian Mafia politician, borrowed billions to buy MGM in the 1990s. Parretti said, 'Everybody is saying it's Mafia money; it's jealousy.' (© Science Faction)

Steven Seagal, who turned to an imprisoned mob boss for help when the Mafia started threatening him. (© Getty Images)

Seagal's producer, Jules Nasso, went to prison for conspiring with the Gotti crime family to extort the star. (© Bolivar Arellano/ Rex Features)

Mafioso Joseph 'Tin Ear' Sclafani boasted of knowing Johnny Depp as well as other stars and producers. In court, his lawyer argued that everything Sclafani knew about the Mafia he gleaned from movies and television, especially *The Sopranos*. (© GangLandNews.com)

Shortly afterwards, Turner began seeing another man, John Steele. Steele had repeatedly phoned Turner, sending her expensive gifts, flowers and records. Then a friend told Turner that John Steele's real name was Johnny Stompanato. He was a gangster who worked for Mickey Cohen. He had been arrested twice but never convicted. Although Stompanato had at various times been a car dealer, owned a pet shop and a furniture store, his main source of income was as a gigolo. According to one actress, he had a reputation for being 'a great lover with a big dong'. Indeed, his nickname was Oscar because his penis was supposed to be the size of an Academy Award statuette. Police regarded Stompanato as an extortionist. He would prey on rich, lonely women and then – like Joe Gillis in Billy Wilder's *Sunset Boulevard* – 'borrow' money from them.

For a time Turner hung up whenever Stompanato telephoned her. Then one night he broke into her bungalow and tried to murder her by suffocating her with a pillow. Just as she was beginning to black out Stompanato removed the pillow and started to kiss her. Turner said later that she found his obsessive passion strangely exciting.

At the time the Bureau of Investigation of the Los Angeles District Attorney's office was keeping Cohen's gang under surveillance. Investigators suspected Cohen was trying to compromise movie stars sexually for blackmail or commercial exploitation. Sound recordings of Turner and Stompanato making love appeared on the market, changing hands for hundreds of dollars a time.

In November 1957, Turner and Stompanato flew to Britain to start filming *Another Time, Another Place*, the first movie made by her independent production company. Stompanato had been keen for Turner to get him a job as a movie executive. Her co-star Sean Connery disliked Stompanato so much that he personally threw him off set. Stompanato then half-strangled Turner again after she refused to give him an executive producer credit. Her vocal cords were so badly damaged that she could only do scenes without dialogue for the next three weeks. Stompanato next threatened to set the mob on an associate producer who urged Turner to go to the police. Turner saw sense and asked the police to deport

Stompanato. Within twenty-four hours police bounced the gangster back to the airport and on to a plane.

When shooting finished in January 1958, Turner flew from London to Mexico via Copenhagen for a holiday. There, waiting on the tarmac at Copenhagen airport, was Stompanato surrounded by reporters and photographers. Turner could hardly create a scene. Instead, Stompanato and Turner flew to Acapulco where they stayed at the Villa Vera Hotel. The hotel manager remembered that Turner was forever trying to have a word with him and his wife in private, but Stompanato was always lurking. Turner later wrote that Stompanato had held a gun to her head forcing her to have sex with him.

Turner was nominated for Best Actress at the 1958 Academy Awards for her part in *Peyton Place*. Stompanato was waiting for her when she returned home on 26 March after the awards ceremony. He beat her up, giving her two black eyes.

A few days later Turner confided to her fourteen-year-old daughter Cheryl how frightened she was of the gangster. Cheryl urged her mother to go to the police, but Turner refused, terrified of the consequences if Cohen's gang found out.

Turner, her daughter and Stompanato moved into a new house in Beverly Hills on 1 April 1958. Three days later, on Good Friday, Turner and Stompanato began arguing again. Shouting could be heard coming from Turner's first-floor bedroom. Turner had found out Stompanato was much younger than he claimed. At thirty-seven she had become sensitive about her age. She did not want to be seen as resorting to paid younger men. At about 9 p.m. Turner told Stompanato that their relationship was over. She told him to get out. Stompanato threatened to disfigure Turner and harm her daughter.

Cheryl was sitting in her bedroom along the landing doing homework. She could hear the fighting through the walls. She got up and ran downstairs to the kitchen. Carmen Cruz, Turner's housekeeper, saw Cheryl leaving the kitchen with an eight-inch carving knife in her hand. Cheryl then ran back upstairs.

Cheryl banged on her mother's door. The argument was still

going on. 'I've just had enough,' Turner was shouting. 'Cunt, you're dead,' Stompanato shouted. Cheryl pounded on the door, which Turner opened. Stompanato was standing behind her with his arm raised. Cheryl thought he was about to strike her mother. In fact, he was holding a shirt and jacket on coat hangers behind his back. According to Cheryl's testimony, Stompanato lunged out and ran on to the knife. The blade punctured his kidney and aorta. The gangster stared at Cheryl in horror. 'My God, Cheryl, what have you done?' he said before making a gurgling sound and collapsing dead on the carpet. Cheryl put the knife down on the dressing table. She ran screaming from the room. It was 9.20 p.m.

One of the first people to arrive at the house was Turner's doctor, Dr John McDonald. He told her to telephone Jerry Giesler, the lawyer who had defended Bugsy Siegel eighteen years earlier.

Mickey Cohen identified Stompanato's body. He said he would arrange for his friend to be buried in his home town of Woodstock, Illinois. 'I don't like the whole thing,' Cohen told reporters. 'There's a lot of unanswered questions about how Johnny was killed. I'm going to find out some of those answers – no matter what happens.' Cohen was right. There were a number of puzzling forensic details. First, there were no identifiable fingerprints on the knife. Second, there was no blood in the bedroom except for small drops on the pink carpet. Cohen believed that either Cheryl or Turner herself had murdered Stompanato while he was asleep. 'When I heard how Johnny was killed cold chills went through me. It's a fantastic way for a man like Stompanato to die.'

Meanwhile, the receptionist at the hotel in Westwood where Stompanato kept his things heard about the stabbing. He let himself in to Stompanato's room with a pass key. He found the lights on and the bathroom window forced open. The maid said later that a leather washbag stuffed with letters was missing from its usual place above the washbasin. Cohen sent the letters to the *Los Angeles Herald*, claiming that Stompanato had given them to him before his death. Cohen said he wanted the letters published to show how Johnny was not stalking the actress, as Turner was claiming, and how deeply in love they were.

Stompanato's forty-five-year-old brother Carmine arrived from Illinois to reclaim the body. He too told the press that he did not believe Cheryl's story. He wanted Turner to take a lie-detector test. How, he wondered, could a fourteen-year-old girl who had never wielded a knife before murder an ex-marine? Carmine Stompanato also suggested that his brother had been asleep in bed when he was murdered. Former Beverly Hills police chief Clinton Anderson later wrote that the most ironic aspect of the Stompanato investigation was organised crime's refusal to accept that a teenager could murder one of its own.

Carmine Stompanato was accompanied by two underworld associates, Max Tannenbaum and Ellis Mandel. All three were anxious to get hold of Stompanato's personal belongings, especially a box containing, among other things, a revolver and reels of negatives from snapshots of actresses photographed nude in compromising positions. Police handed the box over. In front of the actress Turner's lawyers burned other rolls of film containing shots of her naked in bed.

Stompanato's inquest was shown live on television on 11 April 1958. Hundreds of fans lined the pavement to watch Turner arriving at the downtown Hall of Records Building, looking severely elegant in a grey Italian suit with her hair cut in a mannish style. More fans and 150 reporters packed the eighth-floor courtroom. In the words of Turner's make-up man, Del Armstrong, Geisler coached Turner to give what some suggested was the performance of her life. She gave evidence for just over an hour, underplaying and speaking very deliberately. It was never 'Johnny' but always 'Mr Stompanato'. The inquest decided on a verdict of justifiable homicide.

One member of the public, however, stood up and denounced the inquest as a whitewash. Many believed that Turner discovered Stompanato was also having an affair with her daughter. Mother and daughter were both in love with Stompanato, the spectator shouted.

District attorney William B. McKesson did not prosecute Cheryl for manslaughter. Tellingly, given Turner's alternately controlling and distant mothering, the court made Cheryl a ward of court. She spent three weeks in Juvenile Hall before being sent to live with her grandmother. Cheryl tried to commit suicide twice, once after Turner incorrectly told her that she was to continue to be under the authorities' control.

Turner hid herself away at 730 North Bedford Drive. Stompanato had warned her the mob would take revenge should anything happen to him. There had been death threats, menacing phone calls and hate mail. A police car circled the block day and night.

Turner was now deeply in debt to her lawyers and MGM and frightened she would never work again. Then producer Ross Hunter approached her to star in a remake of the 1934 film *Imitation of Life*. The plot blatantly cashed in on the Stompanato scandal, being partly about a self-absorbed movie star who alternately spoils and ignores her daughter. Both mother and daughter are in love with the same man. Turner and Hunter split the profits from the film. *Imitation of Life* made Turner a millionaire.

Eric Root, a former hairdresser and dancing instructor who lived with Turner from the 1970s onwards, said that in April 1985 Turner confessed to him that she and not Cheryl had murdered Stompanato. 'I killed the son of a bitch and I'd do it again,' Turner told Root. In a book Root wrote after Turner's death he gave a different version of events of the night of 4 April 1958. Giesler arrived at the house with private detective Fred Otash before the police. They persuaded Turner to let Cheryl take the blame for the stabbing. Otash wiped Turner's fingerpints off the knife. Root quoted Otash as saying, 'the bed looked as if a hog had been slaughtered in it'.

Author Patricia Bosworth has described the Stompanato murder as 'a power struggle of competing narratives – a mystery which continues to grow in its endless complications'. Actress Esther Williams said that nobody would ever know the whole truth about Stompanato's death. 'The bottom line is there have always been cover-ups here because Hollywood protects its own.'

CHAPTER SEVEN

Surreal and Sordid

By the late 1950s, New York Mafia kingpin Frank Costello had become so infuriated with former RKO Studios boss Joseph Kennedy that he was threatening to have him killed. Kennedy had been appointed US ambassador to Britain before the Second World War, resigning because of his opposition to America entering the conflict. Some said he was a Nazi sympathiser. In the late 1940s, Kennedy was a regular at the casino Costello co-owned with Meyer Lansky, the Colonial Inn in Miami Beach. Lansky said that at one time Kennedy was coming four or five times a week. Kennedy reminded the casino's publicist Harold Conrad of being 'a priest on the cheat'.

In the mid-1950s, Kennedy and Costello had fallen out over a Manhattan property deal. In his vaunted position, Kennedy was no longer returning Costello's calls; Costello wanted to call in some favours. 'You had the sense,' a friend of Costello's said, 'that they were close during Prohibition and then something happened. Frank said that he helped Kennedy become wealthy. What happened between them I don't know. But the way Frank talked you had the feeling that in later years he had tried to reach Joe Kennedy for something and that he was completely ignored. Frank didn't mind if somebody said no to him. He could understand that. But nothing made him angrier than to be just ignored, as if he didn't exist.' Costello sent word to Kennedy that the mob was going to murder him. Kennedy panicked and begged Sam Giancana, who had inherited control of the Outfit from Tony Accardo and Paul Ricca in 1955, to intercede. Giancana also distrusted Kennedy for having come too far from his roots; for getting 'uppity', as he put it. Kennedy knew Giancana through his ownership of the Merchandise Mart Building in Chicago, which had once housed a block-long speakeasy. After a conversation with Costello, the contract was called off.

Kennedy was convinced that his son was going to become president of the United States. Towards the end of 1959, he made several calls to Giancana asking for his help. Kennedy promised the mob would have his son's ear if it supported Jack Kennedy's presidential campaign. The Outfit could still deliver many votes in Democratic Party wards. Giancana had his own favour to ask in return. The ambassador's second son, Robert, was chief counsel to the Senate committee investigating union racketeering. Bobby Kennedy had grilled Giancana that June about corruption. Giancana pleaded the Fifth Amendment thirty-four times, declining to answer questions on the grounds that he might incriminate himself. His father assured Giancana the spotlight would be turned off the mob if the Mafia could deliver the Democratic Party vote in marginal wards.

But Giancana did not trust Kennedy and set about luring both Kennedy sons into a 'honey trap'. Knowing both Kennedy boys shared their father's promiscuous behaviour, Giancana decided to dig up enough dirt on the Kennedys to use as a bargaining tool if they did not keep their side of the deal. This would lead to an extraordinary nexus in American history where the head of the Chicago mob shared a mistress with the president of the United States. And the man who was going to triangulate Hollywood, the Mafia and Washington was Giancana's friend Frank Sinatra.

Sinatra first met John F. Kennedy in 1955 when the singer addressed a Democratic Party rally. They met again the following year at the Democratic convention in Chicago. Adlai Stevenson had been nominated for president. He had left it up to delegates to decide who they wanted for vice-president. Kennedy was campaigning for the vice-presidency against the wishes of his father. In the end Kennedy lost the vice-presidential nomination to Estes Kefauver, still riding the publicity of his exposé of organised crime.

One of Sinatra's friends was Peter Lawford, the English-born actor who had married Jack Kennedy's sister Pat in 1954. The Lawfords had their own associations with organised crime. They were friendly with former Paramount starlet Bea Korshak, the wife of Sidney Korshak. Bea Korshak also knew Sinatra and stayed at his rented villa in Acapulco in 1957. The Lawfords were being watched by the FBI when they had dinner with Bea at the Mocambo restaurant in Los Angeles in the summer of 1958. It was the Lawford connection that drew Sinatra towards the Kennedys.

Both Sinatra and Jack Kennedy were obsessed with women. Apparently, when Kennedy was with Sinatra the talk was never about politics but high-grade gossip. Kennedy said that he wanted to sleep with every woman in Hollywood. During the Second World War he had gone out with actresses including Sonja Henie, June Allyson and Gene Tierney. Grace Kelly was another conquest. By the time he entered Congress in 1946, his Hollywood friends included producers Sam Spiegel (*On the Waterfront*) and Charles Feldman (*A Streetcar Named Desire*). It was at one of Feldman's parties in 1954 that he met Marilyn Monroe for the first time.

Lawford said later that the basis of the relationship between the three men was that he would procure girls for Sinatra, while Sinatra would find girls for Kennedy. 'I was Frank's pimp and Frank was Jack's,' Lawford said.

Sinatra first met Joseph Kennedy at the end of 1959 at the Kennedy family house in Hyannis Port, Massachusetts. It was the first time Sinatra had ever been invited to the compound. Over lunch Kennedy asked Sinatra to talk to their mutual friends in the Outfit about helping Jack win the presidency. In particular, Joseph Kennedy needed the Outfit's help in swinging West Virginia and Illinois behind the Democrats. Sinatra felt ambivalent about Kennedy but the former ambassador, like the Devil tempting Jesus with the panoply of the world, dangled the possibility of the singer becoming America's ambassador to Italy.

In November 1959 Jack Kennedy extended a trip to Los Angeles by two days to stay with Sinatra at his house in Palm Springs. Actor Richard Burton wrote in his diary that when Kennedy stayed with Sinatra the Palm Springs house was like a brothel.

Just as Sinatra was becoming closer to Jack Kennedy so the singer's friendship was deepening with Sam Giancana.

A police official once described the Outfit boss as 'a snarling, sarcastic, ill-mannered, ill-tempered, sadistic psychopath'. The army draft board also summed up Giancana as a 'constitutional psychopath', although the gangster later admitted having played up to avoid the draft. Yul Brynner's son remembered Giancana as 'scary, so profoundly ugly it was hard to look at him. His ugliness, unlike most people's, seemed to reflect his soul.' According to Lawford, Giancana was

> really an awful guy with a gargoyle face and weasel nose. I couldn't stand him but Frank idolised him because he was the Mafia's top gun. Frank used to love to talk about 'hits' and guys getting 'rubbed out'. And you better believe that when the word got around town that Frank was a pal of Sam Giancana, nobody but nobody ever messed with Frank Sinatra. They were too scared. Concrete boots were no joke with this guy. He was a killer.

Despite his aggression and violence, Giancana's hobby was collecting Dresden figurines, Meissen china and silver tea services.

Giancana was present on set during the filming of *Some Came Running* in the summer of 1958. Sinatra's co-star, Shirley Mac-Laine, had no idea who Giancana was. One night she jokingly aimed a water pistol at the gangster when he kept winning at gin rummy; Giancana responded by aiming a very real .38 handgun at her. When police arrested Giancana that same year for carrying a fake driver's licence they found Sinatra's telephone number in his wallet.

Gangster and singer became even closer at the beginning of the 1960s. Sinatra regarded Giancana as his mentor when it came to business. The singer owned 9 per cent of the Sands casino, awarded him by Jimmy 'Blue Eyes' Alo, and he wanted to understand how the business worked. Giancana would mentor Sinatra when they met in Chicago, Miami or Hawaii. Meyer Lansky once described Giancana as 'the only Italian who handles money like a Jew'. Sinatra even invited Giancana to dinner at his parents' house in New Jersey. When Sinatra sang 'My Kind Of Town' it would be with a nod to Giancana if he was in the audience. It was Sinatra's way of acknowledging the mob.

The Rat Pack phenomenon gelled in 1960. Sinatra and his cronies Dean Martin, Sammy Davis Jr and Peter Lawford would sing songs and clown around on stage. The whole thing could be seen as an encomium to the joys of drinking – one long advertisement for booze sold in bars and nightclubs controlled by the Mafia. The whole surreal and sordid interweave of Hollywood starlets, the Rat Pack, politics and the Mafia was beginning to converge.

Lawford and his wife Pat had obtained the rights to a Las Vegas heist novel, *Ocean's Eleven*. Sinatra thought it would be a good vehicle for the Rat Pack. Warner Bros agreed to fund the $2.8 million movie, which would also feature pals including George Raft and actress Angie Dickinson. The idea was that the movie would shoot around Sinatra, Davis and Martin in the dead of night once the stars had finished their live act. Filming began on 11 January 1960. The movie follows Danny Ocean and his men as they plan and execute an implausible heist on four Las Vegas casinos. One shot shows Sinatra robbing his own casino, the Sands. The money is smuggled out of Las Vegas in garbage trucks. In reality, of course, the mob would have fed Ocean and his gang head first into a wood chipper long before they had even reached the city limits.

According to Dickinson, *Ocean's Eleven* reflected the upbeat feeling of America at the time. The movie's scotch-on-the-rocks cool was in step with the swingin' prospect of a new young president. Indeed, Kennedy visited the production on 7 February 1960, staying at the Sands. Sinatra organised a private party for Kennedy in the early hours of 8 February. Los Angeles private detective Fred Otash – the same man who is said to have tidied up Johnny Stompanato's body after his supposed murder by Lana Turner – told the FBI that Kennedy, Sinatra and Lawford had been 'involved in some sort of indiscreet party' during the senator's visit. During the party Lawford took Davis aside and told him if he ever wanted to know what a million dollars in cash looked like he should go to the wardrobe and open the brown leather satchel inside. It was a present from the mob to Kennedy's election campaign. Davis begged off. 'I was also told there were four wild girls scheduled to entertain him and I didn't want to hear about that either and I got out of there. Some things you don't want to know,' he said later.

During this visit Sinatra introduced Kennedy to a twenty-six-year-old high-class call girl called Judy Campbell. She portrayed herself as a free-spirited artist but in fact had met Sinatra through Jimmy Van Heusen, Sinatra's songwriter and fellow hellraiser. Sinatra's valet, George Jacobs, described Van Heusen, who wrote the songs 'All The Way' and 'Come Fly With Me', as another 'whore wrangler'. Van Heusen had a whore wrangler of his own, Murray Wolfe, who in turn was friendly with a Los Angeles madam called Joyce. This madam kept a list of Hollywood starlets who needed extra money and were amenable to going on the game. Nothing was ever overt – just a hundred-dollar bill slipped inside a thank-you card. Campbell had been a starlet under contract at MGM, Universal and Warner Bros whose previous boyfriends had included actor Robert Wagner. She was also friendly with Angie Dickinson. The former model had stayed with Sinatra in Palm Springs before Christmas 1960. Other guests included the Lawfords and gangster Johnny Formosa, an associate of Giancana. In fact, Joseph Kennedy had already slept with Campbell before his son (Marlene Dietrich said that Jack Kennedy was obsessed with whether his father had been with women before he had). Sinatra too had slept with Campbell, trying to introduce her to three-way, interracial sex. She pretended to be asleep while a black prostitute performed oral sex on the singer.

According to Lawford's agent Milt Ebbins, Campbell introduced herself to the Kennedy party that Sunday night during the floor-show at the Sands. Campbell and Kennedy went upstairs when the show ended. Lawford told Ebbins that Campbell was a hooker paid $200 ($1300 in today's money) to entertain the senator.

Sinatra arranged for Campbell and Kennedy to have lunch together in the singer's hotel suite. By the time Kennedy left Las Vegas, the couple had already arranged to meet in New York. Immediately after Kennedy left, a team arrived to destroy photographic evidence of any indiscretions.

In her memoir Campbell portrayed herself as a naïf who would do anything for love. Sinatra first introduced Campbell to Sam Giancana in Miami in March 1960. Campbell was under the impression that Giancana, who was calling himself Sam Flood, was a lonely widower. The gangster was apparently smitten and began sending Campbell yellow roses every day. But the Sands' casino dealer Guido Deiro said that Campbell was already known as Johnny Rosselli's girlfriend. Indeed, Rosselli later testified that he had known Campbell since she was seventeen. Rosselli told a Senate committee that he and Campbell had dated after her divorce. Sinatra's friend Brad Dexter told Sinatra biographer Anthony Summers that Rosselli and Campbell had a sexual relationship. Rosselli himself said that he saw Campbell together with Giancana before 1960. So it appears that Campbell was far from naïve. Rather, the indicators are that the starlet was set up by the mob to embarrass the man tipped to be the next president of the United States – or as Peter Lawford put it, 'Judy was a mob moll.'

By April 1960 the presidential election was under way. Sinatra inveigled cronies such as Sammy Davis to perform at Kennedy fundraisers and also roped in Judy Garland, Tony Curtis, Angie Dickinson and Janet Leigh. That same month Kennedy asked Campbell to carry a bag of money to Giancana.

At one point in *Ocean's Eleven* Lawford remarks, 'I think I'll buy some votes and go into politics.' Being Jack Kennedy's brother-in-law, this got a big laugh from audiences. What moviegoers were unaware of in the summer of 1960 was that this is exactly what happened. The nexus of the mob's involvement in Kennedy's political career came in May, when Giancana told Skinny D'Amato, owner of the 500 Club in Atlantic City where Sinatra sang every year, to spread cash around West Virginia, even forgiving gambling debts. Giancana is thought to have borrowed $50,000 from the Teamsters Pension Fund. 'We're gonna have to buy every fucking vote in the state,' he told D'Amato. West Virginia voted for Kennedy on 10 May 1960. The way was now clear for him to accept the Democratic nomination.

Kennedy was so nonchalant about being nominated for president that during the Democratic convention in Los Angeles in July he spent his evenings cosying up to Campbell and Monroe. On the night of 11 July, Kennedy tried to get Campbell to take part in a threesome with another woman but Campbell walked out in a huff. The next night Kennedy had dinner with Monroe at Puccini, the Beverly Hills restaurant Sinatra owned with Lawford. Presidential aide Kenny O'Donnell, who had driven Campbell home the previous night, remembered Monroe joking about how 'penetrating' Kennedy had been with her earlier in the day.

During the Democratic convention Joseph Kennedy stayed at a house lent to him by silent movie star Marion Davies. Joseph Kennedy was in love with Davies and kept a photograph of her on his bedside table in Hyannis Port – the only photograph in his bedroom.

That same year, Kennedy revisited a favourite family holiday destination, the Cal-Neva Lodge on the California/Nevada border. Although the hotel was in California, the adjacent casino was in Nevada. Kennedy brokered a deal for Sinatra to buy the Cal-Neva for $2 million – $1.5 million of which was lent by the Bank of Nevada with the other $500,000 supposedly coming from Sinatra. However, Sinatra's equity was in fact Giancana's money. Although Sinatra's company Park Lake Enterprises owned the Cal-Neva, the singer was fronting for the mob.

Sinatra performed at the Cal-Neva in the summer of 1960, inviting the cast of *The Misfits*, which was filming nearby in Reno, to watch him sing. Marilyn Monroe and her husband Arthur Miller stayed at the lodge. Sinatra played the concerned friend to Monroe during the breakdown of her marriage to Miller. He gave her a white poodle that she named Maf, as in Mafia. Sinatra, Kennedy, Giancana, Monroe and Rosselli were all now circling around each other. The Rat Pack's tails were becoming intertwined – and the more any of them tried to pull away, the more fused their tails were becoming.

Giancana, meanwhile, was also seeing actress Phyllis McGuire, one of the singing McGuire Sisters. McGuire, who was engaged to comedian Dan Rowan (later famous for *Rowan and Martin's Laugh-In*), began seeing Giancana after the gangster cancelled nearly $100,000 of gambling debts she had run up at the Desert Inn in Las Vegas. Once, at the Cal-Neva, Giancana beat up McGuire's manager while Sinatra and another man tried to restrain him. McGuire later co-starred with Sinatra in *Come Blow Your Horn* (1963). Giancana was a regular visitor on set. McGuire admitted later that her affair with Giancana had hurt her career.

John F. Kennedy was elected president of the United States in November 1960. That same month he asked Campbell to arrange a meeting with Giancana in Miami. He also asked her to convey messages about Cuban dictator Fidel Castro. Kennedy had decided the mob should be used to assassinate the Cuban leader. He also asked her to carry documents to Giancana relating to the assassination plot. Campbell was asked to set up another meeting in her New York apartment, where Kennedy brought cash to the mob boss. There was a follow-up meeting at the Ambassador East Hotel in Chicago. Campbell sat on the edge of the bath while the two men talked in the bedroom.

Johnny Rosselli, who executive-produced the anti-Communist diatribe *Invasion USA*, was training Cuban exiles planning to reinvade Cuba. He was still involved on the fringes of Hollywood, trying to produce a movie titled *Las Vegas at Night*. In Miami Rosselli introduced Bob Maheu to Giancana. Maheu was a private detective connected to the CIA who was the intersection in this Venn diagram of intelligence workers, Mafiosi and right-wing Cubans. Giancana was sceptical about any Castro assassination attempt. He just wanted to con money out of the government.

Giancana asked the private eye to investigate whether McGuire was cheating on him with Rowan. Dollars earmarked for the Cuba invasion were spent on bugging equipment and hiring another investigator. The whole thing descended into farce on 30 October when the private detective employed by Maheu bungled his surveillance operation. The police arrested him and Rosselli had to stand bail for $1000.

Joseph Kennedy, meanwhile, sold the film rights to *The Enemy Within*, his son Bobby's account of his Senate committee crusade against organised crime, to Hollywood. Producer Jerry Wald, the model for movie producer Sammy Glick in Budd Schulberg's novel *What Makes Sammy Run?*, bought the rights for 20th Century Fox. Paul Newman was attached to star. Schulberg, who had written *On the Waterfront* – another screenplay about Mafia intimidation of unions – began work on the script. But Wald began receiving threatening phone calls. 'Are you the SOB who is going to photograph *The Enemy Within*?' asked one caller. Then Jimmy Hoffa, the corrupt head of the trucking Teamsters union, won a court injunction to stop the movie being made – and threatened to sue Fox for millions if it ever went into production.

Meanwhile, as Warner Bros was planning its own film about Jack Kennedy's supposed wartime heroics, studio head Jack Warner began receiving anonymous hate mail. One letter warned that the president was 'a sex pervert, with many mistresses' and that 'the scandals soon coming up for air will kill your picture and you'.

Bobby Kennedy was appointed attorney general in December 1960. Presumably, Giancana assumed he was immune to prosecution with his secret deal intact. In February 1961 he put another favour in his Kennedy goodwill bank. Los Angeles restaurateur Peter Fairchild was planning to name Jack Kennedy, Frank Sinatra, Dean Martin and comedian Jerry Lewis as men his starlet wife Judi Meredith had slept with during their marriage. Fairchild hired Fred Otash to gather evidence against Meredith for the divorce. Campbell turned to Giancana. The Outfit boss asked Rosselli to muzzle Otash and destroy any files. According to Otash, he met Rosselli on several occasions, once with Giancana as well. Otash explained that

Meredith was holding out for $100,000 as a divorce payoff from her husband. Fairchild was loath to give her anything, considering the pain his wife had caused him. Otash, Fairchild and Meredith's lawyers were in the judge's chambers on the day of the divorce proceedings when the payoff happened. A cheque was handed to Meredith's lawyers. Satisfied with her payoff, she went quietly.

The FBI was keeping Rosselli under surveillance, intrigued as to the connection between the gangster, a CIA associate like Maheu and television comedian Dan Rowan. FBI director J. Edgar Hoover was finally able to connect the dots in January 1961, when Rosselli was observed leaving Romanoff's restaurant in Los Angeles with Campbell. The FBI had recorded phone conversations between Campbell and Kennedy and Campbell and Giancana. The president was having an affair with a woman who was also friendly with the head of the Chicago mob – the very same man whom the president's brother had made a name for himself interrogating during his Senate investigation into organised crime. (During the committee hearing Bobby Kennedy humiliated a nervous Giancana on television by telling him only little girls giggled.) Not only that, but while publicly deploring organised crime, the Kennedys had used the mob to help swing marginal elections and were now planning to use the Mafia to spark a *coup d'état* in a foreign country. The hypocrisy was breathtaking.

Hoover wrote to Bobby Kennedy on 27 February 1961 telling him what he knew about the connections between Sinatra, Giancana and the president. But Bobby Kennedy already had misgivings about Sinatra. Marilyn Monroe told her friend reporter Sidney Skolsky that one night during a party at the Lawfords' she had seen Robert Kennedy tell his brother he couldn't afford to associate with Sinatra.

President Kennedy and Hoover had lunch together in March 1961, three days before Kennedy was due to stay with Sinatra in Palm Springs. The singer had refitted his house, even installing a helicopter pad. Alone during lunch for a short time, Hoover laid out all he knew about Giancana, Campbell and the president. That afternoon Kennedy began to distance himself from Campbell. He instructed Lawford to tell Sinatra he would not be staying with him. Sinatra went berserk and began throwing things around the house. He never forgave Lawford for what he saw as his friend's betrayal.

That summer, Joe Kennedy invited Sinatra and his Rat Pack to his villa in Antibes on the French Riviera. But Joe then turned around and announced there wasn't enough room following a visit from Bobby.

Over the summer the FBI increased the pressure on Giancana. His nemesis was an ex-marine and former college boxing champion called Bill Roemer. On one occasion Roemer served Phyllis McGuire with a subpoena to appear before the grand jury when the singer and Giancana arrived at Chicago's O'Hare Airport. Giancana threatened to have his bodyguard murder Roemer there and then. He also intimated that he was ready to divulge the Cuban conspiracy to Bobby Kennedy. On another occasion Roemer and his FBI colleagues were keeping Giancana's headquarters under surveillance when a mob associate, Chuckie English, ran up to their car. He told them that if Bobby Kennedy wanted to meet Giancana, he knew who to go through. 'Sinatra?' Roemer asked. 'You said it,' replied English. (On hearing this, Murray Humphreys observed, 'For Christ sakes, that's a cardinal rule. You don't give up a legit guy. He tells Roemer that Sinatra is our guy to Kennedy?')

The pressure of being under constant surveillance was getting to Giancana. 'This is like Nazi Germany and I'm the biggest Jew in the country,' he said in his high, almost girlish voice. Giancana decided to ask for Sinatra's help. Alone with Bobby Kennedy, Sinatra wrote Giancana's name down on a piece of paper and passed it across to the attorney general. 'This is my buddy. This is what I want you to know, Bob,' said Sinatra.

What Giancana could not have foreseen was Joseph Kennedy having a cerebral haemorrhage on a golf course in Palm Beach in December 1961. With his father incapacitated, Bobby Kennedy was completely free to go after organised crime. In effect, Bobby Kennedy was now trying to handcuff the hand which had helped get his brother elected. All government agencies were told to pool intelligence and coordinate investigations. Bobby Kennedy indicted 350 gangsters in 1962 alone, of which 138 were convicted. One of Kennedy's victims was Skinny D'Amato, who was prosecuted for income tax evasion. The *Wall Street Journal* called it 'the most sweeping undertaking against gangsters, labor racketeers and vice overlords that the country has ever seen'.

By now even Giancana realised his strategy of building up favours with the Kennedys to be traded in at a later date had been a waste of time. 'If I ever get a speeding ticket none of these guys would ever know me,' he told Rosselli in December 1961. Rosselli was overheard to advise Giancana to change strategy. Rather than try and cosy up to the Kennedys, Giancana should show them his dark side. In another wiretap, Johnny Formosa suggested murdering Sinatra but Giancana rejected this. 'Let's show 'em. Let's show those fuckin' Hollywood fruitcakes that they can't get away with it as if nothing's happened,' said Formosa, who also offered to kill Dean Martin, Peter Lawford and take out Sammy Davis's other eye for good measure. But Sinatra was the one celebrity Giancana liked, describing him as 'a real stand-up guy, too good for those bums in Hollywood'. Later, Giancana told his half-brother that it wasn't Sinatra's fault that 'the Kennedys are assholes. But if I didn't like [Sinatra] you can be goddamned sure he'd be a dead man.'

Yet the FBI never actually arrested Giancana. Years later, former assistant attorney general criminal division Will Wilson testified that Bobby Kennedy stopped Giancana's arrest. According to Wilson, Hoover told him in 1971 that Kennedy had run into the FBI director's office just as agents were about to collar the gangster. 'He knows too much,' Kennedy told Hoover.

Marilyn Monroe, meanwhile, had spent time in psychiatric hospital. In February 1961 she was admitted to the Payne Whitney Psychiatric Clinic in New York Presbyterian Hospital – Cornell Medical Center. Under observation Monroe took off all her clothes and threw a chair through a glass door. George Cukor, who later directed her in the abandoned *Something's Got to Give* with Dean Martin, said she belonged in an institution rather than on a movie set. Monroe was addicted to prescription drugs. She blamed herself for the failure of three marriages and two miscarriages. However, she was still having occasional sex with Jack Kennedy. The couple met from time to time in Los Angeles or New York during 1960 and in Palm Springs in 1962. One FBI report quoted an unnamed informant claiming that Monroe, Lawford and Jack and Bobby Kennedy took part in 'sex parties which took place at the Hotel Carlisle [sic] in NYC'. But according to Monroe's hairdresser Mickey Song, the actress met Bobby Kennedy properly backstage at Madison Square Garden on 19 May 1962 – having been introduced to him four months previously. It was the night she sang 'Happy Birthday, Mr President' for the president's forty-fifth birthday. Jack Kennedy broke things off with Monroe that night after one final tryst at the Carlyle. On the rebound, Monroe threw herself into her affair with Bobby Kennedy, telling friends he was going to leave his wife for her. She told her friend Robert Slatzer that Bobby had disclosed the mob's involvement in the assassination attempt on Castro. However, the romance quickly soured. As a young woman Monroe had been complex and fascinating – by the age of thirty-six, however, she came across as downright unhinged. Under orders from his brother, Bobby Kennedy stopped returning Monroe's calls. Monroe herself was told not to make contact again. Feeling betrayed, she telephoned Lawford and told him she was going public with everything. She told Slatzer that she might hold a press conference if Bobby continued to avoid her.

Meanwhile, Bobby Kennedy had ordered his own investigation into Sinatra's links with organised crime. Preliminary reports were finished on 15 May and 2 July 1962. A more comprehensive study was completed on 3 August. Written by Dougald D. MacMillan, an attorney working in the new organised crime and racketeering section of the Justice Department, the nineteen-page final report concluded, 'Sinatra has had a long and wide association with hoodlums and racketeers which seems to be continuing. The nature of Sinatra's work may, on occasion, bring him into contact with underworld figures but this cannot account for his friendship and/ or financial involvement with people such as Joe and Rocco Fischetti – cousins of Al Capone – Paul Emilio [Skinny] D'Amato and Sam Giancana, all of whom are on our list of racketeers. No other entertainer appears to be mentioned nearly so often with racketeers. Available information indicates not only that Sinatra is associated with each of the above named racketeers but that they apparently maintain contact with one another. This indicates a possible community of interest involving Sinatra and racketeers in Illinois, Indiana, New Jersey, Florida and Nevada.'

At the end of July 1962, Monroe stayed at the Cal-Neva Lodge as a guest of Giancana's. Johnny Rosselli and Jimmy Alo were also present. Over dinner Lawford watched Monroe drinking heavily and confiding in Giancana. 'I've been nothing more than a piece of meat for Jack and Bobby,' she was overheard to say. Lawford said that after dinner Monroe went upstairs with Giancana. Monroe told Jeanne Carmen that she slept with Giancana that weekend. Later, Giancana was sarcastic about Monroe's body when bragging about his conquest to gangster cronies and, according to Milton Ebbins, about her ability in bed. Bill Roemer remembered a since-disappeared wiretap during which Rosselli told Giancana, 'You sure get your rocks off fucking the same broad as the brothers, don't you?' – although he may have been talking about either Monroe or Judy Campbell. Alo described the debauch that weekend as disgusting. Sinatra and Lawford kept Monroe drugged, the gangster claimed. Later, photographer Billy Woodfield said the singer showed him a contact sheet of photographs taken that weekend. One photo showed Monroe on all fours being straddled by Giancana, while another showed her with what looked like vomit on her dress. The photographer urged Sinatra to destroy the contact sheet.

Former FBI assistant director Courtney Evans admitted to Monroe's biographer, investigative journalist Anthony Summers, that organised crime put pressure on the presidency, the closest the US government has ever come to admitting that the Mafia tried to blackmail the Kennedy brothers. Bobby Kennedy arrived in California on 3 August 1962. It is believed he made a flying visit to Los Angeles the next day. In his 1973 biography of Monroe, Norman Mailer wrote:

For anyone who wished to embarrass the Kennedys profoundly, and begin perhaps a whispering campaign which would destroy them by '64, how perfect a move [it would be] to kill Marilyn in just such a way as to make it look like suicide in the first reports. As a suicide, however, it is so clumsily staged that by the second week every newspaper would be hinting at murder. That could do the Kennedys an unholy damage. Given the force of underground gossip . . . who would believe they had nothing to do with it?

Marilyn Monroe died in the early hours of 5 August 1962. Her housekeeper raised the alarm by calling Monroe's psychiatrist. She had not left her bedroom all night, which the housekeeper thought odd. The actress was declared dead by her doctor. The coroner decided cause of death was 'probably suicide'. Her liver contained 13 milligrams per cent of pentobarbital – the chemical identified in the sleeping pill Nembutal – ten times the normal dose. Her blood also contained 8 milligrams per cent of sleeping pill chloral hydrate – up to twenty times the amount recommended for sleep. However, Monroe's autopsy did not find any residue of sleeping pills in her stomach, which was odd. Sometimes fragments of gelatine capsules are found digesting, and sometimes intact, undigested pills.

The Los Angeles District Attorney's office took part in the official investigation. According to his family, district attorney investigator Frank Hronek died still believing organised crime was behind Monroe's supposed suicide – and specifically Sam Giancana and Johnny Rosselli.

Hank Messick, crime author and former consultant to New York's Joint Legislative Committee on Crime, believed that the Mafia tried to blackmail Kennedy by manipulating a drugged Monroe into calling Bobby Kennedy for help. Messick pointed out that in 1961 the mob had also injected a local politician with chloral hydrate, put his drugged body into bed with a woman and then taken photographs with which to blackmail him. Messick believed the plan was to compromise the married Kennedy by providing evidence of him alone at night in Monroe's bungalow.

But the plan backfired when Kennedy hardened his heart and refused to come to Monroe's rescue, leaving her to die alone. Messick said his theory was based on unattributable interviews with sources at the US Justice Department and within organised crime.

According to another version of events, Giancana – aware that Monroe was thinking of going public about the mob's involvement in the Castro assassination attempt – planned to murder Monroe and implicate Bobby Kennedy in her death. Giancana supposedly instructed four gangsters to plan the hit. One arrived in Los Angeles accompanied by another man. Two more assassins arrived the same day, one from Kansas, the other from Detroit. The four men listened to what was going on in Monroe's bungalow. Private detective Fred Otash had installed bugging equipment on Teamster boss Jimmy Hoffa's orders. Hoffa said later he hid a tape of one of the Kennedys with a woman, which he described as 'filthy stuff'. Bobby arrived at Monroe's home accompanied by a doctor. When the actress became hysterical the doctor injected her with a sedative. Kennedy and the doctor then left. The assassins supposedly broke into the house. Monroe was still groggy from the injection. They held her down on the bed and taped over her mouth. Then they inserted a Nembutal and chloral hydrate suppository into her anus. Monroe was quickly unconscious. They ripped off the tape and left.

In 2005, former Los Angeles County deputy district attorney John Miner – who watched Dr Thomas Noguchi perform his autopsy of Monroe – said he was almost certain that she was murdered by a poisoned enema. Miner's theory is that the actress took or was given chloral hydrate to make her unconscious – possibly in a soft drink – before somebody then dissolved Nembutal in water and gave her a lethal enema. Miner said his argument was backed up by shorthand notes he made after listening to tape recordings Monroe made for her psychiatrist Dr Ralph Greenson. Not only was Monroe clearly not suicidal, said Miner, but she also used enemas for sexual pleasure. But Miner's credibility has been undermined by his inability to produce these contemporaneous notes. Instead, he has relied on his memory of tape recordings that nobody has ever heard.

Supposing all the conspiracy theories about Monroe's murder are true, her bedroom that night must have resembled the ship's cabin in the Marx Brothers' movie *A Night at the Opera*, given the number of Mafiosi, politicians and doctors clambering over each other.

According to Murray Humphreys's second wife Jeanne, the Outfit was just as curious as everybody else to know if Monroe had been murdered. The gangsters wondered if the Kennedys were behind her death.

The most plausible explanation remains that Monroe took an accidental overdose after being rejected by Bobby Kennedy. She had previously had her stomach pumped after taking overdoses on numerous occasions. She made suicide-watch pacts with various people, including her acting teacher, Lee Strasberg, to call if either party were feeling suicidal. The British poet Edith Sitwell predicted that Monroe would kill herself, having only met her once. As Los Angeles police chief Daryl Gates said in September 1985, announcing the public release of police files on Monroe's death, 'She committed suicide by barbiturates – that is the reality, and there is nothing very special about it except for the fact that she was Marilyn Monroe.'

A fellow barbiturate addict, Judy Garland, put it another way. 'You take a couple of sleeping pills, and you wake up in twenty minutes and forget you've taken them,' said Garland. 'So you take a couple more, and the next thing you know you've taken too many.'

Judy Campbell discovered she was pregnant with Kennedy's baby in December 1962. She told Giancana and he offered to marry her. Campbell decided to have an abortion and Giancana collected her from Chicago's Grant Hospital on 28 January 1963. Campbell was being harassed by the FBI, who kept questioning her about people she knew but stopped short of asking her to testify in front of the grand jury. Campbell suspected that the Justice Department was pulling its punches because she knew too much.

That summer Sinatra was busy trying to sell his loss-making record company to Warner Bros. Back in 1961 he had fallen out with his record label, Capitol. He decided to found his own company, Reprise (as in *reprisal*). During the second half of 1963 Sinatra began negotiating with Jack Warner for Warner Bros to buy the company, but Warner made clear that he wanted nothing to do with the mob if the deal went through. He told Sinatra to stop seeing Giancana, sell the Cal-Neva and cash in his 9 per cent share of the Sands. In exchange Warner Bros was offering Sinatra $2 million ($13 million in today's money) for his label. Sinatra would be obliged to spend $500,000 buying one-third of the stock in the new Warner Reprise record company. The other $1.5 million he was allowed to pocket. In effect, Sinatra was swapping sole ownership of an unsuccessful company for 33 per cent of a successful one.

In addition, Sinatra's two movie companies, Artanis – 'Sinatra' spelt backwards – and Park Lake Enterprises, were offered sweet production deals. Warner Bros guaranteed to pay Sinatra $250,000 for each movie he appeared in plus 15 per cent of the gross. He was given offices on the Warner Bros lot and the title 'special assistant to Jack Warner'.

The way Sinatra's lawyer, Milton 'Mickey' Rudin – described by one senior Los Angeles police intelligence officer as a 'hoodlum lawyer' – structured the deal would make the singer even richer when a mob-associated parking and funeral services company bought Warner Bros five years later.

Sinatra duly dropped Giancana, leaving the gangster both bewildered and hurt. Coming on top of the Kennedys reneging on their part of the 1960 election deal and the loss of the Cal-Neva in October 1962, Giancana wanted to have Sinatra murdered in 1963. A Giancana family member told investigative journalist Gus Russo that only the intercession of the East Coast mob prevented that from happening. Even so, he still talked about having Sinatra killed. By the spring of 1965 Giancana was being ground down by legal problems, having been ordered to testify before a grand jury investigating organised crime in Chicago. But the Justice Department never cross-examined Giancana in court for reasons that have never been explained. Chicago-based US attorney Edward Harkson said that Washington told him not to prosecute the gangster. The grand jury then offered Giancana immunity if he talked freely. Giancana was now seeing a dilemma – either tell all and face retribution or go to jail for contempt. Giancana kept *omerta* and was sent to prison for a year, after which he settled in Mexico, having lost control of Chicago.

On 22 November 1963 President Kennedy was assassinated. Sinatra wondered if Giancana had had anything to do with the assassination. He knew Giancana had been friendly with Lee Harvey Oswald's killer, Jack Ruby, through the strip club circuit. Ruby had grown up in Chicago and told people the mob had ordered him to move to Dallas. When associates of Giancana gathered in Dallas to discuss betting operations a few months before the assassination, they met at Ruby's Carousel Club. (Co-incidentally, one of Giancana's favourite movies – which he kept a 16mm copy of in his Chicago home – was *The Manchurian Candidate*, the assassination thriller about a plot to murder the president.)

Jack Warner's assistant Richard Gully went further, claiming that Johnny Rosselli assassinated Kennedy. Hollywood gossip columnist Jimmy Starr told Rosselli's biographer that the gangster put together the team that assassinated the president. Rosselli himself claimed that Harry Cohn's old assistant, Jonie Taps, told him the news, telephoning him from Hollywood just after the assassination. Years later, prison convict Robert L. Russell wrote to the Senate committee investigation into the assassination that he had met a woman named Cindy who in turn claimed she had worked for Ruby. According to Russell, Cindy said that on 22 November she had dropped off Rosselli and a second man – a marksman who had flown in to Dallas from Miami – at the far end of Dealey Plaza. As the president's motorcade approached, the sniper squeezed off two rounds, handed the rifle to Rosselli and disappeared into the crowd. Cindy then drove Rosselli and the rifle away from the scene. Gully said that the reason Rosselli was found butchered in an oil drum in Florida on 29 July 1976 was because he had started boasting about his part in the assassination. Ironically, one year before his murder, Rosselli had pitched a movie idea to his old friend, producer Bryan Foy, about a patriotic gangster who becomes involved in a plot to invade Cuba but whose plans are derailed when Castro organises Kennedy's assassination. Foy dismissed the movie idea as too far-fetched.

Judy Campbell went into shock after Kennedy's assassination. Rosselli had checked her into a Beverly Hills hotel two days before the president's death. After Kennedy died, Campbell's drinking spun out of control. She also became addicted to injecting amphetamine, prescribed by New York doctor Dr Max Jacobson – the same man who supplied speed shots to Jack Kennedy and his wife Jackie, Johnny Mathis and Andy Williams. Eventually Campbell was hospitalised with amphetamine psychosis, convinced that the FBI was trying to make her kill herself.

Robert Blakey, former chief counsel of the House Select Committee on Assassinations – which investigated Kennedy's murder – come to the conclusion that the mob was involved in the assassination. Blakey once wrote: 'As in Greek tragedy, there was in the President's character a fatal flaw, a *hamartia*, one that left him vulnerable to assassination by organised crime.'

Author Stephen Fox has written that without Bobby Kennedy's dogged pursuit of gangsters, and without Joe Kennedy's long-standing underworld connections, John F. Kennedy would never have been killed. 'In that sense,' wrote Fox, 'brother killed brother, and father killed son.'

Nevertheless, given how difficult it is for people to keep a secret, it is implausible the assassination conspiracy did not leak out immediately after Kennedy's death. If one has to choose between conspiracy or a bizarre alignment of people and events to explain the Kennedy assassination, one is bound to choose the latter. Despite the number of exiled Cubans, rogue CIA agents and vengeful Mafiosi milling around in downtown New Orleans, even Lee Harvey Oswald's biographer Norman Mailer has concluded that Oswald worked alone.

Regardless of whether the mob was involved in Kennedy's assassination, in a sense his death achieved what the Mafia wanted. Bobby Kennedy lost his gangbusting zeal after his brother was murdered. He resigned as attorney general in the summer of 1964.

Sinatra was not the only mob associate who worked his way into the Democratic Party machine. Sidney Korshak became such an important contributor to party fundraising that later he would be the first person introduced to presidential nominee Jimmy Carter when he visited Los Angeles. By the 1960s, Korshak was best friends with Universal MCA chief executive Lew Wasserman, the man once described as 'the Zeus of the Mount Olympus known as Hollywood'. Both Korshak and Wasserman were Democratic Party stalwarts, inviting each other to fundraising events. MCA agent Harris Katleman described Korshak and Wasserman as being joined at the hip. Wasserman was introduced to Korshak in 1939 shortly after the MCA agent arrived in Los Angeles. MCA was nicknamed 'the Star-Spangled Octopus' after the Second World War because of its hold over every aspect of show business. Not only did it represent every actor or singer of note, but it was also the only talent agency allowed to make television programmes – taking a producer's fee and 10 per cent of its clients' earnings. In 1958 it bought the Universal backlot and then leased it back to the studio. The government tried to build an anti-competition case against MCA but it came to nothing because of Wasserman's political connections. MCA bought Universal from Decca Records in 1962. Universal MCA began building its new corporate headquarters, 'as alien and menacing as a spaceship' in the words of producer Saul David, at Universal Studios on the edge of Hollywood. The fourteen-storey Universal MCA headquarters became known as the Black Tower and, according to one former secretary, MCA chairman Jules Stein let Korshak use his office for private meetings with Meyer Lansky as late as 1965. Johnny Rosselli's actress god-daughter, Nancy Bretzfield, said that Korshak and Wasserman were two of the five people who controlled Hollywood. 'They controlled all the moves,' she said.

By the 1960s, former Los Angeles organised crime division head A.O. Richards considered Korshak almost untouchable because he was so well insulated. Korshak admitted to the FBI on 23 October 1963 that his friends included Kirk Douglas, Dinah Shore, Cyd Charisse and Debbie Reynolds.

According to former Screen Actors Guild executive director Chester Migden, Wasserman used Korshak as a 'fixer'. The studios had a lot of money invested in actors, directors and writers and they used Korshak when talent got into trouble, said Migden.

The FBI recorded one conversation between Los Angeles Mafia member Jimmy Fratiano and Johnny Rosselli, during which Rosselli explained how Korshak worked. 'One thing you've got to keep in mind with Korshak. He's made millions for Chicago and he's got plenty of clout in LA and Vegas. He's really burrowed in. He's real big with the movie colony, lives in a big mansion in Bel Air, knows most of the big stars,' said Rosselli. 'He calls himself a labour-relations expert but he's really a fixer. A union cooks up a strike and Sidney arbitrates it. Instead of a payoff under the table, he gets a real big fee, pays taxes on it, and cuts it up. All nice and clean.'

One of Korshak's union clients was the truckers' union, the International Brotherhood of Teamsters. Movie production involves manhandling heavy equipment – there is much more of a 'blue collar' input than most people assume. The Teamsters control everything that has to be driven to and from the movie set: cameras, lighting, props, food, portable toilets, even film stock itself. The Teamsters later tried to take over the Producers Guild of America and other film-production trade associations. The truck drivers' cooperation is critical, especially in the television business, which follows a strict timetable. If the Teamsters go on strike then a film or television series collapses. Moreover, Teamsters were so feared that few would dare to cross their picket lines. Korshak provided Wasserman with a connection to the truckers' union. Wasserman was the only studio head with whom Korshak had such a close relationship, said former Western Conference Teamsters head Andy Anderson. In turn, Wasserman represented Hollywood in union negotiations. Wasserman bent over backwards to accommodate the unions, sometimes to a bewildering extent. It could be argued that Wasserman helped put Hollywood out of business by making it too expensive to shoot in California – the state has been crippled by the volume of subsequent 'runaway production' due to high employment costs.

Wall Street analysts once questioned Wasserman about his friendship with Teamsters boss Jimmy Hoffa. Towards the end of the 1950s Bobby Kennedy, chief counsel on a Senate committee investigating Mafia union corruption, called Hoffa and his Teamsters 'a conspiracy of evil'. Kennedy said that Hoffa had defrauded his own union and put gangster cronies in key positions. Analysts were nervous about a Hollywood mogul having such a close relationship with such a notorious figure. Wasserman, however, defended the friendship. Considering Universal MCA hired about 15,000 Teamsters each week, Wasserman said, he would rather do business with somebody he knew than somebody he didn't.

One reason why Wasserman may have been so keen to keep the Teamsters on side was that he was borrowing money from their pension fund. In 1955 Hoffa consolidated scores of small pension funds in twenty-two states into the Central States, Southeast and Southwest Areas Pension Fund. With the studio system disintegrating and Mayer on his way out, MGM was shedding most of the stars it had under contract. Korshak arranged for Wasserman to borrow from the Teamsters Pension Fund to lock in talent for Universal MCA.

The mob also borrowed money from the fund. In the 1950s Moe Dalitz borrowed $1 million to build a hospital in Las Vegas. The hundred-bed Sunrise Hospital was the brainchild of Irwin Molasky and his partner, Mervyn Adelson. Adelson used his share of hospital profits to build a television production company, Lorimar. In the 1980s Lorimar would produce *Dallas*, *The Waltons* and movies including *An Officer and a Gentleman*.

Despite the years Chicago spent embedding Korshak in Hollywood, he was not above the mob reminding him who was boss. Once Korshak found a dead fish in his mailbox while trying to settle an argument between the Los Angeles Mafia family and the Teamsters about the union not paying kickbacks.

Another of Korshak's clients was Charles Bludhorn, chairman of Gulf & Western Industries. Bludhorn was an Austrian immigrant who had parlayed a Michigan car bumper manufacturing business into a group whose interests spanned finance, manufacturing and mining. Bludhorn acquired Paramount Pictures in October 1966, according to one Hollywood mogul's widow, with the sole purpose 'to get laid – it was that simple'.

At the time Korshak was having an affair with actress Jill St John while she was dating Henry Kissinger, national security adviser to President Richard Nixon. St John was introduced to Kissinger at a dinner party given by Kirk Douglas, one of Korshak's oldest friends in Hollywood. In 1968 Korshak arranged for St John – who once said of herself 'I was a woman at six' – to buy shares in Las Vegas casino operating company Parvin-Dohrmann Inc. On 23 January 1969 Parvin-Dohrmann bought the Stardust casino from Moe Dalitz. The Denny's restaurant chain acquired Parvin-Dohrmann shortly afterwards. St John walked away from the deal a wealthy woman. Audiences watching her in the James Bond movie *Diamonds Are Forever* (1971) – on which Korshak worked as an unaccredited consultant – were unaware that the actress had co-owned some of the Las Vegas casinos the movie was filmed in.

Bludhorn, meanwhile, was looking for somebody to run Paramount Pictures. Korshak first met former actor Robert Evans at the Palm Springs Racquet Club in the late 1950s. According to former Paramount president Frank Yablans, Evans reminded Korshak of Bugsy Siegel. Korshak recommended Evans, who had yet to produce his first film, to work for Paramount, initially running its European business from London. Evans was appointed senior vice-president in charge of worldwide production at Paramount at the beginning of 1967.

One of Evans's first green lights was to hire Roman Polanksi to direct *Rosemary's Baby*. Polanski had chosen Mia Farrow, an inexperienced actress who had just got married to Frank Sinatra, for the lead. The Polish director was stretching Farrow to the limit, putting her through as many as thirty takes in an effort to elicit an appropriately tortured performance. Early in the shoot, a Sinatra emissary paid a visit to Paramount executive Peter Bart, warning him that he would have his legs broken unless Polanski confined himself to one or two takes.

In March of that year Evans paid nearly $100,000 ($574,000 in today's money) for the movie rights to a sixty-page outline of a novel. Its author, Mario Puzo, had been to see Evans previously, telling him, 'Thinkin' of writin' an inside story on the boys, the organisation – part real, part fiction – callin' it *Mafia*.'

Puzo decided to change the title of the book he was working on. *The Godfather* would go on to become arguably the greatest gangster movie ever made.

CHAPTER EIGHT

Apelike Men in Silk Suits Selling Popcorn

In November 1966 Frank Sinatra's lawyer, Mickey Rudin, read that seventy-four-year-old Jack Warner was in talks to sell his controlling share in Warner Bros to television company Seven Arts for $32 million or $20 a share. One observer told *Variety* he was puzzled by the deal; Warner could have held out for a lot more than what he was getting. Rudin realised that everybody had forgotten about Sinatra having control over the sale. Back in 1963, when Sinatra sold his record company Reprise to Warner Bros, Rudin had inserted a clause in the contract giving his client veto over any change in ownership.

In 1953 investment banker Charles Allen, who later became chairman of the parent company of Columbia Pictures, met former tyre dealer Eliot Hyman. Howard Hughes still wanted to sell RKO Pictures despite the bad publicity of the controversial takeover attempt the year before. Allen lent Hyman $11 million ($79 million today) to buy the studio in July 1955. Hyman's company sold off RKO's back catalogue in 1955 and the studio closed down three years later.

Hyman, however, went into business with former agent Ray Stark, whose clients had included Marilyn Monroe, Lana Turner and Kirk Douglas. Stark once described business as the eighth art – the art of making money. Hyman and Stark acquired Canadian television distributor Seven Arts, which licensed programming to broadcasters. Seven Arts' founder and chairman was Louis Chesler, described by one former US prosecutor as 'just another bagman for Meyer Lansky'. Chesler had met Lansky and gangster Mike 'Trigger' Coppola when on holiday in Miami. Coppola became a shareholder in one of Chesler's companies, while Seven Arts was used to move cash backwards and forwards between Canada, the USA and the Bahamas. Seven Arts laundered money for the mob over a ten-year period before Hyman and Stark acquired it.

Charles Allen joined the board of Warner Bros in 1956 and approved the studio selling its library of pre-1948 films to Seven Arts to license to Canadian broadcasters that same year. Allen also became a shareholder, giving him leverage over any future sale.

In 1964 Hyman and Stark decided to take Seven Arts public and float on the American Stock Exchange, the second largest financial market in the USA. Stringent US Securities and Exchange Com-Mike mission (SEC) reporting rules meant that Seven Arts would have to lose its mob connections. Chesler was asked to step down as chairman.

Mickey Rudin decided to keep quiet about Sinatra's veto over any sale until the Seven Arts deal acquired a momentum of its own. Seven Arts bought Warner Bros for $84 million in June 1967. Sinatra pocketed another $9 million and retained 20 per cent of Warner Reprise. He also hung on to his veto of any future sale of the merged Warner Bros–Seven Arts.

Just such an acquisition of Warner Bros was talked about in Miami the following summer. A group of executives from Kinney National Services met in Florida to discuss strategy. Kinney was a corporation whose activities included parking lots, funeral homes, pest control and building maintenance. Kinney's president, Steven J. Ross, now wanted to move the company out of bricks and mortar and into the media business. Ross was something of a visionary who foresaw the rise of cable television, and with it the opportunity to sell goods and services through the television set. But he also knew that he would need a Hollywood studio such as Warner Bros to provide content for the interactive pipelines he envisaged.

Kinney, through Ross, had deep associations with the mob. The company's founder used to rent garages in New Jersey to mob boss

Longy Zwillman for him to store bootleg alcohol in. Zwillman's rent money was used to buy the sites in New York that formed the basis of Kinney. Indeed, Zwillman may have been a silent partner in Kinney; his widow told one suitor he could expect to own shares in Kinney should they ever get married. In the 1940s Joey Adonis paid Kinney to allow the Mafia to park limousines in one of its parking lots.

Ross acquired control of Kinney Parking in March 1962, having started out running his father-in-law's funeral home. Ross was rumoured to have his own ties with more than one of New York's five Mafia families.

By the end of the Miami strategy session Ross and his executives had identified three possible acquisitions – ABC, MGM and Warner Bros–Seven Arts. ABC and MGM said they were not interested, while Warner Bros–Seven Arts was polite but noncommittal.

On 28 January 1969 Commonwealth United, a Los Angeles-based conglomerate of insurance, oil and property companies, announced it was in talks to buy Warner Bros–Seven Arts. The share swap deal valued the studio at $400 million. Ross decided that Commonwealth United was basically a shell company fuelled by share dealing – the more one pushed one's finger into it, the less there really was. A few hours later Kinney announced it too was bidding for the Hollywood studio. Each company revised its offer twice at the beginning of February. The Warner Bros board accepted Kinney's $400 million offer in March and the deal closed in July 1969. Kinney renamed the studio Warner Communications in keeping with its plans to reinvent Warner Bros as a multimedia content provider.

In June 1970, *Forbes* magazine ran a profile of Warner Communications which said rumours had long circulated about its parent company Kinney's links with the Mafia. Grubby underworld connections were embarrassing to Ross, who by now saw himself as a spokesman for Hollywood – a Lew Wasserman *manqué*. He decided to distance Warner Communications from the parking lots and their unsavoury past by spinning them off into a separate company, National Kinney Corp. But Warner Communications was canny enough still to hold on to the money-making parking lots. Warner Communications eventually sold National Kinney Corp. off completely at the end of 1978. The Genovese Mafia family was still supposed to own shares in Kinney, having inherited some of Longy Zwillman's stake. Nine years later, Kinney System, Inc. chairman Daniel Katz was found dead in his car with a shotgun wound in his chest. He was supposed to have killed himself. At the time, Katz was under investigation for making illegal payments to Local 272, the Mafia-controlled New York chapter of the parking and garage employees' union.

Warner, meanwhile, was investing alongside the Gambino crime family in an upstate New York theatre that had millions embezzled from it before it collapsed. The studio was mixing its own cash with mob money to buy shares in the mob-owned concert venue. Because of its greed for cash – supposedly to finance a secret company slush fund – Warner, through certain executives, was laundering money for the New York Mafia. The cash fund is thought to have been used to buy cocaine for film and rock stars.

At the beginning of 1972, New York stockbroker Eliot Weisman and his colleague Leonard Horwitz were raising money to build a concert venue in upstate New York. Weisman and Horwitz both worked for stockbroker Ferkauf, Roggen. Horwitz was trying to sell $150,000 of shares in the new venture. The money would be used to secure some land in Tarrytown, Westchester County, and also to cover other start-up costs. One of the first people he approached was Ross's lieutenant, Jay Emmett, vice-president of Warner Communications. Emmett belonged to an investment club that Horwitz ran for four pals. The Warner Communications executive agreed to buy $15,000 of stock in Westchester Premier Theatre as a personal investment.

But the Mafia was the main backer of the venture. Individual investors included Salvatore Cannatella, a Genovese family associate who eventually invested $1.4 million in the theatre. Another investor was Thomas Marson, a plumbing business entrepreneur whose Rancho Mirage, California, home was considered by the FBI to be a meeting place for the Los Angeles mob. Toledo-based bookmaker Irving 'Slick' Shapiro told Jimmy 'the Weasel' Fratiano that Marson represented $1.4 million of investment in the Westchester – $400,000 of Marson's own money, plus another $800,000 from a Detroit gangster and $200,000 from a Toledo dentist. The scheme was the brainchild of Carlo Gambino and his second in command Paul Castellano. Gambino family member Gregory De Palma and Richard 'Nerves' Fusco, who was linked to the Colombo crime family, were also involved. The Westchester Premier Theatre scam was to be a simple 'bust out' operation. The theatre's owners would skim ticket sales while leaving creditors unpaid.

But by the late spring of 1973, the public stock offering was faltering. Even with Mafia seed money, the share offer did not look as if it was going to reach the minimum needed to float. Horwitz went to see Emmett at Warner Communications' headquarters with a proposal. Horwitz suggested to Emmett that he borrow $50,000 in cash from the theatre's owners and add $25,000 of his own money to buy $75,000 of stock. Presumably, Horwitz's thinking was that facilitating Emmett's investment would get the share offer past the minimum subscription, allowing Westchester Premier Theatre to go public. Mixing Mafia cash with Emmett's own money would launder Gambino's investment through the share offering. Horwitz even had $50,000 in cash on him in a brown paper bag. Emmett said he was not interested but described Horwitz's proposition to Ross. According to Emmett, Ross said Horwitz should go and see Warner Communications' assistant treasurer Solomon Weiss, who was also Ross's private accountant. Horwitz later testified that Weiss said a company like Warner Communications always had a need for ready cash. After counting the $50,000, Weiss left the room, presumably to confer with Ross. On his return Weiss told Horwitz that the company would buy not 10,000 but 20, 000 shares. The stockbroker would have to come up with another $50,000 in cash to bring the total up to $100,000. Between 1974 and 1977 Warner bought another $150,000 worth of stock in Westchester in exchange for a further $100,000 in cash. In doing so, Warner Communications may have unwittingly laundered mob money. Marson told Fratiano that the Mafia was getting officers of corporations to buy stock with company money at inflated prices in exchange for getting kickbacks.

Despite pump-priming by Gambino and others, the theatre was $3.5 million in debt by the time it opened two years after it was supposed to. Skimming was incessant. Money was taken from the box office cashbox to repay some of the high-interest 'shylock' money the mob had borrowed to help finance the theatre. The gangsters also dipped their own fingers in the till. One scam was installing sixty-four 'phantom seats' the theatre's accountants were unaware of. These seats were always the first to be sold. About $4500 in cash would be put in a separate envelope and split between Gambino and the others.

Mafia hoods also ran the day-to-day business of the theatre. Mobsters in silk suits patrolled the aisles selling popcorn. One gangster watching a performance of *The Nutcracker* was overheard to ask, 'Hey, how come there's no talkin' in this thing?' Concertgoers were bewildered when parking lot attendants greeted them with, 'Get the fuck out and I'll park this fucking piece of shit.'

Another cash drain was the amount Westchester paid entertainers. Performers were paid top dollar for appearing. Diana Ross, for example, received $225,000 for one week's engagement. Another entertainer who demanded to be paid $150,000 in cash brought along her own armed bodyguards. When they pointed their guns at Fusco and De Palma the gangsters pulled out their own guns, disarming the bodyguards.

Early in 1976, Marson was overheard telephoning Sinatra from a Palm Springs hotel, ordering him to perform at the Westchester. Another version of events has Sinatra appearing at the Westchester at the behest of Louis 'Louie Domes' Pacella, a gangster who worked for the Genovese crime family. According to the Drug Enforcement Administration (DEA), Pacella was a heroin dealer and capo reporting to family boss Frank 'Funzi' Tieri. Philip Leonetti, a senior Mafioso turned federal informant, told the FBI that Pacella took over as Sinatra's Mafia handler after Giancana was murdered in 1975. Sinatra performed at the Westchester for ten nights in April 1976, nine nights in September and October that same year, and eight nights in May 1977. Later, Jimmy 'the Weasel' Fratiano implicated Sinatra in the skimming of the Westchester. Fratiano, who was inducted into the Mafia by Johnny Rosselli, said that De Palma paid Sinatra between $50,000 and $60,000 in cash under the table to play the venue, thereby avoiding income tax. The FBI recorded De Palma saying that Sinatra's lawyer Mickey Rudin was also given a cut of money skimmed off the top from sales of Sinatra concert merchandise.

Fratiano wrote that Sinatra agreed to extend his run at the Westchester specifically to raise cash to feed the families of imprisoned Mafiosi. In exchange, Sinatra's friend Jilly Rizzo came back with a message from the singer. Sinatra wanted the Mafia to break the legs of a former security guard who was selling stories to gossip magazines.

The Westchester Premier Theatre went bankrupt in the second half of 1977. It is estimated that the Mafia embezzled $9 million before the theatre collapsed. However, the FBI managed to bug the theatre's offices while it was still open. Federal agents also wiretapped De Palma's home phone line. In September 1977, an FBI agent knocked on the door of Horwitz's home in Norwal, Connecticut. The FBI said it wanted to talk to Horwitz about the closure of the Westchester. Horwitz immediately phoned Emmett, who by now was co-president of Warner Communications. Horwitz told him about the FBI coming to his door. Emmett told Horwitz not to say anything. One month later Horwitz was offered a $75,000-a-year job with Warner Communications in exchange for his silence.

Federal prosecutors were convinced they had a strong case against the financiers of the Westchester. The Justice Department was determined to prove that everybody involved knew the Westchester was a scam. In June 1978 Emmett, Horwitz, Weisman and seven others were charged with twenty-six crimes including defrauding investors and looting the theatre while it was in bankruptcy proceedings.

At the pre-trial hearing in November 1978 the prosecution submitted as evidence a photograph of Sinatra in his dressing room at the Westchester. Exhibit 181 showed Sinatra smiling with his arms around two men. Six others were crowded around him. Bunched together for the photographer were Carlo Gambino, his nephew Joseph Gambino and Paul Castellano. Also posing was Jimmy 'the Weasel' Fratiano. Sinatra later told gambling officials that he had not known the men herding together. He did admit, however, to having met Fratiano once before in the early 1970s – even then, Sinatra only knew the man as 'Jimmy'. Fratiano later contradicted this, saying he had known Sinatra since the 1950s. As with the Lucky Luciano photographs back in the 1940s, Sinatra passed the whole thing off as an occupational hazard for an entertainer. Lots of people wanted to have their photograph taken with him, he said. Sinatra told the Nevada Gaming Control Board that he knew nothing about the backgrounds of the men in the photograph – which was odd, considering that, according to Fratiano, Sinatra greeted Carlo Gambino like an old friend, giving him a hug and a kiss on both cheeks.

The first trial of Emmett and his co-defendants ended in a mis-trial. The whole process would have to be gone through again. Several defendants, presumably unable to face a second trial, hoped to reduce their sentences by admitting their guilt. But Emmett and Warner Communications treasurer Solomon Weiss held out. When the second trial began in March 1979 they pleaded the Fifth Amendment. After a two-month trial Horwitz, Weisman and Cannatella were all found guilty. Emmett was found not guilty.

The US Attorney's Office smelled the blood in the water. Nathaniel Akerman was convinced the seam of corruption inside Warner Communications extended right to the top of the company. His office trained its legal firepower on Steve Ross, certain that he knew about mob money laundering. Ross insulated himself from proceedings, telling lawyers that he knew nothing about the Westchester. Furthermore, he had never investigated the scandal himself because Warner's lawyers told him this was the job of the company's audit committee. According to Ross, Emmett alone hired Horwitz as a consultant, Emmett alone knew why Horwitz was hired and only Emmett knew what Horwitz's actual job was at Warner Communications. Ross's strategy was to use Emmett as a buffer, protecting himself at all costs. In effect, he was throwing Warner Communications' second in command to the wolves.

In September 1980 Emmett was charged with accepting bribes to induce Warner Communications to buy stock, misappropriating company funds and creating fraudulent documentation to hide the theft. Weisman promised to testify against Emmett providing what was left of his seven-year sentence was reduced to eighteen months. Horwitz, who had already been convicted of defrauding investors and skimming money from the Westchester, went on trial again, this time for bribing Warner Communications executives. Emmett and Horwitz both pleaded guilty on 9 February 1981, the day their trial was due to start.

Akerman, who by now had been promoted to federal prosecutor, was still not satisfied. He was aligning crosshairs on Ross, using the same strategy he had used to convict Emmett. If he could send Warner Communications' treasurer Solomon Weiss to prison, then the accountant could be turned against Ross in exchange for a reduced prison sentence. Weiss was indicted and put on trial in November 1982. He was charged with laundering mob money and issuing fake cheques to cover money laundering over a five-year period. Weiss was also accused of overseeing a secret cash fund at Warner, although it was never spelt out what this money was for. However, under cross-examination Weiss maintained his innocence. The only part he played in the scandal, he said, was to prepare cheques at the behest of Emmett. In the end, Weiss was found guilty on seven of the thirteen charges brought against him, including racketeering and perjury. Weiss avoided being sent to prison, however. He was fined $58,000 and placed on probation for five years, doing full-time community service. The trial broke Weiss's health and he never recovered. Akerman failed in his attempt to put Ross on trial. Ross carried on running Warner Communications for another eleven years until his death in December 1992.

The Gambino crime family may have made millions from the Westchester Theatre scandal, but it was small change compared with the cash the Colombo crime family made from its involvement with what has been called 'the other Hollywood' – pornography.

CHAPTER NINE

An Even Deeper Throat

By 1970 the New York Mafia was financing the growing film pornography business. It put up the money to make five-minute stag reels shown in peep booths in Times Square sex shops. One of the directors of these stag reels was Gerald Damiano, who has been called the Scorsese of porn because of the amount of Catholic imagery in his work. One day Damiano had an idea for a new movie. He had just met porn actress Linda Lovelace, who showed the director her party piece – her ability to swallow a man's erect penis to the hilt. Damiano went home and dashed off a script starring Lovelace as a woman unable to achieve orgasm in the conventional way because her clitoris is in her oesophagus. The former hairdresser from Queens then went off to pitch the idea to his producer and financier.

Gerald Damiano Film Productions was two-thirds owned by Louis 'Butchie' Peraino, whose father Anthony and uncle Joseph were both members of the Colombo crime family. Law enforcement officials nicknamed Peraino's father and uncle 'Big Tony' and 'Joe the Whale' respectively. Each of them weighed nearly 300 pounds. The Peraino brothers' father Giuseppe had been murdered during the Castellammarese war in 1931 (see Chapter Two). Anthony Peraino was sixteen when his father died and his brother Joseph just five. The orphans were brought up mainly by the Colombo crime family. Anthony was first charged with murder the same year as his father died but avoided conviction, as he would for his next six arrests. Over the years Anthony Peraino would be charged with various crimes including gambling, tax evasion and knocking down and killing a pedestrian with his car, but he was never convicted.

His son Louis was considered to be a Mafia associate rather than a full-blown member, or 'made man'. Many of those interviewed for a 1982 *Los Angeles Times* profile of the Peraino family said that Louis, like Michael Corleone in *The Godfather*, was driven by a desire for respectability. Porn actor Fred Lincoln said that all Peraino wanted to be was a legitimate movie producer. 'It's kind of a sad story,' said Lincoln. 'Here's this mobster's son who wants to be an auteur, you know? Butchie Peraino did nothing but make movies – that's all he ever wanted to do. He didn't extort from people, he didn't hurt people – he made movies. That's what he did, that's what he always wanted to do and that was his love.' On the other hand, one investigator pointed out that Louis Peraino's grandfather, uncle and father were all involved in organised crime, 'so he's in it – that's the way it is. You don't get out.'

Louis Peraino borrowed the $22,000 needed to make the film from his father. According to Linda Lovelace, Anthony Peraino would come into the office 'with his own small army, all wearing dark suits and trenchcoats, looking like they were trying out for an Edward G. Robinson movie'. Anthony Peraino drove Lovelace down to Miami where the movie was going to be shot over six days. All they needed now was a title. 'Why doncha call it *The Sword Swallower*?' said Peraino. But Damiano came up with something much better – *Deep Throat*.

Peraino had not wanted Lovelace in the lead but the actress's boyfriend and manager, Chuck Traynor, frightened at the thought of losing her $1200 fee, forced Lovelace to perform oral sex on the gangster every day in order to secure the part. Lovelace described Peraino as 'heavy and sloppy. What I remember most about him was his loud mouth. He was always yelling at somebody about something.' Traynor tried to foist Lovelace on Anthony Peraino as well until the old man lectured him on the importance in Italian culture of monogamy. At least, Lovelace thought, he had some values, some code of behaviour. Lovelace said later that her performance had been coerced at gunpoint. She said that a gun was held to her head during filming. Cast and crew did nothing when her manager beat her up in an adjoining hotel room, she said. Indeed, bruises are visible on Lovelace's legs in the film. 'When you see the movie *Deep Throat*, you are watching me being raped,' Lovelace told the Congressional Meese Commission investigation into pornography in January 1986. 'It is a crime that movie is still showing. There was a gun to my head the entire time.'

But Traynor denied that the mob financed pornography, telling the *Los Angeles Free Press*, 'People say, "It's the Mafia." That's bullshit. I was production manager on *Deep Throat* and people said that was a Syndicate film. It's not.'

Deep Throat opened in New York in June 1972 at the New World Theatre on 49th Street. It caught the public mood of greater freedom in film and on television. *Deep Throat* opened against *Cabaret* and the sequel to *Shaft* and went on to earn more than both. Celebrities went to see it. Sammy Davis Jr rented the Pussycat Theatre in Santa Monica and invited Hollywood friends including Shirley MacLaine to a screening. Louis Peraino later introduced Lovelace to Davis and the two of them had an affair. Lovelace claimed that Davis also had sex with her boyfriend and manager Chuck Traynor. Even former US vice-president Spiro Agnew watched *Deep Throat* at Frank Sinatra's home in Palm Springs. Men and women from every stratum of American society rushed to see the film, a phenomenon the *New York Times* dubbed 'porno chic'. According to *Variety*, a typical Friday afternoon audience included elegant, unaccompanied ladies, middle-aged couples and at least three silver-haired matrons.

Hollywood sat up and took notice. Louis B. Mayer once said that the only measure of artistic success was how much cash a movie earned at the box office. The studios have always seen movies primarily as a moneymaking opportunity with some artistic potential. Porn actress Annie Sprinkle said that Damiano was convinced Hollywood was about to start making conventional films with hardcore sex scenes. Indeed, MGM wanted to sign up

Damiano, indicating that the studio was indeed contemplating such a move. Apparently, Damiano's contract stipulated the number of sex scenes each movie would have and in what order. Damiano turned MGM down, claiming that he could not work to a formula. Others said he was frightened of moving into the mainstream.

Deep Throat was still at number 11 on the box office chart two years after release. The Perainos' accountant, Chuck Bernstene, was overheard on an FBI wiretap saying that $150,000 was coming into his office each week. The Perainos did not know what to do with all the money they were making. Dallas distributor Fred Biersdorf remembered the atmosphere in the Perainos' New York office at 630 Ninth Avenue: 'I was like a kid in Disneyland. Everything was strictly cash. I mean, if somebody wanted a mink coat, they'd just walk into Bonwit Teller and plop down $18,000 or $20,000 in cash.' Joseph Peraino told his nephew that Louis's eight children and his grandchildren would be financially secure for the rest of their lives. One informant working in the Perainos' lawyer's office in Wilton Manors, Florida, told the FBI that so much money was coming in they did not bother to count it any more. They just weighed it.

It has been estimated that the Perainos' $22,000 movie went on to earn $600 million worldwide. The movie grossed $127 million in North American box office and $86 million internationally. It generated another $385 million through home video, both rentals and more than three million units sold. Assuming the Perainos skimmed 15 per cent of cash off the top, the gangsters earned $90 million through their investment. Mafia custom dictated that half of that money flowed down the deeper throat of the Colombo crime family. 'Here were a couple of guys from Brooklyn who never had much money before and all of a sudden they're millionaires,' a lawyer who represented the Perainos told the *Los Angeles Times*. 'The amount of money coming in was frightening. Nobody could have handled it. Whatever you've heard about how much *Deep Throat* earned, it's underestimated.'

Trying to make money out of the movie business has been

compared to holding a bucket of water full of holes. The holes in the bucket are the number of commissions and cash deductions taken out along the way before the investor gets any money. By the time the cinema, the distributor and other financiers have all taken their cut, most of the water has drained out of the bucket. The Perainos circumvented this by employing their own people to count the number of customers filing into each cinema. They would then skim a percentage of the box office and the cash would be transported back to the Perainos' office. The Perainos would probably have earned even more cash had they used a legitimate film distributor. The people they employed to check patrons going into porno cinemas were easily corruptible. A lot of cash owing to the Perainos was itself skimmed by their so-called 'checkers'.

Damiano owned one-third of the production company that made *Deep Throat*. By rights he was due one-third of the film's profits. But when Damiano went to see one of the Perainos asking for more money, he was told the only thing he was going to get on top of his $15,000 director's fee was two smashed kneecaps. Damiano sold his interest in *Deep Throat* to Louis Peraino shortly after the film opened for just $25,000. When a *New York Times* reporter pressed the director as to why he had accepted such a rotten deal, Damiano replied, 'You want me to get both my legs broken?'

Of course, in refusing to give the director any more money just because a movie was a hit, Peraino was aping the actions of a legitimate Hollywood producer. Unless above-the-line talent such as an actor or the director has negotiated a share of net profits beforehand, filmmakers are just paid a fee.

The rest of the Mafia quickly realised that pirating porn films was even more profitable than investing in them. The Mafia made millions of dollars from porn movies without ever putting up the money. One exhibitor in Hartford, Connecticut, complained that a rival cinema was playing a pirated version of *The Life and Times of Xaviera Hollander*. He was warned that unless he shut up his cinema would be bombed. Arthur and James Mitchell, the San Francisco-based brothers who produced porn hit *Behind the Green*

Door, were visited by two representatives from the Gambino family. *Behind the Green Door* became a hit after it was revealed that Marilyn Chambers, the woman at the centre of an orgy in the film, was the model portraying a mother snuggling a baby on boxes of Ivory Soap washing powder. The Gambino men said they wanted to release the movie through their Florida-based film company. They offered to split proceeds equally with the Mitchell brothers. Arthur Mitchell explained that the film had already been licensed theatrically. The Mafiosi warned Mitchell that unless he handed over the negative, the market would be flooded with pirate copies within a week – which is what happened. Illegal copies of *Behind the Green Door* played in cinemas in cities around America including Dallas, Las Vegas and Miami.

In 1974 a cinema projectionist suspected of pirating another porn hit, *The Devil in Miss Jones*, was found shot dead in his car in Youngstown, Ohio. Police surmised the Mafia killed him before he could turn informant.

Deep Throat was the most popular movie to pirate. The joke about organised crime being anything but organised rang true. Small-time Mafia hoods unaware of its producer's connection to the Colombo family copied the film. But Louis Peraino turned the piracy to his advantage. His representatives would tell cinema owners they had to split proceeds from pirated copies equally with the Perainos. That way Louis and 'Big Tony' and 'Joe the Whale' did not have to spend money striking fresh prints or on advertising campaigns. They could just piggyback on the cinema's marketing campaign.

A 1975 Los Angeles police memo said that the success of *Deep Throat* had prompted many New York mob figures to move to California. In a moment of naïvety, the LAPD warned that, once established in porn, the Mafia's next move would be into the legitimate movie business. As we have seen, the history of the Mafia and Hollywood had been fused since the 1930s. In fact, the Colombo crime family had already established a new beachhead in Beverly Hills by the time of the 1975 police memo. Louis Peraino capitalised on the success of *Deep Throat* by launching his own legitimate movie company. Over the next two years Bryanston Film Distributors would become the most successful releasing company outside the studios.

Peraino established Bryanston in July 1971 shortly after creating Gerald Damiano Film Productions. According to a joint company prospectus prepared for a New York bank, Bryanston and the *Deep Throat* producer were 'twin companies engaged in the financing, acquisition, production and distribution of motion picture film products of every kind, nature and language'. In 1973 the trade press announced that 'two New York businessmen' – Louis and Joseph Peraino – had established 'a major new film production and distribution company' called Bryanston. Peraino told the trades that he planned to make at least ten feature films over the coming year. Bryanston's finance director was one Joseph (Junior) Torchio, a former car thief described by police as not having 'an IQ above room temperature'.

The Godfather producer Al Ruddy said it was fairly common knowledge that Bryanston was controlled by organised crime. Despite this, Louis Peraino was liked by the industry, even if, as one producer put it, when you negotiated with him you never knew whether you were negotiating for your movie or your life. But one studio executive was rattled when a *Los Angeles Times* reporter cold-called him asking about his experience with Bryanston. 'No way,' the executive said. 'As far as I'm concerned, this phone call never happened.' Then he put the phone down.

Bryanston's staff also turned a blind eye to where the money was coming from to pay their salaries. 'I didn't want to know anything more than I needed to do my job,' said one employee. 'I didn't ask people who came into the office their business.'

According to Ruddy, Peraino's history as a pornographer counted against him when negotiating for films. Most producers did not want a company with Bryanston's porn associations releasing their movies. Instead, Bryanston carved out a niche distributing violent titles including *The Texas Chainsaw Massacre, Andy Warhol's Frankenstein* and Bruce Lee kung-fu flick *Enter the Dragon*. Peraino bought the rights to all three films for less than $1 million but earned $30 million from them. Between 1973 and 1976 Bryanston released twenty movies in total, including cult science-fiction comedy *Dark Star*. In 1974 alone Bryanston earned $20 million in film rentals – the amount left after the cinema owner has taken his cut – or, as *Variety* put it, 'Bryanston Boffo!'

The FBI realised that Hollywood could not care less where money came from to finance its movies. One FBI agent told the *Los Angeles Times* that the morals of movie producers were on a par with those of pornographers:

> We have a set of standards about how to finance motion pictures in Hollywood that is incredibly lax. In the last ten years or so, we've made six or seven efforts to try and ferret out allegations of organised crime in the movie business. And we got zero support from the industry. They don't view it as a threat. It's good money to them. It's a way of life, condoned – even embraced. Nobody wants to expose it.

Tobe Hooper, director of *The Texas Chainsaw Massacre*, did not want to talk to the *Los Angeles Times* about his dealings with Bryanston. 'All I know is that about two months after Chainsaw was released, I heard a rumour that Bryanston was a Mafia operation. If these guys are behind door number one, then who's behind door number two or door number three?'

Louis Peraino threatened to throw one cinema owner who owed him money out of a window. The exhibitor sent round the money that afternoon. Sandy Howard, producer of the Jodie Foster film *Echoes of a Summer*, was told his nose would be broken and his ears torn off during one argument.

Most movie companies tire of releasing other people's films and move into production themselves. This is to ensure they have enough product of the kind they want to release. Peraino gave speeches to exhibitor conventions, telling theatre owners that Bryanston was going to start making family movies, including one about the Pope. The first movie it started shooting in November 1973 was a $600,000 comedy based on the making of *Deep*

Throat. Part of the filming took place in the Rampart-Parthenon Theatre in Los Angeles, which had also been used to shoot actual porn movies. *The Last Porno Flick* follows two Italian cab drivers who borrow $22,000 from friends and relatives to make a pornographic film. They tell their families they are making a religious movie. Complications arise when the cab drivers' wives decide they want to star in it. Then, as with Mel Brooks's *The Producers*, the porn movie becomes a hit. *The Last Porno Flick* even features a Brando-esque Godfather character. Bryanston's finance director, Junior Torchio, was credited with writing the film's story. It was to be Torchio's only screenplay credit as he was knocked down by a car shortly afterwards in what police suspected was a Mafia hit. Retitled *The Mad, Mad Moviemakers*, Bryanston's first production was released in August 1974 to poor reviews.

In 1975 Bryanston released *The Devil's Rain*, a horror film starring Ernest Borgnine which gave John Travolta his first on-screen appearance. It also released *Coonskin*, an animated feature satirising the vogue for 'blaxploitation' movies such as *Shaft* and *Foxy Brown*. The cartoon was fully financed by Paramount and produced by Al Ruddy. Tongues wagged that Paramount had given Peraino *Coonskin* as a payoff to the Mafia for its cooperation over *The Godfather*.

By the beginning of 1976 Bryanston was top of the California Justice Department's list of companies thought to be controlled by the Mafia. Then, in the spring of 1976, Louis Peraino, his father Anthony and uncle Joseph were arrested for transporting obscene material across state lines. Anthony Peraino jumped bail and fled to Europe to escape conviction. Louis and Joe went on trial with nine others, including actor Harry Reems, on 1 March 1976 in Memphis, Tennessee. The trial proved controversial because the prosecution argued that as an actor Reems was just as responsible as the Perainos for trafficking obscenity. Celebrities including Warren Beatty and Jack Nicholson allied themselves with Reems, who thought his new friends would help him get established in Hollywood. The prosecution led the jury through *Deep Throat*'s financial maze step-by-step based on evidence from the FBI, the IRS and two US Justice Department organised crime taskforces. The trial lasted for two months, at the end of which the Perainos and Reems were found guilty. Louis Peraino and his uncle were sent to prison for a year and fined $10,000 each ($34,165 in today's money). *Deep Throat*'s distribution company was also fined $10,000. Reems's conviction was overturned but his Hollywood friends evaporated. In June 1975 Bryanston closed its Beverly Hills office, disappearing as quickly as it had come. In addition to owing $750,000 in unpaid taxes, Bryanston owed millions to suppliers and even more to filmmakers, who never saw most of the cash they were owed. For example, the makers of *The Texas Chainsaw Massacre* were due 35 per cent of its gross earnings of $25 million. They only ever received $5734. Despite being sent to jail, Louis Peraino assured the trade press he would bounce back: 'Don't worry about it. I can't say any more now but I'll be back in business,' Peraino told *Variety*.

Louis and Joe Peraino were arrested in February 1980 for distributing pornographic titles, including *Hot and Saucy Pizza Girls*. They were not charged with film piracy, despite the police finding more than fifty Hollywood movies in their offices along with VHS pirating equipment. Pirated videotapes confiscated included *Animal House, Kramer vs. Kramer, The Sting, Star Wars* and *The Godfather*, parts one and two. Both men were convicted in Miami on 2 December 1981. This time Louis Peraino was sent to prison for six years. He died of lung cancer in 1999.

By the 1980s pornography had lost its éclat. The mid-1970s era when middle-class couples and society matrons went to see porn movies turned out to be a brief fad. Feminists picketed sex shops protesting that porn degraded women. Lovelace's Congressional evidence as to how she was forced to make *Deep Throat* got wide publicity. The business itself changed with the arrival of videotape, which slashed profit margins. When the retail price of porn VHS tapes plummeted from $100 each to just $3.99, the Mafia turned the business over to Israelis and Sri Lankans. The market was flooded with 'killer and filler' videos, featuring a pretty girl on the cover and not much else inside. Filmmakers too lost interest in hardcore pornography. Some Hollywood directors, Wes Craven (*Scream*) among them, had got their first break directing porn. The business moved away from comparatively expensive theatrical movies such as *Deep Throat* to cheaply made videos. The arrival of Aids in the early 1980s terrorised an industry that has been called the playpen of the damned.

Back in 1972, however, another film was playing across the street from *Deep Throat*. *The Godfather* remains the most influential film ever made about the Mafia. It changed the way the Mafia regarded itself and, for many, rehabilitated gangsters into men of honour instead of what they really were – pig-ignorant, violent-sentimental goombahs. It perpetuated the myth of honour among thieves at a time when the real Mafia was being eaten away by rat-informants more concerned about saving their own skins than keeping *omerta*.

CHAPTER TEN

A Fairy Tale for Grown-ups

On 12 April 1971 Marlon Brando was in the Little Italy district of New York filming *The Godfather* – the scene where gunmen working for rival crime boss Sollozzo shoot the godfather. Brando was looking around a fruit stall, testing some oranges. Behind the camera, two real Mafiosi were critiquing his performance. According to *New York Times* reporter Nicholas Pileggi, neither was much impressed. Brando was too shabby for their liking. 'He makes the old man look like an iceman. That's not right. A man like that had style. He should have a diamond belt buckle. They all had diamond belt buckles – and a diamond ring and the clasp. Those old bosses loved diamonds. They all wore them.'

In the next scene, actor gangsters broke into a run, shooting Brando with flame-stabbing pistols. Brando slumped forward, ending up in the gutter. This too met with the gangsters' disapproval. Brando's assassins were holding their guns the wrong way. 'They hold pieces like flowers,' sniffed one.

At this point, a third Mafioso came up and whispered something. Apparently, one of the characters whom Brando was based upon was sitting right around the corner. The two Mafiosi became as excited as the rest of the neighbourhood was about catching a glimpse of Brando. They walked quickly towards Grand Street before stopping on the corner. One popped his head round and whispered back excitedly, 'He's there. He's there. I see his car. I see Paul's guy.'

The old man, Carlo Gambino, was sitting in a Grand Street café, sipping coffee from a glass. He had arrived some moments before with his brother Paul and five bodyguards. Gambino projected the air of a benevolent patrician, something captured by Brando in the movie. It belied his career as a pornographer and drug dealer. Jimmy 'the Weasel' Fratiano said that Gambino reminded him of a bird that perches, waiting for somebody to die. Now he was re-enacting a tradition from eighteenth-century Sicily in 1970s New York. It was his custom – as well as his duty as head of a New York Mafia family – regularly to hear the woes of dishonoured fathers, deportable husbands and other people beseeching his help. They were ushered before him, one at a time, from a waiting area in a restaurant across the street. Gambino, just like Brando in *The Godfather*, was being asked to dispense justice.

Mario Puzo was forty-five when he wrote *The Godfather* and, in his own words, tired of being an artist. He had written two critically acclaimed but poorly selling novels. By 1968 he owed $20,000 – $110,000 in today's money – to various relatives, banks, finance companies and loan sharks. He told his publisher he wanted to write a bestseller. 'It was really time to grow up and sell out, as Lenny Bruce once advised,' Puzo remembered.

Puzo's indebtedness was not helped by his gambling addiction. He was a gambler who took as much pleasure in losing as he did in winning; sometimes it seemed to him as if he willed himself to lose. The perverse pleasure he took in losing was part of the reason he was so in debt when he wrote *The Godfather*. Following the novel's publication, Puzo found that a Las Vegas gambling debt he had run up had been settled. When Puzo protested he was told, 'It's a certain party's pleasure.' On other occasions, bottles of champagne would arrive unordered at his table. Multisyllabic names would be whispered in his ear by reverential head waiters. Men wearing sunglasses and diamond rings would wave from across dimly lit restaurants. The Mafia was pleased that somebody had romanticised its past. Now the mob had its own *Gone With the Wind*. For *The Godfather* was a nostalgic yarn, harking back to the glory years of a racket whose best days were long behind it. It promulgated the myth that the Mafia was not involved in drugs. It romanticised and exaggerated the mob's wealth and its political influence. In short, *The Godfather* satisfied America's sweet tooth for fantasy.

Although Puzo had southern Italian roots he had no actual experience of organised crime. He did, however, have some child-hood memories he could draw on. 'Stories about crime were part of the culture,' he recalled. 'A couple of things I saw when I was a kid ended up in *The Godfather*.' As a child, Puzo once glimpsed a man passing guns to his mother from the window of the next-door apartment. And his mother once asked the local godfather for a favour when the Puzo family was facing eviction – the threat of being turned out into the street evaporated.

But Puzo had never met a real-life Mafioso. Instead, he based everything in *The Godfather* on what he had read. For example, Puzo consulted the testimony of Mafia soldier Joseph Valachi, who disclosed the workings of the New York Syndicate to a Senate committee in 1963. Because of Puzo's research there are numerous parallels between the fictional *Godfather* and mob history. Las Vegas casino operator Moe Greene is murdered in a barbershop just like Albert Anastasia; shot through the eye like Bugsy Siegel. There are fictional versions of the Castellammarese war and the Night of Sicilian Vespers. And most of the characters are inspired by real people too. Although Don Vito Corleone was based on Puzo's idea of what a Mafia boss should be like, one inspiration was Frank Costello. Like Costello, Corleone's power derives from the number of politicians, judges and police officers he has in his pocket. Like Costello, Corleone is opposed to getting involved with drugs. His resistance to using his political contacts to help fellow Mafiosi deal narcotics sparks the gang war. Ironically, Costello would not have Puzo's book in his house. He claimed to be shocked by the dialogue. 'This book here,' Costello said, 'is a dirty book.'

Puzo's novel had already sold twenty-one million copies by the time Paramount produced it as a film. Paramount's original idea was to cash in on the book's success, making a contemporary movie cheaply for about $1 million. The first draft of Puzo's screenplay even featured hippies in an attempt to make the Mafia seem relevant in the era of make-love-not-war and levitating the Pentagon. Conventional wisdom was that gangster movies did not make money, Martin Ritt's *The Brotherhood* (1968) being a case in point – audiences stayed away even though the film had starred Kirk Douglas. Gangster movies, it was felt, were the preserve of exploitation filmmakers: Roger Corman had just made a low-budget Ma Baker flick, *Bloody Mama* (1970). Paramount interviewed about thirty directors for *The Godfather*, including John Frankenheimer (*The Manchurian Candidate* (1962)), Sidney J. Furie (*The Ipcress File* (1965)) and Lewis Gilbert (*You Only Live Twice* (1967)). They all rejected the project, not wanting to be seen romanticising the Mafia. Only Sam Peckinpah said he wanted to make *The Godfather*, presumably because of the scope it offered for his trademark violence.

It was Paramount vice-president of production Peter Bart who first suggested Francis Ford Coppola to his boss Robert Evans. Despite Coppola's reputation for being difficult, Bart argued that he would bring an Italian sensibility to the project. At first, Coppola did not want anything to do with *The Godfather*. He too thought that glamorising the Mafia was immoral and he wanted nothing to do with rehabilitating a secret society that had blackened his Italian heritage. On the other hand, he did owe a lot of money. What persuaded him was watching Aggie Murch – wife of his sound editor, Walter – one afternoon during the summer of 1971 sitting some way off from the others at a barbecue, reading. Murch was engrossed in *The Godfather*. Coppola figured that if somebody was so gripped by a book that they did not want to eat there must be something in it.

Coppola told Paramount he would do the movie on two conditions. First, it would not mention the words Cosa Nostra or gangsters. Second, it would not contain any violence. Instead, Coppola saw *The Godfather* as a family chronicle. The Corleones – like Coppola's own family would become in time – were an American royal family. Don Corleone is the king who has three sons, each inheriting a different characteristic of their father.

Alfredo Corleone inherits his sweetness, Sonny his temper and Michael his cunning. By the end of the movie, Michael Corleone becomes head of the family, having avenged the deaths of his father and brother Sonny. Bart felt that somewhere between Coppola's muted approach and Peckinpah's blood-and-gore had the makings of a good movie.

Evans convinced Paramount chairman Charles Bludhorn to hire Coppola, arguing that the reason every Mafia movie had failed until now was because they had been made by Jews. With *The Godfather*, audiences were going to 'smell the spaghetti', as Evans put it, and only an Italian could do this. Evans later dismissed his argument as 'bullshit reasoning' but at the time it swayed Bludhorn.

Orson Welles campaigned for the part of Don Corleone. Other actors considered included Laurence Olivier and Edward G. Robinson, but Paramount vetoed Coppola's choice for Don Vito – Marlon Brando – because of his appalling reputation. Brando had behaved so badly on sets in the past that no studio wanted to work with him. Bludhorn changed his mind after seeing an off-the-cuff screen test Coppola made at Brando's home. Bludhorn was won over when Brando stuffed his cheeks with toilet paper and affected a hoarse, groping whisper. The physical transformation was remarkable.

But Paramount put its foot down about the unknown Italian Coppola wanted for the lead. Evans was pushing for his pal Alain Delon to play Michael Corleone but Coppola was adamant. He threatened to quit unless Al Pacino was given the part. Evans called Pacino's agent only to be told that Pacino had grown so frustrated waiting that he had accepted another film at MGM instead. Evans called MGM head Jim Aubrey, who treated the Paramount production boss – as Evans put it later – 'like I had just given his daughter Aids'. Evans then telephoned his mentor Sidney Korshak and explained his problem. Korshak agreed to intercede with Kirk Kerkorian, owner of MGM. Kerkorian had bought the studio so that he could attach the MGM brand – and its association with the movie *Grand Hotel* – to a hotel he was building in Las Vegas. The MGM Grand Hotel remains the largest hotel in the world with

5005 rooms. Twenty minutes after the conversation with Korshak Evans's phone rang again. Aubrey was on the line. 'You no-good motherfucker, cocksucker. I'll get you for this,' was all he said. 'The midget's yours; you got him.' Korshak later told Evans he had intimated to Kerkorian he might have union problems with his hotel unless he released Pacino.

Before filming began Puzo warned Coppola that he might be approached by the Mafia, 'because in a way they're fans too – and they want to be your friend and hang out'. Puzo said this would not be a good idea because sooner or later they would feel close enough to ask Coppola a favour. Puzo's advice was to be pleasant and friendly but keep them at a distance. Otherwise, Coppola would be sucked into their world, which, of course, was their intention.

In 1970 Joe Colombo, head of the Colombo crime family, founded the Italian American Civil Rights League. The organisation protested against the stereotyping of Italian-Americans as hoodlums and gangsters. 'Is it *possible* in New York that only *Italians* have committed crimes?' Colombo asked. 'I wasn't born free of sin but I sure couldn't be all the things people have said – I got torture chambers in my cellar, I'm a murderer, I'm head of every shylock ring, of every bookmakin' ring. Who are they kiddin' and how far will they go to kid the public?' Colombo claimed that the Mafia did not exist – it was a racial slur exploited by the FBI on behalf of the Establishment. Thousands picketed the FBI's headquarters in New York. To everybody's surprise, the FBI agreed to the league's demands and in July 1970 attorney general John Mitchell banned the terms 'Mafia' and 'Cosa Nostra' from all FBI press releases.

Next the anti-defamation organisation trained its guns on *The Godfather*. The league staged a rally in Madison Square Garden at which Frank Sinatra appeared. The event raised $600,000 to stop filming on *The Godfather*. The league wrote to Paramount, complaining that *The Godfather* stigmatised all Italian-Americans. Instead, the studio should make films about great Italians such as Garibaldi, unifier of Italy, or Marconi, inventor of the radio. (Coppola subsequently mocked the league by having a corrupt senator spout the same argument during Mafia corruption hearings in *The Godfather Part II*.)

The mob, meanwhile, had threatened to kill Evans's baby son unless the project was scrapped. One day Evans got a phone call. 'Get out of fuckin' town, or your kid won't be alive,' said the voice on the phone. Evans protested that he was not the producer of the movie. 'When you wanna kill something, you go for the head,' said the voice.

Al Ruddy, the movie's actual producer, also received death threats and his secretary even had the windows of her car shot out. Ruddy did not think the Mafia would actually hurt anybody making *The Godfather*, but filming would be made impossible. There would be union problems, pickets, sabotage and suchlike. Ruddy decided to have a 'sit down' with Joe Colombo. The two arranged to meet at the Park Sheraton Hotel – where Coppola had an apartment – on 25 February 1971. But when he got to the hotel he was taken aback to see about six hundred league members picketing the meeting. Then it dawned on Ruddy that league members did not want to shut the movie down so much as get bit parts and extra work themselves. Cheering broke out when Ruddy began pointing to people in the crowd, promising they would be in the movie if filming went ahead. One friend of Colombo's who got a part was Gianni Russo, an actor with little previous experience who was given the important role of traitorous son-in-law Carlo Rizzi. 'Certainly Joe's, um, influence helped some,' admitted Russo.

A meeting was arranged with studio owner Charles Bludhorn in his office at the Gulf & Western Building on Columbus Circle. Paramount agreed to certain conditions in exchange for the league's cooperation. Ruddy promised Colombo that the movie would refer to 'the five families' and other non-Italian phrases rather than use the terms 'Mafia' or 'Cosa Nostra'. He also offered to give the movie a charity premiere to benefit a hospital or charity of the league's choice. According to Ruddy, Colombo then turned around to his men and asked, 'Look, do we trust this guy?' The Mafiosi nodded and the deal was done. Ruddy said later he would rather do business with Colombo than some of the people he met in Hollywood.

But when the league issued a press release announcing honour had been satisfied, the *Wall Street Journal* ran a story disclosing that Paramount had caved in to Colombo. Shares in Gulf & Western fell. Ruddy told the press that his job was not to support Gulf & Western's share price; his job was to get the movie made. Bludhorn was incensed and fired Ruddy. Only Coppola's intervention got him his job back.

The league held another public meeting on 19 March, where Ruddy reassured them that his being Jewish meant he knew what prejudice and bigotry felt like.

But Senator John Marchi wrote to Ruddy telling him that giving in to the league was 'a monstrous insult to millions upon millions of loyal Americans of Italian extraction. Apparently you are a ready market for the league's preposterous theory that we can exorcise devils by reading them out of the English language. Yes, Mr Ruddy, there just might be a Mafia, and if you have been reached, I have only the feeling that the Italian-Americans as well as the larger community have been had.'

The *New York Times* supported Senator Marchi's stance, pointing out that the vast majority of Italian-Americans did not need to pretend the Mafia did not exist in order to maintain their self-respect and high standing in the community. It was an insult to imply that their reputation was so fragile that merely mentioning the words 'Mafia' or 'Cosa Nostra' threatened it.

Shooting began in April 1971 on location in Manhattan. Ruddy and his assistant, Gary Chasen, would sometimes join Colombo associates for drinks and dinner. Some league members had been given crew jobs, while others were awarded walk-on parts in the movie itself. James Caan, who played Sonny Corleone, would study Mafiosi hanging around the set. He said that it helped his characterisation. For Caan, this was the start of an association that would last many years.

Caan grew up in Brooklyn and as a teenager belonged to a street gang. He admitted that some of his old friends from the neighbourhood were 'not exactly bakers'. On set he watched how Mafiosi behaved, noticing, for example, that gangsters never bought drinks by the glass but always by the bottle. To indicate to another that somebody they both knew had been killed, one wiseguy raised his hands in front of him, pointed his fingers like guns and aimed them at the ground. 'BabadaBOOM!' he said and they both laughed. Caan told Nicholas Pileggi that copying the way gangsters moved was easy, 'but their language, that's something else. They repeat certain words, like "Where you been, where?" They have a street language all their own. It's not Italian, certainly, and it's not English.'

Caan's infatuation with the Mafia grew after *The Godfather* finished shooting. In November 1985, Caan was subpoenaed to give evidence at the trial of Andrew Russo, whom the FBI said was a high-ranking member of the Colombo crime family. Caan had known Russo for fifteen years and always denied his friend had anything to do with violent crime. Russo was on trial for bribery and extortion. He had only recently been released from a four-year prison sentence for bribery and conspiracy to evade taxes. Coming into the courtroom, Caan kissed Russo's co-defendant Carmine 'the Snake' Persico, head of the Colombo crime family, Mafia-style on each cheek. 'I thought he was killed at the toll booth,' quipped federal prosecutor Rudolph Giuliani in reference to *The Godfather* when he saw Caan. Giuliani himself had seen *The Godfather* so many times that he knew the dialogue off by heart. Persico and eight others were convicted of labour racketeering in June 1986.

Caan videotaped a character reference for Russo that was shown during another trial in 1999. This time Russo was accused of jury tampering and obstructing justice in the trial of his son, Joseph Russo, who was accused of racketeering. Andrew Russo was found guilty.

In 1988 Caan put his home up as collateral for the $10 million bail of a mob-connected drug dealer. Joey Ippolito had already been in prison for three years for marijuana smuggling when he opened CentAnni, a fashionable Italian restaurant in Malibu, California. Federal law enforcement sources said that Ippolito was a member of the DeCavalcante crime family of New Jersey.

The restaurant was a front for the cocaine business Ippolito ran with Ronnie Lorenzo, an associate of the Bonanno crime family. In 1993 Caan attended Lorenzo's trial. Caan said at the trial that Lorenzo was his best friend. Both Ippolito and Lorenzo were found guilty and sentenced to ten years in prison. As late as December 1998, Caan was spotted by FBI agents attending a Christmas party given by the Colombo crime family at a restaurant in Little Italy.

Caan became a heavy cocaine user himself, buying drugs from Los Angeles Mafioso Tony 'the Animal' Fiato. Fiato was known as Tony Rome after the 1967 Frank Sinatra movie of the same name. Ironically, part of the gangster's income came from pirating video-tapes, one of which was *The Godfather*. Caan used Fiato for various strong-arming jobs he wanted done. Once he asked Fiato to send some muscle to collect from an actor who owed him money. Caan also used Fiato to try and muscle in on the lead role in *The Pope of Greenwich Village* (1984). Fiato and another mobster intimidated the movie's producer, who explained that shooting had already started with Mickey Rourke in the lead. (Rourke himself visited Gambino family head John Gotti's trial in 1991, kissing the mob boss's ring.) On another occasion, Caan received a phone call from a gang saying it had kidnapped his brother, Ronnie. The gang wanted $50,000 for his release. Fiato and his gang ambushed the kidnappers and gave them a severe beating. 'I am a consequence man,' Fiato wrote in his autobiography. 'I am a consequence to the people that fuck me.' It emerged that Ronnie Caan, who was addicted to free-basing cocaine, staged his own kidnapping to steal money from his brother. James and Ronnie Caan were shouting at each other driving away from the ambush when they were stopped by police. Ironically, one of the police officers told Caan how much he loved him in *The Godfather* before letting both of them drive off. Caan only stopped using drugs some years later when he witnessed his son taking a baseball bat to his cocaine dealer.

Like Al Capone, Joe Colombo became addicted to publicising himself. He wanted to stage another rally outside the Gulf & Western Building protesting against Italian-American stereotyping, despite having reached a deal over *The Godfather*. Other Mafia dons sitting on the Commission were becoming nervous about the publicity. The Italian American Civil Rights League was little more than a skimming operation itself. Colombo was stealing donations made by patriotic Italian-Americans and splitting the cash with other Mafia bosses. All this self-promotion could attract some unwelcome press attention. Carlo Gambino told Colombo to stop courting publicity and cancel the rally. Colombo, his ego presumably inflated with press coverage, refused and the protest went ahead in Columbus Circle. On 28 June 1971 – the sixty-sixth day of filming *The Godfather* – Colombo was shot three times in the back of the head by a hired assassin. The shooting had been organised by 'Crazy Joe' Gallo, one of Albert Anastasia's killers. The black gunman, Jerome Johnson, was killed by Colombo's bodyguards. Colombo survived but was left paralysed and unable to speak. Coppola said: 'Would you believe it? Before we started working on the film, we kept saying, "But these Mafia guys don't go around shooting each other any more." We thought one of our problems was to make the film relevant.'

The following year, Joey Gallo was himself shot to death at a restaurant in Little Italy. Gallo used to spend hours watching old gangster movies of Jimmy Cagney and Edward G. Robinson, making sure he got the body language right. On the night of his murder, he spent the evening with an actor who was about to play Gallo in a movie. The actor kept asking Gallo questions about how to walk and talk like a gangster, little knowing that Gallo had learned most of it from television. The barrier between the Mafia in reality and movie fiction had grown increasingly permeable over the years. Art was imitating life imitating art.

Singer Al Martino, who played Johnny Fontane in the film, said that Paramount was afraid Sinatra would slap an injunction on *The Godfather* to stop filming. The studio agreed with Sinatra to cut the Johnny Fontane part down as much as possible in order to placate him. But Sinatra was still unsatisfied and, according to Martino, 'tried to have me muscled out of the part, but I had muscle of my own. Phyllis McGuire called Sam Giancana for me, and Sam told Frank to back off and that was the end of it.'

Once shooting on the movie was finished Ruddy stopped returning calls to the mob. He said he never wanted to hear from some of the people he had been dealing with ever again, 'and I'm not talking about Brando or Coppola'. Neither was the mob invited to the premiere on 14 March 1972, with guests including Henry Kissinger, to the chagrin of one Genovese family soldier. 'Look, if some picture company did the life of Audie Murphy, he'd be invited to the premiere. If the movie was about the military, they'd turn out the generals. So when they do one about us, we should be there too.'

Interviewed by *Life* magazine, Brando said that *The Godfather* was a useful commentary on corporate thinking in America. He suggested the tactics the Don used were not so different from the way General Motors treated consumer champion Ralph Nader. 'I mean, if Cosa Nostra had been black or socialist, Corleone would have been dead or in jail. But because the Mafia patterned itself so closely on the corporation – and dealt in a hard-nosed way with money and with politics, it prospered. The Mafia is so *American*.'

The Godfather's close-knit family, ruled by a tough but caring patriarch, united against the world, struck a chord in an America reeling from conflict between parent and child during the Vietnam War. People wished they could turn to a Don Corleone to solve their problems with a wave of his hand. As Joe Bonanno, head of the Bonanno crime family, pointed out, *The Godfather* was not really about organised crime or gangsterism. It was about family pride and honour. Author Stephen Fox has pointed out that part of the appeal of the Mafia is that at a time when society has atomised into particles of free-floating individuals, the Mafia underlines the importance of family. The myth of modern America is that people can endlessly reinvent themselves; the Mafia reminds you that you cannot change your roots.

According to Ruddy, *The Godfather* earned more than $100 million during its initial theatrical release (the equivalent of $465 million today). Coppola and Ruddy each had 7½ per cent of net profits, while Puzo had 2½ per cent. One percentage point would eventually be worth $1 million. *The Godfather* went on to win three Academy Awards, including best picture. 'Funny thing is,' mused Coppola, 'I've never been very interested in the Mafia.'

Just as *The Godfather* proved a hit with audiences, so it influenced how the Mafia itself behaved. Former US attorney Rudolph Giuliani said that you could tell the difference between surveillance tapes recorded before and after the movie came out. Gangsters began talking like characters out of the movie. For example, Puzo invented the term 'godfather' for head of a crime family; it had never been used by the Mafia itself. But once *The Godfather* was a hit gangsters began calling each other 'godfather' and reviving moribund customs such as kissing the don's ring. Nino Rota's theme music was played at the wedding of one Sicilian don's daughter, while Joe Adonis's son kept asking for it to be played again in a New York restaurant. A horse's head was found in the car of three building contractors near Palermo. One Mafia soldier working for Gambino family crime boss John Gotti referred to his hitman as 'my Luca Brasi'. Another Gambino soldier said he tried to go straight but went back into organised crime after watching *The Godfather* because it made him feel 'terribly homesick'.

The Godfather's romanticised view of the Mafia angered organised-crime writer Nicholas Pileggi. 'They're not Sonny Corleone,' he said. 'They're not those characters in movies. There's nothing noble about them. They're quite loathsome.' Rather than honour and loyalty, the underworld runs on betrayal and treachery, said Pileggi. 'The romantic notion of that world is *so* far from the truth. It's a career filled with pain, much of it inflicted on others.'

Film critic David Thomson has also noted that *The Godfather* became a role model not only for mobsters but for movie executives as well. Phrases such as 'this isn't personal, it's business' and 'the one who brings you the message will be the betrayer' became part of the vocabulary for Hollywood studio executives.

Paramount urged Coppola to make a sequel but he turned the studio down six times, saying he was bored of gangsters. Instead, he suggested another Italian director, Martin Scorsese, whose *Mean Streets* (1973) followed a hoodlum and a would-be priest in Little Italy. Paramount had no choice but to issue a press release announcing that Coppola would not be making the sequel. But Bludhorn was tenacious and his greatest pleasure was negotiating. He pointed out that the money Coppola would make from a follow-up would subsidise his work far into the future. He flattered Coppola, telling him he would make history by creating a sequel better than the original. It was as if the director had discovered the formula to Coca-Cola, Bludhorn emolliated. In the end, Coppola's head was turned. His terms were $1 million to write, direct and produce *The Godfather Part II*. Bludhorn guaranteed creative freedom plus a share of the gross – as opposed to net profits, which have a habit of receding the closer one gets to them.

Coppola spent a year researching *The Godfather Part II*. On 9 June 1972 he wrote to Peter Bart telling them that Sidney Korshak's son Harry had been hired as a consultant. Harry Korshak was a producer at Paramount who had never actually made a film before joining the studio. One day Sidney Korshak simply told Bart that his son was becoming a producer. Coppola's thinking was that having Korshak's son on board would provide a link to the Mafia, albeit at one remove proving snippets of interest which could be used in the script. Coppola also read transcripts of the Kefauver hearings. This time around he decided to focus on Meyer Lansky, renaming him Hyman Roth in the film. Everything said in the film by Roth, played by Lee Strasberg, was supposed to have been said by Lansky. For example, Roth, like Lansky, describes the mob as 'bigger than US Steel'. Another character, Senator Pat Geary, was based on Nevada politician Pat McCarren who was thought to have ties to organised crime. Mafia informant Frank Pentageli was based on Joseph Valachi, the Mafioso who had given evidence to the McClellan committee in 1963. Like Valachi, Pentageli decides to commit suicide by hanging himself in the shower. Unlike Valachi, Pentageli succeeds in falling on his sword like the Roman generals he so admires – again, a character trait taken from 1930s Mafia boss Salvatore Maranzano.

Coppola had been stung by accusations that the first movie romanticised the Mafia. Certainly, it promulgated some myths about the mob – that they only kill each other, for example, and have nothing to do with drugs. *The Godfather Part II* would show Michael Corleone's succumbing to evil, culminating with ordering the murder of his brother Fredo. Coppola decided that, to an extent, being a second-generation Italian-American, Michael Corleone represented America itself. By the end of the movie, Corleone would become isolated, imperial and self-righteous – just as America was in the 1950s.

Like all good art, the second film would also to a degree be a self-portrait of its creator. Corleone's middle initial is 'F' for Francis, Coppola's Christian name. Like Corleone, Coppola had an elder brother, August, whom people assumed would be the one to succeed. Instead, Coppola was the brother who became famous. Coppola may have been acting out his triumph over his brother when Michael has Fredo murdered. 'To some extent I have become Michael in that I'm a powerful man in charge of an entire production,' Coppola admitted.

The Godfather Part II would go on to win six Academy Awards, including best picture, and, as Bludhorn predicted, is a sequel better than the original. It tells two parallel stories, that of how Vito Corleone joined This Thing of Ours and the utter corruption of his son Michael, taking in the Mafia's rise to power in Las Vegas.

Between them *The Godfather* and *The Godfather Part II* have earned nearly $1 billion in combined theatrical, video, television and licensing revenues.

Sidney Korshak, meanwhile, was coming to Paramount almost every day helping to run the studio. Always immaculately attired in a dark grey suit, the tall, sombre Korshak was constantly on the phone to Bludhorn or conferring with Evans. Bart found Korshak to be impeccably polite but utterly humourless. Years later, when one former Paramount executive was overheard grumbling that studios were not as well run as they used to be, his wife interjected that was because Korshak was not around telling him what to do every day.

Korshak was instrumental in founding what remains the world's biggest international film company, United International Pictures

(UIP), which releases DreamWorks, Paramount and Universal movies globally. At the beginning of the 1970s both Universal and Paramount were wasting hundreds of thousands of dollars each year duplicating one another's offices overseas. The obvious thing was to merge their back-office operations – accounting, personnel and so forth. There were also substantial tax advantages to be had by establishing a separate international business. Korshak put Bludhorn at Paramount together with Lew Wasserman at Universal and picked up a $50,000 fee for doing so. Cinema International Corporation (CIC) became operational in April 1970. MGM was next brought into the fold. Mini-major United Artists had been acquired by Kerkorian, whose MGM released its own films internationally. But United Artists was contracted to release its slate through CIC. In October 1973, Korshak persuaded Kerkorian over lunch to put MGM's slate through the joint venture too. Bludhorn described negotiations with Kerkorian as 'very, very tough'. He said the deal would have collapsed without Korshak's help. The mob lawyer invoiced CIC for another $250,000 once MGM joined the group.

Korshak's friend Evans, meanwhile, had enjoyed a run of successes with *Love Story*, *The Godfather* movies and *Chinatown*. But the production head's growing cocaine habit meant he was often too hung-over for work. Despite his affection for Evans, Bludhorn had no choice but to drop him. Again, Korshak interceded for his client, negotiating an eight-year, twenty-four-movie production deal with Paramount in 1974. Six years later Evans – along with his brother Charles and brother-in-law Michael Shure – pleaded guilty to buying five ounces of cocaine from undercover narcotics agents. Evans obeyed his brother's wishes and, against his better judgement, did not ask for Korshak's help this time. The former Paramount production chief was sentenced to a year's probation. But worse was yet to come. For Robert Evans the magic carpet on which he had ridden with such success in the 1970s was fraying into wired cocaine paranoia.

CHAPTER ELEVEN

Gangsters, Music, Pussy

Imagine that you are Hollywood producer Robert Evans in June 1983. For more than a year you have been trying to get a project called *The Cotton Club* off the ground. Texas oilmen, Arab arms dealers and other would-be financiers have traipsed through your Beverly Hills home listening to your sales pitch. '*The Godfather* with music' is how you describe it – or, more pungently, 'gangsters, music, pussy'. But bullshit rather than money has done the talking. Then your limousine driver introduces you to Lanie Jacobs, a thirty-something divorcee who says she is in the jewellery business. In turn, Jacobs introduces you to a New York-based show promoter called Roy Radin. He says he is going to finance *The Cotton Club* using Puerto Rican money. You and Radin shake hands, cutting Lanie out of the deal. Lanie goes ballistic when she hears this and demands to be made an equal partner. Then Radin disappears. Lanie flies to New York where you are setting up the movie; she tells you Radin has been murdered. It turns out Lanie Jacobs is not a Texas divorcee but a cocaine dealer connected to organised crime in Miami. And unless you cut her back in on *The Cotton Club* you are going to be her next victim.

By the early 1980s Hollywood had changed. Armani-suited agents had ousted showmen like Evans as the ones with the almost mystic ability to 'green light' a production. The centre of power had shifted to the Beverly Hills talent agencies. Agencies such as Creative Artists Agency were presenting studios with readymade packages of talent, known as 'packaging'. Manager Bernie Brill-stein realised things had changed when he saw moguls including Lew Wasserman queuing to pay their respects to agent Michael Ovitz at a testimonial dinner. Ovitz acknowledged their good wishes much like Don Corleone greeting supplicants in *The God-father*. 'The only thing missing was the kissing of the new don's ring,' observed journalist Nikki Finke.

Evans's *Cotton Club* nightmare began in 1980 at the Cannes Film Festival. The arrival of home video in the early 1980s bloated the movie business. Home video's impact on the film industry was like dumping pure heroin on the street when junkies had made do with methadone for years. Producers gorged themselves – investors were handing over money on the basis of little more than a script and a salesman's enthusiasm. It looked as if anything could get made, knowing it could be sold to the VHS market. Slowly the patchwork of cash advances, or 'pre-sales', would be sewn to-gether, pushing the film into production.

Evans presented distributors with a black and gold and silver poster he had designed. Beneath the title 'The Cotton Club' was an illustration showing gangsters, musicians and whizzing bullets. Underneath were the words 'Its violence startled the nation – its music startled the world.' It was as if, through the sheer alchemy of his salesmanship, he was going to bring the poster to life. Film critic Alexander Walker noted that Evans's handshake was like the touch of a spark plug.

The Cotton Club was a speakeasy with a floorshow that became famous in the 1920s. White celebrities and society people would venture uptown to Harlem to watch black dancers and singers. Duke Ellington was the house bandleader. Seven hundred social-ites, Hollywood stars and gangsters would sit at tiny tables ar-ranged in a horseshoe around the stage. No blacks were allowed as customers. The Cotton Club belonged to George Raft's gangster mentor, Owney Madden. On any given night customers might include movie producer Samuel Goldwyn, Lucky Luciano, Charlie Chaplin, Dutch Schultz and Fred Astaire.

Evans raised $8 million in foreign pre-sales on the back of his poster. Now he needed to find another $12 million to get the movie into production. The clock was already ticking before negotiations with arms dealer Adnan Kashoggi soured. Pre-production costs were running at $140,000 a week. Evans had already rented a townhouse in New York, where *The Cotton Club* was to be filmed. But all he had was a screenplay by Mario Puzo nobody was enthusiastic about and Richard Gere apparently committed to play the lead – which he was trying to wriggle out of. The producer sold the last of his Paramount stock to feed the daily cash burn.

It was at this point that Evans met Jacobs and Radin. The touring show promoter was spending time in Los Angeles, re-inventing himself as a movie producer. Back east, a television actress said she had been beaten and raped during a cocaine party at Radin's Long Island mansion. Radin was trying to distance himself from his past. Jacobs had moved to California the year before, in 1982. She had a baby son by Milan Bellechasses, a Cuban immigrant. According to police, Jacobs was being sent 10 kilos of cocaine every six weeks or so. Jacobs's job was to sell it on at $60,000 a kilo.

Indeed, the real source of conflict between Jacobs and Radin was not some imaginary share of profits in a movie that at the moment was no more than a poster. Rather, Jacobs suspected Radin of having something to do with the theft of 10 kilos of cocaine from her home and $270,000 in cash. At the very least, Jacobs thought Radin knew the whereabouts of the thief. She was terrified of what her supplier would do to her when he found out the drugs and money had been stolen.

Evans met Jacobs in Miami in April 1983. On the same trip she introduced the producer to lawyer Frank Diaz. The lawyer also tried to help Evans raise money for *The Cotton Club*. Three years later Diaz would be sent to jail in Brazil for helping drug smugglers launder money through shell companies in the Dutch Antilles.

On 13 May 1983 Jacobs and Radin arranged to have dinner at Beverly Hills restaurant La Scala to settle their differences over *The Cotton Club*. Jacobs arrived outside Radin's hotel in a limousine. One witness noticed she was wearing a gold lamé dress. Radin was so nervous about the meeting that he had asked a friend to follow him to Beverly Hills. He was last seen alive getting into Jacobs's car.

The limousine was driven by Robert Lowe, a security guard employed by pornographer Larry Flynt. Jacobs's car was being followed by another vehicle. In this car were two more *Hustler* magazine employees, Jacobs's boyfriend William Mentzer and his associate Alex Marti. The limousine was also being followed by a third car, this one being driven by the friend of Radin's who was supposed to keep watch. But Radin's friend lost the limousine en route to Beverly Hills. Inside the limo Radin and Jacobs got into an argument. The limousine pulled over, presumably at a prearranged spot. Jacobs got out of the car. Mentzer and Marti got in with their guns drawn.

Phone records showed that Jacobs telephoned Evans shortly afterwards in New York. She and one of the assassins then flew by private plane from Miami to confront Evans. After the meeting – the substance of which has never been disclosed – Evans phoned Woodlands, his Beverly Hills home, making sure it was locked up. Then he fled to Las Vegas to stay with Lebanese casino owners Frederick and Edward Doumani. According to a detective involved in the case, Evans told the Doumanis that Jacobs had arranged Radin's murder – and that he would be next.

One month later police discovered a body in a dry stream bed in a national park north of Los Angeles. The desert sun had shrunk the corpse to 69 pounds. A Gucci loafer dangled from the end of one shrivelled leg. Twelve bullets had been fired into the back of the victim's skull. His genitals were missing and his face had been blown off to prevent the corpse being identified by dental records. A stick of dynamite had been placed in his mouth. At first police listed the body as a 'John Doe' – an anonymous victim. Only later did they identify him as Roy Radin.

Back in Los Angeles, Evans asked a friend, producer Scott Strader, to drive him and his girlfriend of the time to Palm Springs. Paranoid that he was being watched, Evans asked Strader to drive his butler's car. Evans and his girlfriend lay on the floor of the back seat until they were safely away from Woodlands. The journey was uneventful until the car began to play up near Cabazon on the way to the desert resort. Strader had no option but to pull over on the side of the road. Evans began shouting that he was being set up. Suddenly the car was surrounded by the sound of gunfire. 'I told you they were going to kill me,' Evans screamed, throwing himself on the floor. Strader had inadvertently pulled over next to a firing range.

Meanwhile, Evans convinced his friends the Doumanis to take over Radin's position in *The Cotton Club*. The Doumanis brought in another investor, Victor Sayrah. The budget was set at $20 million. The Doumanis owned the El Morocco casino in Las Vegas. They admitted knowing underworld associate Joe Agosto and reputed mob figure Joey Cusumano. These loose associations had got the Doumanis into trouble with both the Nevada and New Jersey state casino regulators. The Nevada Gaming Control Board in particular was unhappy about the Doumanis lending millions of dollars to Agosto, who was the key witness in the trial of Kansas City Mafia bosses convicted of skimming Las Vegas hotel profits. Cusumano, on the other hand, was friendly with the Chicago Outfit's enforcer in Las Vegas, Anthony 'the Ant' Spilotro – the snarling Punchinello portrayed by Joe Pesci in *Casino* (1995). Cusumano, who would later become one of the producers of *The Cotton Club*, described Spilotro as 'a dear friend of mine'. He accused the FBI of having an overheated imagination: 'Sure I know Spilotro but that doesn't make me a gangster. I also see a lot of heart surgeons around town but that doesn't make me a heart surgeon.' The authorities had been watching Cusumano for a decade but were unable to prove anything. Evans, on the other hand, described Cusumano as 'more comfortable holding a .38 handgun than a Steadycam'.

Evans had been planning to direct *The Cotton Club* – he had grown up in Harlem during the 1930s – but admitted defeat after calling in Francis Coppola to rewrite the script. Coppola, who was strapped for cash, offered to direct as well. He then abandoned the existing script one month before shooting was due to begin and brought in novelist William Kennedy. Coppola and Kennedy concocted a screenplay loosely based on the George Raft story. Jazz trumpeter Dixie Dwyer, the Richard Gere character, saves the life of gangster Dutch Schultz and is rewarded by being taken on the bootlegger's payroll. Schultz is sniffing around Harlem trying to muscle in on the numbers gambling racket. Raft's real-life mentor, Owney Madden, arranges for Dwyer to become his eyes and ears in Hollywood, keeping watch on the gangster's investment in a studio.

Shooting began on 28 August 1983 and was chaotic from start to finish. Rather than gold, Evans's alchemy was turning *The Cotton Club* into something base. The project was hobbled from the start by Gere's insistence that he portray a cornet player. This was somewhat problematic as the Cotton Club only employed black musicians. Coppola and Kennedy came up with two parallel stories – Richard Gere becoming involved with Dutch Schultz's moll crosscut with the fortunes of a black tap dancer (Gregory Hines) working at the club. Gere failed to turn up on the first day of shooting because he did not have a contract. Coppola appeared to be making the film on the hoof, extemporising like a jazz musician, something you can do in a jam session but not with a movie costing tens of millions of dollars. Locations would be scouted but never used, sets built and then abandoned. Coppola shot one scene that his co-writer had just phoned in from a public telephone booth. Black jazz musicians hired to portray the Duke Ellington Band found themselves miming along to white musicians impersonating the Cotton Club sound. Each of the black jazz musicians had been hired because he was a Duke Ellington expert, but only Richard Gere was allowed to play live. 'They should have called the movie *Tarzan Plays Jazz*,' said one musician.

As costs ballooned, so money ran short. Coppola complained the producers kept telling him to cut 20 per cent of the budget but never told him what the budget was. By the end of the sixth week of shooting Coppola still had not been paid. He quit and flew to London on Concorde. He only came back in the middle of the following week once the Doumanis had agreed to start paying him his $2.5 million fee. Meanwhile, none of the cast or crew had seen any money either. They threatened to go on strike unless they were paid in cash.

Bob Hoskins, the British actor playing Madden, later claimed Las Vegas investors used the production to launder money. Men would turn up unannounced at Evans's townhouse with briefcases full of cash. The money would be in irregular amounts, making predictable cash flow impossible. There was also a lot of cocaine in evidence.

The Doumanis had grown fed up with what they saw as Coppola's profligacy. Having failed to make him responsible if he went over budget, the Doumanis called in their old friend Joey Cusumano to oversee production. At this point *The Cotton Club* was haemorrhaging $1.2 million a week. Ed Doumani told the *New York Times* that he wanted somebody with 'real street savvy' to keep an eye on his investment.

Cusumano would arrive on set each morning and stand silently off to one side. The Las Vegas enforcer never said a word all day – he just stood there. Cusumano later explained why he rarely spoke: 'Before I open my mouth, I want to know something. My father said, "Fishes only get caught when they open their mouths."' Coppola, perhaps intimidated by Cusumano's presence, arranged for a director's chair to be placed next to his. The word 'Joey' was stencilled on the back. Coppola, whom Evans has compared to Machiavelli in his cunning, turned an enemy into an ally. In a situation reminiscent of the Woody Allen comedy *Bullets Over Broadway* – in which a gangster sent to oversee his boss's invest-ment in a Broadway play starts to direct the production – so Cusumano became protective of Coppola's vision. Posted on set as the investors' guard dog, Cusumano told Ed Doumani to stay away from Coppola. 'Francis doesn't want to hear about budgets,' Cusumano warned. 'He just wants to create.'

The production was by now running on vapour – its fuel tank was almost empty. The daily cash burn had increased to $1.4 million a week and the budget was heading towards $48 million. Some of the underworld characters who had lent Evans money to cash-flow production telephoned the producer, warning him of what would happen if they did not get their money back. 'Bob was visibly shaken by those calls,' said Evans's lawyer, Alan Schwartz. Evans borrowed another $3.5 million from organised crime street lenders – 'shylocks' – at usurious interest rates. He put up his home as collateral, handing over a cheque for $46,000 from a settled insurance claim to street lenders. 'The guys from Vegas were in no mood for creative flack; leaving town was a better bet than testing their sympathy,' Evans wrote. 'Not wanting my life insurance cancelled, I had no choice but to spread my legs.'

Cusumano told Coppola that the bulk of filming had to be finished by 23 December 1983. Cusumano, whom the crew was by now calling 'my favourite gangster', distributed T-shirts with 'December 23, 1983' printed on the back to keep everybody focused. Coppola concentrated on trying to cram the most essential scenes into a three-week shooting schedule. Oddly, the perfectionist director, known for shooting at least seven takes of each scene, managed forty shots in just three days.

Cusumano, who was credited as line producer on *The Cotton Club*, talked about quitting Las Vegas for Hollywood. Like most people, he had a contact high from the movie industry. 'I'll get a house on the beach,' said Cusumano. Coppola wrote a character reference for the gangster. Then in 1987 Cusumano was convicted of conspiring to defraud the Las Vegas kitchen workers' union in an insurance scam. He was sentenced to four years in prison.

Evans, meanwhile, accused the Doumani brothers of threatening him with violence. He relinquished his profit share in *The Cotton Club* in exchange for $1 million in cash and the deeds back to his beloved Woodlands. In hindsight, given *The Cotton Club*'s lukewarm critical reception and sluggish box office, Evans got away lightly. But if Evans walked away from *The Cotton Club* with his finances relatively intact, he walked straight into a legal nightmare.

Police arrested Lanie Jacobs, William Mentzer, Alex Marti and Robert Lowe for the murder of Roy Radin. Jacobs was now called Lanie Greenberger, having married Larry Greenberger – also known as 'Vinnie De Angelo' – supposed to be second in command in a Colombian cocaine operation. What on the face of it was a simple case of murder over a stolen drugs shipment was complicated by the fact that lawyers with political ambitions were desperate to involve Evans with the murder. The state prosecutor wanted to prove the fanciful notion that it was the row over *The Cotton Club*'s profits that lay behind Radin's kidnapping. Only in Hollywood, noted author Joan Didion, could a murder motivation be based on the notion of an interest in an entirely hypothetical share of entirely hypothetical profits from an entirely hypothetical movie – and that somehow this was money in the bank for everybody concerned. But then again, wrote Didion, Los Angeles in the 1980s was itself largely supported by a series of confidence games, a city afloat on motion pictures and junk bonds. Evans's lawyer Robert Shapiro – who later defended O.J. Simpson in his murder trial – nevertheless advised Evans to exercise his right to plead the Fifth Amendment. To this day Evans is unable to talk openly about what happened.

Jacobs/Greenberger and Robert Lowe – the security guard who drove the limousine – were convicted of second-degree murder in 1991. Marti and Mentzer were convicted of first-degree murder. All four received life sentences.

Cocaine remained an integral part of Hollywood. For some the 1980s were the new 1920s, with similar excesses. John Gotti was seen as the new Al Capone and *Time* magazine put an Andy Warhol portrait of the New York gangster on its cover. The joy powder of 1920s Hollywood was just as popular six decades later. According to Evans, everybody in Hollywood used cocaine, from writers to actors to directors. Agents would accept part-payment in cocaine on behalf of their clients. Between 1985 and 1987, the 'cash surplus' in the Los Angeles branch of the Federal Reserve increased by 2300 per cent to $3.8 billion, an indication, observers said, of the volume of cocaine money sloshing through the system. The Justice Department described the Los Angeles economy as an ocean of drug-tainted cash. One notorious cocaine user was producer Dodi Al-Fayed, who later died in a Paris car crash with Princess Diana. Al-Fayed, one of the producers of *Chariots of Fire*

(1981) and *F/X* (1986), bought cocaine from Mike Liszt, an associate of Los Angeles mob enforcer Tony Fiato. It was claimed that Al-Fayed displayed bricks of cocaine at his parties. James Caan told Fiato that Al-Fayed had reneged on a drugs deal with Liszt. 'A lot of people knew Dodi,' wrote Fiato. 'He used people all over Hollywood and left a trail of debts.'

The continuing links between celebrities like Caan and hoodlums like Fiato attracted the attention of federal prosecutor Richard Stavin, who decided to attack organised crime in the film and television industry. For example, the Mafia had planned to murder Hollywood mogul Lew Wasserman in the autumn of 1983 because of his informing federal prosecutors about mob involvement in the music business. Both the Gambino and Gotti crime families invested in Brunswick Records, a former subsidiary of Universal MCA. Mobsters had threatened radio station DJs with violence if they did not play Brunswick records – either that or bribe them with cocaine.

   Stavin, an upright lawyer contemptuous of liberal qualms, spent twelve years in New York as a prosecutor before moving to Los Angeles. There he joined the Organised Crime Strike Force in the Justice Department. Stavin discovered that two FBI investigations into Mafia corruption of the movie business were already under way. The first involved the FBI setting up a fake movie production company; the idea was that the production company would travel around America seeing if it could make a feature without having to use the powerful Teamsters Union, which had links to organised crime. The FBI production company visited Atlanta, Boston, Dallas and Miami seeing whether the Teamsters would have to be bribed if the independent production was to be left alone. The other investigation had begun in the early 1980s looking at the Los Angeles crime families. Over a period of time, federal agent Thomas Gates concentrated on one individual, Martin Bacow, the Teamsters' liaison to the studios. Bacow had written and sold a screenplay about Meyer Lansky to Eugene Giaquinto, head of the home-video division of Universal MCA. What puzzled the FBI about Giaquinto was why he continued to do business with North Star Graphics, a New Jersey-based video packaging company, despite knowing that North Star had defrauded Universal only recently for hundreds of thousands of dollars. In 1981 the government had indicted North Star's managing director, Edward 'the Conductor' Sciandra – an underboss in the Bufalino crime family – for defrauding Universal by invoicing it for work never done. Universal itself estimated that North Star had cost it between $400,000 and $500,000 in false invoices. In the end, Sciandra was convicted for tax evasion. Yet Giaquinto met the Bufalino underboss at least twice after the conviction – once at a video convention and then at a Beverly Hills restaurant. Stavin grew convinced that movie studio executives with Mafia links were fairly commonplace throughout Hollywood.

By December 1986, Stavin decided he had enough to launch a grand jury investigation into Mafia involvement in Hollywood. The grand jury would listen to evidence and then decide whether there was enough to go to full trial. His probe would look at possible union racketeering, extortion and obstruction of justice. Information was to be gathered through wiretaps of Teamster officials and nationwide scrutiny of mid-level mobsters.

Stavin's investigation uncovered that the Mafia was extorting one Warner Bros executive. The federal prosecutor also identified two Hollywood studios that employed Mafia associates as executives. Independent producer Cannon was suspected of inflating budgets of films – putting phantom Teamsters on the payroll and presumably splitting the money with union officials. Stavin and Gates identified three movies that the Mafia had laundered money through, one of which was 1988 Universal release *Screwball Hotel*.

Meanwhile, the FBI were eavesdropping on a conversation between Giaquinto and Sciandra during which the Universal home-video executive disclosed that a mob war was brewing over rival Meyer Lansky projects. Separately to the Giaquinto/Bacow project, the Genovese family was planning its own version of the Meyer Lansky story. James Caan told Los Angeles Mafioso Michael Rizzitello that he and not Giaquinto would be making the Meyer Lansky biopic. Not only did Caan have the support of Lansky's widow Thelma, but also the backing of Jimmy 'Blue Eyes' Alo, second in command to Lansky himself. Giaquinto said he was prepared to 'go to the mattresses' – as *The Godfather* put it – over who was going to make the Lansky story. Obviously there could not be room for both. He told Sciandra that he had persuaded Gambino capo John Gotti to mobilise soldiers to come to Hollywood and stop the Genovese clan. Giaquinto told Bacow in another wiretap that if Alo and the Genovese family wanted war then war is what they would get. In a subsequent conversation with a man transcripts identified only as Tommy, Giaquinto said he would import thirty Gotti soldiers to quash any competition from Jimmy Alo, James Caan or the Genovese mob. However, the threatened mob war never happened. There is a high rate of attrition among Hollywood projects – only one in ten ideas even makes it to script stage, let alone goes into production. Nothing came of either Lansky film. The Gambino family's dream of becoming a Hollywood player evaporated.

Nevertheless, with wiretap transcripts like this, Stavin felt sure his investigation would lead to convictions. But he suspected his confidence was not shared by his managers; he was not being given enough time or resources. Wiretaps were expensive to maintain and the investigation team consisted of just two individuals, Stavin and FBI agent Gates. Stavin grew convinced nobody wanted him looking too closely at Universal MCA. He suspected that somebody within the Los Angeles Police Department was leaking information as to how the investigation was progressing to Bacow. Two LAPD officers were questioned about giving information to organised crime figures – one took early retirement and the other was suspended. Observers wondered if somebody was being leaned on to stop the grand jury probe going any further. Worse, Los Angeles Strike Force chief John Newcomer kept rejecting Stavin's prosecution memo – the document distilling grand jury testimony into evidence aimed at securing indictments. The prosecutor still had not found a single piece of compelling evidence to warrant a full trial. Stavin quit the Justice Department in May 1989 after

Newcomer refused to take the investigation any further. 'It was a good attempt but we weren't given enough resources to make it a full effort,' said Stavin.

Paramount had at one point become a shareholder in an Italian company laundering heroin profits for Cosa Nostra. Despite its involvement with the real Cosa Nostra, the studio was much more interested in its fictional Mafia clan, the Corleones. By the late 1980s Paramount was desperate for a third *Godfather* movie. The studio considered and rejected various directors including Martin Scorsese, Sidney Lumet and Michael Cimino. Paramount head Frank Mancuso eventually persuaded Coppola after promising him $6 million plus 15 per cent of the gross. Coppola was once again suffocated by debt and faced losing the 1400-acre Napa Valley vineyards he had bought with money from the original *Godfather*. Coppola flew to Reno, Nevada, in March 1989 to spend a week developing the script for *The Godfather Part III* with Mario Puzo. The two men spent the week either working in a hotel room or gambling in the casino. Coppola wanted six months to write the screenplay but Paramount only gave him six weeks. The studio was adamant that *The Godfather Part III* would open by Christmas 1990 at the latest. Coppola drew on many literary sources for his script, including *King Lear, Titus Andronicus* and *Romeo and Juliet* as well as the opera *Rigoletto*. But in many ways, Coppola admitted, *The Godfather Part III* was a portrait of the studio which made it.

The Godfather Part III follows Michael Corleone in late middle age attempting to atone for his sins. Coppola felt that, as people get older, being seen as good and doing good things becomes more important. Corleone wants to merge his business interests with those of the Vatican, but the higher he goes inside the Church the more corrupt he realises the institution is. Somewhat adolescently, Coppola called the Catholic Church the real Mafia, the real power, an organisation with immense wealth unaccountable to anybody. In the movie, the holding company through which Corleone wants to legitimise his fortune is called Immobiliare. This was also the real-life name of a company that the Vatican was accused of laundering Mafia money through – which then bought half of the Paramount backlot in 1970 and allowed hardcore porn movies to be shot on its soundstages.

In the early 1970s the Vatican's finances were overseen by Chicago-born Bishop Paul Marcinkus, a man who once said: 'You can't run the Church on Hail Marys.' Marcinkus was in charge of the Vatican Bank, the Istituto per le Opere di Religioni (Institute for Religious Works). The Vatican Bank has subsequently been accused of laundering almost $1 billion of Mafia cash, paying 65 per cent of face value for forged government bonds. Marcinkus and others, it is alleged, received huge kickbacks for laundering proceeds of organised crime. Many believe that the death of Pope John Paul I in 1978, just thirty-three days after his election, happened because he wanted to break the links between the Vatican and its murky financial dealings.

One of Marcinkus's advisers was Sicilian financier Michele Sindona, who was in charge of the Vatican's investments overseas. Sindona was a Sicilian Mafioso of the highest order. At a 1957 conclave of top-ranking Sicilian and American Mafiosi in Palermo, Sindona was appointed the mob's chief banker. He was put in charge of washing profits from transatlantic heroin smuggling. Sindona, who also advised the Gambino crime family on its finances, oversaw money-laundering worth $500 million a year. He ran a construction company, Società Generale Immobiliare, of which the Vatican owned 15 per cent. In mid-1970 Immobiliare bought half of the Paramount backlot for double its worth. In exchange, Paramount became a 10 per cent shareholder in Immobiliare alongside the Vatican, buying fifteen million shares. In its accounts, Gulf & Western valued the Immobiliare shares at one and a half times their market value. Paramount chairman Charles Bludhorn was given a seat on the Immobiliare board. Coppola remembered being introduced to Sindona by Bludhorn in an elevator in the Gulf & Western Building in New York. According to Peter Bart, Bludhorn became fascinated by Sindona, who seemed to have complete access to Europe's wealthy and famous – as well as insider knowledge of the Vatican Bank's arcane finances. Bludhorn bragged that his new European allies – men such as Sindona – were going to provide almost unlimited funds for expansion, enabling Gulf & Western to launch hostile takeovers of supermarket chain A&P and air carrier Pan American Airlines. The question remains whether Bludhorn knew that the owner of Paramount's soundstages was laundering money for the Mafia. Perhaps he envisaged the Vatican Bank with its $1 billion of laundered mob cash becoming Paramount's private banker too.

Meanwhile, according to Bart, Sindona was allowing hardcore porn movies to be shot on Paramount's soundstages. 'The Paramount lot itself would ultimately become a beachhead for the mob, a substantial piece of it owned by a company with shadowy connections to "the boys",' Bart wrote.

US financial regulator the Securities and Exchange Commission accused Gulf & Western of inflating the share price of companies in which it was partners with Sindona. These included Immobiliare and its subsidiary, Paramount Marathon, the company which owned half the Paramount lot. The SEC also accused Sindona and Bludhorn of breaking stock exchange rules by swapping worthless shares back and forth. The two agreed to stop and the Commission dropped the charges.

Sindona's financial empire collapsed in 1974 after the Italian authorities charged him with fraud. He fled to America hoping to avoid extradition. In 1979, Sindona hired a Mafioso to murder the lawyer liquidating his Italian assets. With both the Italian and US authorities closing in on him, Sindona bolted to Sicily where he staged his own kidnapping, pretending to have been abducted by a fictitious left-wing political group. In reality, local Mafiosi were hiding the financier. Sindona arranged to be anaesthetised and then have a Mafioso shoot him in the left thigh as proof of his ordeal. He also began sending blackmail notes, while still in hiding, to politicians he had bribed in the past. Sindona hoped that his cronies would intercede to have his blocked funds – in reality Cosa Nostra's money – released. The plot failed and Sindona turned himself in to the FBI after being set free by his supposed captors. He died in prison in 1986 after drinking poisoned coffee.

One of Sindona's allies was a Sicilian politician, Graziano Verzotto. In 1975 an investigation by the Italian government disclosed that Verzotto accepted bribes to launder money for Sindona. Verzotto also knew Frankie 'Three Fingers' Coppola, the Miami-based gangster who pioneered the Sicilian Mafia's heroin export business to America. Frankie Coppola was friendly with Louis Chesler, former chairman of Seven Arts, the company which acquired Warner Bros in 1967. In addition to his political clout, Verzotto oversaw Sicily's state-owned mining company and owned the local Syracuse football club. He also had a number of non-core business interests, including a hotel, the Villa Politi, in Syracuse, whose management he delegated to his lieutenant, Giancarlo Parretti.

It was Parretti, investigative journalists have speculated, who helped the Sicilian Mafia make organised crime's deepest incursion yet into Hollywood.

CHAPTER TWELVE

Lots and Lots of Pretty Girls

Trying to corroborate even the most basic fact about Giancarlo Parretti is like untangling spaghetti. Indeed, there are at least two versions of almost every aspect of Parretti's life – his own and that of other people. For example, Parretti claimed that he became Winston Churchill's favourite waiter while working at the Grill Room of the Savoy Hotel in London. But the Savoy later said it had no record of employing Parretti. Others said that Parretti met Churchill, if he met him at all, while working as a steward on the *Queen Elizabeth*. Parretti countered that he worked on the *Queen Mary*, not the *Queen Elizabeth*, and not as a waiter but as the ship's restaurant manager – and so forth.

It is probable that Parretti was born in Orvieto, about seventy-five miles north of Rome, on 23 October 1941. He enjoyed telling one story that illustrated his childhood canniness about money. The twelve-year-old Parretti used to earn tips acting as an unofficial guide at Orvieto's cathedral. One day an American tourist tipped Parretti with a five-lire coin from the Mussolini era, impressive to look at but almost completely worthless. Thinking on his feet, Parretti protested that this was far too big a gift for such a small service. Presumably touched by the boy's honesty, the American dug into his pocket and presented Parretti with a five-dollar bill – a small fortune for a boy growing up in Orvieto in the 1950s.

Parretti said he arrived in Sicily in 1966, where, having borrowed 20 million lire from the bank, he bought his first hotel.

According to Parretti, his fortune accumulated from there. He attributed his wealth to hard work and an eye for a sharp deal. Parretti's detractors, on the other hand, said that he was not so much self-made as created. They claimed Parretti was inducted into the Cosa Nostra and that Mafia associate Graziano Verzotto left Parretti in charge of his business interests after the senator was gunned down in public. Sicilians assumed that a Mafia hit squad had tried to kill the politician. In 1975 Verzotto quit Sicily for the then haven of Beirut, once considered the Paris of the Middle East, leaving Parretti in charge of the hotel and the local football club. His critics alleged that Verzotto still controlled things long-distance from Lebanon.

Parretti founded a chain of ten regional newspapers that gave fervent support to the ruling Italian Socialist Party. As a consequence, Parretti began making powerful friends in Italian government.

At about this time, Parretti met Swiss-based financier Florio Fiorini while buying and selling two insurance companies. Fiorini was a protégé of Mafia financier Michele Sindona, who taught him about money laundering and political bribery. Previously, Fiorini had been finance director of Italian oil and gas conglomerate ENI, where he tried to prevent the collapse of Italy's largest private bank, Banco Ambrosiano, in 1982. The Italian bank collapsed with debts of $1.4 billion. It is also suspected of laundering heroin profits for the Mafia. Its chairman, Roberto Calvi, was found hanged on Blackfriars Bridge in London just before the bank's collapse, victim of what many people think was a Mafia killing. It is thought that Calvi was murdered because he was threatening to blow the whistle on the Vatican laundering Mafia cash and political bribery. His former protégé Sindona had informed on him for violating currency exchange controls. Calvi was facing four years in jail unless his friends in the Vatican and in politics intervened. When Parretti met Fiorini, he was managing director of Sasea, a Geneva holding company with interests throughout Europe. By the 1980s Fiorini had become one of the biggest, if not *the* biggest, political briber and money launderer in Europe. 'Fiorini is an expert at barter,' Olivetti chairman Carlo De Benedetti told the *Sunday Times*. 'Fiorini can change a bird into a cow and then into a motorbike.'

In 1983 Fiorini and Parretti became partners in a shell company called Interpart that was floated on the Luxembourg Stock Exchange. The two men set about creating a nebula of shell holding companies that would obscure ownership of all their acquisitions to come. Fiorini's principal vehicle, Sasea, eventually had more than three hundred subsidiaries worldwide, many of them entwined with Parretti's shell companies, which in turn were ultimately controlled by a shadowy entity called Comfinance Panama.

In December 1986 Interpart received a cash injection of $55 million (the equivalent of $98 million in today's money). By this time all of Parretti's businesses in Italy – the hotels, the newspapers and the football club – were either loss-making or bankrupt. It has never been explained where the $55 million came from. Even the independent auditor at the time of the transaction, accountancy firm Arthur Andersen, dryly noted its concern that there was not a single document explaining the origin of the $55 million. Interpart was later removed from the Luxembourg Stock Exchange after failing to provide adequate financial information. The secretary general of the Luxembourg exchange compared Parretti to 'a bar of soap in the water. Every time you try and get a grip, he slips through your fingers.'

In the early 1970s Italian producer Dino De Laurentiis claimed to have invented a new film finance tool, although others would dispute that claim. De Laurentiis persuaded the private Rotterdam-based Slavenberg Bank to lend money against international distribution contracts for his films, a practice subsequently described as 'discounting pre-sales'. The bank would lend a percentage of what the overseas distributor – the end-user – was willing to put up to get a film into production and into its cinemas. Slavenberg Bank, however, had already been the subject of earlier investigations concerning laundering drug money. De Laurentiis laughed off rumours that his films were being financed with Mafia profits, even playing a trick on one reporter; he promised to introduce her to the Mafiosi behind his films but they turned out to be a roomful of stolid Dutch bankers. From Slavenberg Bank's point of view, lending money to independent producers became a profitable business.

At the beginning of the 1980s French state-owned bank Crédit Lyonnais ran a slide rule over Slavenberg Bank with a view to buying it. Founded in 1863 and nationalised in 1945, Crédit Lyonnais had been one of the world's biggest banks for decades. It was, in the words of investigative journalist David McClintick, the gem of France's dirigiste economy. President François Mitterrand lavished Crédit Lyonnais with public money, so much so that the bank functioned almost as an arm of the French government. Its magisterial French Empire headquarters on Boulevard des Italiens remains the largest non-government building in Paris. Crédit Lyonnais, attracted in part by Slavenberg Bank's film-lending 'book', acquired the Dutch banker in 1981. The French bank gave the nod for its Rotterdam branch, renamed Crédit Lyonnais Bank Netherlands (CLBN), to increase the amount it was lending to the movies. Between 1981 and 1987 Crédit Lyonnais lent $775 million to various independent movie companies including Cannon, Carolco, Castle Rock, Gladden Entertainment, Hemdale Pictures, Imagine Films and Nelson Entertainment. Movies financed by Crédit Lyonnais included *Platoon*, *A Room With a View*, *When Harry Met Sally* and *The Fabulous Baker Boys*.

But eyebrows were raised when Crédit Lyonnais's chief film-lending officer, Frans Afman, accepted consultancy fees worth hundreds of thousands of dollars from the very companies he was lending to, which was seen as a conflict of interest. Afman also became a board member of various companies borrowing his employer's money, including Cannon, Carolco and Hemdale, eroding distance between the bank and its debtor. Afman later said that his superior told him to keep a close eye on things and that any consultancy fees went straight back to Crédit Lyonnais.

Nevertheless, one eyewitness said in a declaration filed at the California Superior Court in Los Angeles that Afman accepted an envelope full of dollars from Bruce McNall, owner of Gladden Entertainment – the company behind *The Fabulous Baker Boys* –

on board a yacht during the 1983 Cannes Film Festival, a charge Afman denies. McNall was subsequently jailed for fraud.

It was at Cannes that Afman met Parretti for the first time. To Afman's incredulity, Parretti publicly offered to bribe him at their first meeting. Parretti had come to Cannes hoping to buy Cannon, which by 1987 had become an embarrassment to Crédit Lyonnais. Cannon owed Crédit Lyonnais more than $150 million, which it had no hope of repaying. The company, which had used some of Crédit Lyonnais's money to buy a chain of cinemas in Britain, had made a $22 million loss in its last financial year. Its auditors were refusing to sign off its accounts for the past three years because of irregularities. And Cannon was being sued in the USA by the SEC. Parretti had offered to bribe Afman with a sum equivalent to three times his annual salary because he was in a position to approve a loan to buy Cannon. In effect, Parretti was borrowing more cash from Crédit Lyonnais to get a defaulting debtor off its books. Over lunch Afman's boss, Georges Vigon, approved the deal. Parretti was now the new owner of Cannon. Parretti reduced Cannon's indebtedness by $100 million through selling off some assets, settled the US lawsuit with the SEC and persuaded the company's auditors to approve the accounts.

Parretti now moved in on other struggling film companies, again borrowing more money from Crédit Lyonnais to get them off its books. One such acquisition was the De Laurentiis Entertainment Group. Next Parretti set his sights on venerable French film company Pathé. By the late 1980s Pathé had been reduced to running its chain of cinemas and selling television rights to classic films such as *Les Enfants du Paradis*. Parretti told the press that, should his bid be successful, Pathé would move back into filmmaking. Pathé, he said, would join forces with the Cannon cinema circuits in France, Holland and the UK to become the biggest exhibitor in Europe. Parretti and his French partner, Max Théret, acquired Pathé on 16 December 1988. They paid $81 million for 52 per cent of the company. Théret, a French citizen, was the public face man of the deal, complying with French government demands that Pathé remain in French hands. Forty-two per cent of the company belonged to other shareholders Suez Bank, Lyonnaise des Eaux and Tractebel. The rest of the shares were publicly owned. Suez Bank, which had tried to block the sale, announced it would be pulling out of Pathé following Parretti's acquisition.

By now Parretti had moved to America from Italy after Italian stock market regulations required he disclose his shareholders. Parretti set up in Los Angeles, taking over Dino De Laurentiis's Wilshire Boulevard office. He treated himself to a brown Rolls-Royce identical to the one De Laurentiis drove. De Laurentiis introduced Parretti to Alan Ladd Jr at a dinner party. Known throughout the industry as 'Laddie', Ladd was a former head of 20th Century Fox and MGM. It was Ladd who had approved *Star Wars* at 20th Century Fox. As an independent producer his credits included *Alien, Blade Runner* and *Chariots of Fire*. Ladd had only stepped down as chairman of MGM six months earlier; during his tenure he had overseen *A Fish Called Wanda* and *Moonstruck*. Over dinner Parretti told Ladd that he had $5 billion with which to finance movies, but Ladd was unconvinced when he checked the situation out. Parretti offered Ladd a job as his head of production. Hiring Ladd as a Pathé executive boosted Parretti's credibility in Hollywood.

Like a juggler spinning plates in the air, some of Parretti's deals were becoming unstable. French parliamentary deputy François d'Aubert, who had fought to block Parretti buying Pathé, tried to establish a government committee to investigate where Parretti got his money from. D'Aubert believed that Crédit Lyonnais's bankers were seduced by the glamour of the movie business – presumably they had never met anybody like Parretti before. He could only conclude that Crédit Lyonnais had been beguiled by Parretti's roguish flamboyance. The truth was more prosaic. It emerged later that bank officials had accepted all-expenses-paid trips to Bora Bora in the South Pacific from Parretti for approving loans.

Separately, the French government also let it be known that it too was suspicious about the source of Parretti's money. It was reported that the French Secret Service was investigating Parretti, although the government never went public with the results of any investigation.

In April 1989 Parretti was charged with fraud in Naples for falsifying the accounts of his newspaper chain. Parretti had put the newspapers into fraudulent bankruptcy. He was found guilty and sentenced *in absentia* to three years and ten months in prison.

Concerned about the Rotterdam branch's exposure, the Dutch central bank imposed a lending limit of $200 million on each of its clients or each related group of clients. CLBN had already lent more than $900 million to Parretti. But instead of reducing the indebtedness, Crédit Lyonnais worked with Parretti to make it look as if the loan was being reduced. In one particular manoeuvre, Parretti fabricated the fact that he had paid off nearly $200 million of what he owed the bank. A company called Cinema V, newly incorporated in the Netherlands, bought some of Pathé's cinemas in England and Holland for $184 million. But what the Dutch central bank did not know was that Cinema V was a shell company created by Fiorini. That only added to the confusion. The $184 million was just another bank loan. Parretti and Fiorini controlled both ends of the transaction. Parretti's indebtedness was increasing, not decreasing. He was now like Atlas except that he was supporting an enormous debt on his shoulders.

In June 1989 the French finance ministry blocked the Pathé sale six months after the deal was announced. The government claimed that official permission was always required for non-European Union investors to buy more than 20 per cent of a French company. It argued that Fiorini's Swiss company, Sasea, had acted as guarantor for the Crédit Lyonnais loan. Therefore, Sasea was in breach of the 20 per cent rule as it had sought no such permission. Parretti sold his 52 per cent stake in Pathé Cinema to French company Chargeurs a year later for $90 million. But in scuppering the Pathé deal, the French government unwittingly gave Parretti something that could be just as valuable: he was allowed to use the Pathé name outside France. The Cannon Group was renamed Pathé Communications Corporation and its shares were listed on the New York Stock Exchange. That Parretti's company had nothing to do with the illustrious French company was lost on most American investors.

Two months after the French government stopped the Pathé sale, the chief executive of a Hollywood film company hired a private detective to investigate Parretti's past. In a twenty-eight-page fax marked STRICTLY PRIVATE AND CONFIDENTIAL the detective said that there were persistent reports – originating from Parretti's former associates and Italian government officials – that Parretti was linked to the Sicilian Mafia and had been involved in money laundering.

Similarly, the Dutch central bank wrote to Crédit Lyonnais's Paris-based chief executive, Jean-Yves Haberer, at the beginning of 1990, warning him that Parretti and Fiorini's companies were being used to launder 'dirty money'. But the Crédit Lyonnais head did nothing about this written warning from Dutch banking officials.

Meanwhile, Las Vegas-based airline entrepreneur Kirk Kerkorian was trying to sell the MGM/UA studio he owned. Despite several changes of management, MGM/UA was still making a loss. Kerkorian had bought MGM back from CNN founder Ted Turner to stop him selling it to Cannon. Its only two franchises – the repeat business which the studios are mainly in – were the James Bond and the Pink Panther films. Despite slashing overheads, making MGM the studio of last resort, nothing had pulled it out of its nosedive. At the end of 1989, the studio disclosed it had made a $75 million loss during the last financial year. Qintex, an Australian television production company, had offered $1.9 billion for MGM but could not come up with its initial $50 million down payment. Talks with Rupert Murdoch's News Corporation had come to nothing. To one observer, Kerkorian resembled an ageing croupier stuck in a never-ending poker game.

Like Parretti, Kerkorian had been linked to the Mafia, in his case New York and Las Vegas hoods as opposed to Sicilian Mafiosi. In 1961, the FBI recorded Kerkorian agreeing to pay New York gangster Charles 'the Blade' Tourine $21,300 for unspecified purposes. In the wiretap, Kerkorian was overheard promising Tourine that he would send him a cheque made out to actor George Raft. Raft would cash it and hand the money to Tourine. Kerkorian warned Tourine not to cash the cheque himself 'because the heat is on'. Later, Kerkorian – who already owned Bugsy Siegel's Flamingo Hotel – bought the land he built his MGM Grand on from Moe Dalitz. When an interviewer pointed out during one of the few interviews Kerkorian has ever given that Dalitz had a criminal past, Kerkorian replied, 'What's wrong with Moe?'

In March 1990 Hollywood jaws dropped as industry executives opened their morning *Variety* to read, 'MGM/UA: Europe's Gain or Parretti's Pipe Dream?' Pathé Communications had offered to buy MGM for $1.25 billion. According to Alan Ladd Jr, MGM was the only studio Parretti was interested in buying; he had dreamed about owning MGM since he was a child. As an Italian, the MGM lion had great symbolic value for Parretti. Under the terms of the deal, he had to pay Kerkorian $50 million each month towards the eventual purchase price. To help pay for the bid, Parretti hoped to sell MGM's library of one thousand feature films including *West Side Story, Annie Hall* and the Rocky sequels to Time-Warner, the new name of Steve Ross's Warner Communications. Time-Warner agreed to pay $650 million for the right to license MGM's back catalogue. 'The Pathé rooster [company's logo] will marry the MGM lion,' Parretti promised reporters. Pending the takeover, Parretti attended a soirée at the White House, chatting with President Bush and his wife Barbara.

One thing that Parretti could count on was plenty of press coverage. By the 1980s, it seemed as if the colour and charisma had gone out of most movie moguls. Studio executives had either been to law school or business school, rather than pushing a handcart like Louis B. Mayer or Harry Cohn. Parretti, on the other hand, could be counted on for good copy. In the words of one reporter, Parretti's linguistic melange of Italian, English and French alarmed even the most cosmopolitan of international dealmakers. According to his business card, he lived in many places – Los Angeles, New York, Rome, Madrid and Paris. Parretti boasted of his $9 million mansion in the part of Beverly Hills known as the Platinum Triangle. The two-acre property had once belonged to Barbara Stanwyck and featured a seven-bedroom main house, a two-bedroom guesthouse, an Olympic-sized swimming pool and tennis court. Parretti and his wife spent another $2 million on renovations. The paintings on its walls – Picassos, Goyas and Mirós – were picked, apparently at random, from an auction house catalogue. He boasted of his twelve-room apartment within coin-tossing distance of the Trevi Fountain in Rome; of the Ferrari he kept at his third home in Paris; and of the Gulfstream executive jet which served as his flying office.

Peter Bart, editor-in-chief of *Variety* and a former MGM executive himself, has compared the installation of a new regime at a movie studio as reminiscent, in nuance and in ritual, of the transfer of power within a powerful Mafia clan. The *consigliere* hovers close by as the new capo receives a succession of ceremonial visitors. Supplicants position themselves in the corridors, Bart has written, awaiting some impromptu dispensation. The atmosphere crackles with high expectations, mixed with an undercurrent of fear. In Parretti's case, following the handover of power, his most pressing concern was to meet actresses. On taking control of MGM, he told Alan Ladd Jr, 'Laddie, you make the pictures, I fucka the girls.' Florio Fiorini later remembered the high point of Parretti's mogul-dom as a harem. Parretti put at least three Italian 'actresses' on the payroll, buying them $1 million-worth of jewellery in exchange for personal favours. The girls would visit his office in the afternoon, during which time his door would be closed. There was Carla from Milan, Marina from Venice and Cinzia from Rome. According to a report by a former FBI official, Cinzia alone – who once won third place in the Miss Universe contest – was paid more than $387,000 over a two-year period.

But even as the lawyers were finessing the paperwork on the MGM acquisition, *Business Week* magazine was accusing Parretti of money laundering. MGM's new owner had 'close ties with Sicilian crime families', said the magazine. Ladd dismissed talk of Parretti's links with the Mafia as nonsense. Parretti denied the allegation and told the *Wall Street Journal*, 'Everybody is saying it's Mafia money. It's jealousy. There's a list of people involved in the Mafia and my name isn't on it.' Nevertheless, comedian Billy Crystal got his biggest laugh at that year's Oscar ceremony when he said that Leo the Lion, MGM's famous trademark, would no longer roar but instead plead the Fifth.

In truth, Parretti defrauded Crédit Lyonnais to make his first $50 million payment to Kerkorian. He fraudulently borrowed cash on twenty-three separate occasions before the initial 10 March 1990 deadline. Parretti claimed one loan was needed to pay $500,000 to actor Charles Bronson. Another $2.3 million was supposedly to pay for the running costs of the MGM jet. Parretti forged the loan requests by cutting out the required signature of an MGM executive from other documents, pasting it on to phoney loan applications and faxing the photocopied forms to Crédit Lyonnais.

The new chairman of MGM managed to alienate the rest of the Hollywood community – a business which, as Joan Didion has pointed out, is run on the same corporate lines as General Motors despite the glamour of its product – within a few months of taking over the studio. One reporter asked whether Hollywood talent agencies such as CAA and William Morris, gatekeepers of talent such as actors and directors, were being helpful to Parretti's plans to revitalise the studio. 'CAA, CIA, ICM . . . all this bullshit,' said Parretti. He made a pass at actress Meryl Streep that was rebuffed. One story that did the rounds had Parretti meeting Clint Eastwood and his agent at the Cannes film festival. Parretti introduced himself, saying, 'Mr Eastwood, I've always admired your work' – unfortunately addressing the agent rather than the actor. Things only got worse when Parretti hosted a dinner for the press in his home town of Orvieto. He introduced Yoram Globus, former head of Cannon, saying that both of them belonged to the Mafia. 'Yoram is from the Jewish Mafia and I'm from the Italian Mafia,' joked Parretti. There was complete silence in the room, except for Florio Fiorini, who was laughing uncontrollably. In an interview with Italian Communist Party newspaper L'Unità, Parretti described the Jews and the Japanese as his enemies – somewhat intemperate given that Japanese companies owned both Universal Pictures and Columbia TriStar and that he was trying to raise $650 million from Steve Ross, the Jewish head of Time-Warner.

Time-Warner pulled out of the deal to license the MGM/UA

library for $650 million because it decided that Parretti was un-
willing to keep his side of the bargain, which was to bring another
$600 million of equity to the table. All he could come up with was a
further $370 million of bank borrowing, which did not satisfy
Ross. Time-Warner then turned around and sued Parretti for $100
million, alleging three breaches of contempt, fraud and negligence.
Parretti countersued Time-Warner for $500 million for supposedly
reneging on promises made.

MGM's cash-flow problems were beginning to affect its relations with the Hollywood community. Several cheques to actors
including Dustin Hoffman and Sylvester Stallone bounced. Some
MGM staff had their paycheques returned because there was not
enough money in the bank to clear them. Payments to Sean
Connery, star of MGM production *The Russia House*, were late
– and Parretti's attempt to mollify Connery by offering to send a
private jet to whisk him to London from his home in Marbella for
the premiere only made matters worse. There was no plane when
Connery arrived at the airport and he was bundled on to a Spanish
charter flight. Within months of the takeover, a group of MGM's
creditors, including producer Roger Corman, who said he was
owed $6.1 million, was trying to force the studio into liquidation.

The depth of the crisis became apparent on 4 February 1991.
Alan Ladd Jr had to postpone the release of as many as thirty films,
including Ridley Scott's *Thelma and Louise*. MGM did not have
enough money to pay for prints and advertising. Its display
advertising accounts with newspaper publishers were hopelessly
overdue. There was not enough cash even to pay laboratory bills
for processing prints of movies to show in cinemas. Ladd wrote to
Parretti in Rome, 'Production funds have been made available on a
consistently sporadic and late basis. My contract is breached every
single day Pathé fails to provide funds or fails to pay a valid bill.
While it may not bother you, these failures to pay have caused good
people to lose their homes.'

Ladd had no choice but to go behind Parretti's back and contact
Crédit Lyonnais directly. He telephoned the bank to alert it to the
crisis but officials did not bother to return his calls. By now, Crédit

Lyonnais had lent almost $1.3 billion to Parretti, excluding the $800 million left to pay off the MGM acquisition price. Ladd persisted in trying to warn Crédit Lyonnais. Paris-based bank officers eventually flew to Los Angeles to meet Ladd, who told them the studio was burning cash at a rate of about $1 million a day. He said that Parretti claimed Crédit Lyonnais was on the verge of approving another $250 million loan, which was news to the bankers. Crédit Lyonnais forced Parretti to step down as chairman and chief executive, blaming his 'complete disregard and contempt for his legal and contractual obligations'. Ladd hired Charles Meeker, a corporate lawyer at Crédit Lyonnais's law firm White & Case, to help him run the studio. Ladd was promoted to chairman and chief executive. Meeker in turn hired the retiring head of the FBI's Los Angeles office, Lawrence Lawler, to investigate Parretti. By this time, the Los Angeles Police Department's organised crime intelligence division was also investigating Parretti. But a friend warned Meeker that in accepting the job he had put his life in danger. Indeed, Parretti confronted Meeker on 6 June, warning the new MGM president that he was 'really crazy. I want you to understand I am really dangerous. I am very dangerous.'

Ladd, however, doubts Meeker was ever in physical danger from Parretti. 'Parretti may have had some peripheral dealings with the Mafia but in the main he was out to bilk the bank out of billions of dollars,' said Ladd.

But journalists covering the MGM–Pathé story did receive threatening phone calls. Italian journalist Sergio di Cori, who quoted Parretti as saying 'the Jews are ganging up on me' in *L'Unità*, was told in one phone call that his family would be harmed unless he stopped writing about Parretti.

Parretti was ordered to leave the USA in September 1991 following the withdrawal of his entry visa. The reason given was that he had failed to reveal his conviction for fraud when he had first applied for a visitor's visa back in 1982. However, the US immigration authority later apologised to Parretti for saying that he had lied. Parretti was only convicted in 1989. He returned to Italy but was arrested on 27 December 1991 at Rome airport while trying to board a private jet bound for Tunisia. Sicilian police said that Parretti was accused of 'associating with criminals', an official euphemism for working with the Mafia. Sicilian magistrates were investigating thirteen of Parretti's companies based in Sicily involved in film production, car sales, property, hotels and agriculture. Parretti was also under investigation for tax fraud amounting to 120 billion lire ($150 million in today's money) between 1984 and 1988. Pending his trial for tax evasion Parretti was sent to prison. One Italian politician said publicly that he hoped Parretti would not be poisoned in jail like Sindona.

Meanwhile, Crédit Lyonnais went to court to try and wrest control of MGM back from Parretti. The studio had been incorporated in Wilmington, Delaware, which is where proceedings took place. Parretti flew back to America for the hearing. Both Ladd and Meeker testified that he had siphoned money out of the studio into other companies he owned with his wife. According to Lawrence Lawler's investigation, Parretti had misappropriated about $100 million, either directly or indirectly, from MGM and Pathé Communications. The judge awarded continuing control of MGM–Pathé back to Crédit Lyonnais on 30 December 1991. Judge William Allen said that Parretti had lied under oath and produced fake evidence to the court.

Florio Fiorini was arrested in Switzerland on fraud charges stemming from the bankruptcy of his company Sasea. European press reports said that he had squirrelled away millions of dollars after falling out with Crédit Lyonnais. In 2001 Fiorini pleaded guilty to US federal charges relating to the purchase of MGM. He was sentenced to forty-one months in prison.

Crédit Lyonnais poured another $700 million into MGM following Parretti's ousting, eventually hiring Frank Mancuso – the former Paramount executive who had shepherded *The Godfather Part III* – to run the studio. In 1996 Crédit Lyonnais sold the studio back to Kerkorian for $1.3 billion, the same price it had paid for it. In 2004 Kerkorian sold MGM to a Sony Pictures-led investment consortium for $5 billion.

The bank continued to make huge losses as a result of its portfolio of bad debts. The French government was forced to intervene in the early 1990s, and French taxpayers had to bail out Crédit Lyonnais for $18 billion-worth of loans that had defaulted, including Parretti's. In 1993 Crédit Lyonnais chairman Jean-Yves Haberer, the man who had ignored the Dutch central bank's warning about Mafia money laundering, resigned. Shortly before Crédit Lyonnais was privatised in 1999, US federal prosecutors indicted some of the same bank officials who had lent money to Parretti. Crédit Lyonnais bankers were indicted for the fraudulent acquisition of a California insurance company and its junk bond portfolio. On 30 July 2003 the federal grand jury in Los Angeles indicted Crédit Lyonnais and executives, including Haberer, with crimes including conspiracy, fraud and money laundering. Far from being Parretti's unwitting dupe, it was alleged that Crédit Lyonnais was complicit in Parretti's rape of MGM and Pathé. 'A lot of people feel that bankers were lining their own pockets with all the scams that were going on. Crédit Lyonnais seemed to be complicit with Parretti siphoning off money from the studio,' said Ladd.

In July 1996 Parretti skipped bail in the USA and fled back to Italy just days before he was due to be sentenced to an expected ten years in prison. In October that same year he was convicted of evidence tampering and perjury for altering a document relating to his MGM acquisition during the Delaware court case. Parretti continues to be a fugitive from US and French authorities. He is currently running for political office in Orvieto.

Sifting through the wreckage of the MGM catastrophe, California Superior Court judge Irving Shimer – the man presiding over the Crédit Lyonnais grand jury investigation – observed that the bankers who lent Parretti and other movie financiers billions were not 'interested in making movies. They were interested in getting girls on the yacht. That's why bankers come to Hollywood – lots and lots of pretty girls.'

CHAPTER THIRTEEN

All on the Fade

On 3 March 1999 the FBI secretly recorded a conversation between Anthony Rotondo, a soldier in the DeCavalcante crime family of New Jersey, and fellow mobster Joseph 'Tin Ear' Sclafani as they were driving. Sclafani – nicknamed 'Tin Ear' because he wore a hearing aid – boasted of knowing Johnny Depp and other stars and producers. The two men were discussing a television programme they had watched the night before, admiring it for its accuracy. 'Hey, what's that fucking thing *Sopranos*?' asked Sclafani. 'What the fuck are they? Is it supposed to be us?' Rotondo admitted, 'Every show you watch, more and more you pick up somebody. One week it was Corky, one week it was, well, from the beginning it was Albert G.' Sclafani, however, felt he was being ignored – the perennial anxiety of a mobster in the sticks. 'I'm not even existing over there,' he wailed.

The show the DeCavalcante hoods were admiring, *The Sopranos*, premiered on cable channel HBO on 10 January 1999. *The Sopranos* melds two genres, the gangster movie and the soap opera. The result is the only television series ever to have been given a retrospective at New York's Museum of Modern Art. Its first three series were nominated for fifty-six Emmy Awards and won six for acting and writing. The show follows Tony Soprano, under boss of a New Jersey crime family, who goes into therapy unable to cope with his failing marriage, domineering mother and disintegrating family. Series creator David Chase, whose real name is

DeCesare, was born in Naples but grew up in North Caldwell, New Jersey. Chase said he was inspired to write the show by his own relationship with his mother. He described her as 'a crank of a woman'. He would tell funny stories about her and his friends would urge him to write them down. Chase tried to sell *The Sopranos* as a movie, without success. Then in 1996 television production company Brillstein-Grey hired him to create a *Godfather*-style series. The Fox television network, which commissioned *The Sopranos*, rejected the pilot, as did rival networks CBS and NBC – but HBO picked it up, to widespread critical acclaim. Writing in the *Guardian*, John Patterson compared Chase to 'a New Jersey Balzac or Dos Passos, delving ever more deeply into the overlapping milieux – suburban America and "this thing of ours" – that he's staked out'. *The Sopranos* was, for Patterson, 'an Italian-American symphony with four movements, a quartet of great American novels, a quadruple-decker wedding cake iced with the dried blood of dead wise guys'.

One of the attractions of the show, apart from the quality of its acting and writing, is its valedictory air. By the 1990s, the mob had been pulverised from without and eaten away from within. The mob had grown sclerotic, its salad days long past. *The Sopranos* reflects this. Even the scams Soprano and his crew get up to – fake phone cards, selling used car airbags and stealing telephone cable – seem small beer compared with the Outfit's plan to own Hollywood itself. Chase has said the mob has been decapitated in so many places that for him it echoes, in comedic terms, a nervous breakdown. 'The way things are in America, it seems like everything is falling apart. The mob is no different,' said Chase. Tony Soprano sits in his den, like Joey Gallo, watching old gangster movies from the 1930s. Or, as he tells his therapist, 'Lately, I get the feeling that I came in too late, that the best is over', to which his therapist replies that a lot of Americans feel the same way.

Indeed, in another DeCavalcante wiretap one gangster's complaints sounded almost as plaintive as Tony Soprano's. Joseph 'Joey O' Masella was overheard grumbling that the FBI had served his mother with a subpoena, that his ex-wife – who had run off with her plastic surgeon – had thrown his clothes on to the lawn, his daughter needed a therapist and his girlfriend – who was smoking too much marijuana – wanted breast implants, neither of which he could afford. On top of this Joey O, who worked as a driver for New Jersey mob boss Vincent 'Vinny Ocean' Palermo, owed $100,000 to various gangsters. Fatherhood was also driving him mad. In another wiretap, Joey O telephoned his ex-wife and begged her to take the children off his hands. 'Come and get your daughters. I can't take it no more,' he said. 'You left me this responsibility. I'm fifty years old. I can't fuckin' breathe. I'm dyin' over here.'

The FBI first began eavesdropping on the DeCavalcantes in the early 1960s, when agents planted a bug in the offices of mob boss Simone Rizzo DeCavalcante. The New Jersey gang boss was nicknamed 'Sam the Plumber' on account of his plumbing supply business. DeCavalcante was supposed to be another inspiration behind Don Vito Corleone. The FBI recorded DeCavalcante expressing such patriarchal sentiments as 'I'd give my life for our people.' Even then, you get the sense that the mob's influence was not all it was thought to be. DeCavalcante said that his crew had about thirty-one or thirty-two soldiers, most of whom were old and not earning much. In another tape, he sounded like a salaried municipal worker calculating his pension. 'If I can continue for another two or three years, I will be able to show $40,000 or $50,000 legitimately and walk out. Then my family situation will be resolved,' he explained.

There are so many parallels between the DeCavalcantes and the Sopranos that one FBI agent wondered if the show's writers were talking to the New Jersey crime family directly. 'They've got to have somebody over there,' he said. Just as Tony Soprano owns the Bada-Bing strip club, so Vinny Ocean owned Wiggles, a lap-dancing club in the borough of Queens. Various scams that the Mafia was involved with in the late 1990s turned up in the show, sometimes before the scams had even been made public. In January 1998 John A. (Junior) Gotti, son of Gambino crime boss John Gotti, was indicted for selling fake long-distance phone cards. Just as on television, a real doctor was caught recommending healthy patients for expensive treatment at a mob-owned medical company – the Mafia was bilking insurers for millions of dollars' worth of fake medical tests. In New York City, groups of black and Latino construction workers would picket white-controlled sites demanding jobs. Nobody was quite sure how these so-called coalitions managed to do this in a business controlled by the mob. Again, mirroring an episode of The Sopranos, it emerged that the Mafia controlled some of the protest groups. The coalition would picket the building site, at which point the Mafia would step in offering to make the problem go away – for a fee. The mob would then pocket the property developer's cash after paying off the coalition leader. In short, it was a protection racket updated in the era of affirmative action.

Joey O was found murdered in a Flatbush golf course parking lot on 10 October 1998. There were bullets in his pancreas, stomach, spleen and intestines. As Joey O put it shortly before he died, 'The whole fucking life. Who the fuck wants it? I don't.' Joey O's murder was the justification the authorities needed to smash the DeCavalcantes. The New Jersey crime family was decapitated in three organised crime sweeps between December 1999 and March 2001. Tens of Mafiosi were arrested including Vinny Ocean and Joseph Sclafani. Vinny Ocean was charged with sanctioning Joey O's murder. In court, Sclafani's lawyer tried to argue that any talk of murder and extortion the FBI might have overheard was just Tin Ear recycling stuff he had heard on television and in the movies. Attorney Francisco Celedonio argued that his client was just as infatuated with mob lore as everybody else. Everything Joseph Sclafani knew about the Mafia he had gleaned from The Sopranos and Mario Puzo novels, said Celedonio. Clearly, by the late 1990s any difference between organised crime reality and the fictional Mafia had blurred. If in the 1920s the Mafia's only contact with Hollywood was Al Capone going on a studio tour, and in the 1940s it was George Raft showing gangsters how to dress, by the 1990s even wiseguys were having trouble telling the difference between truth and fiction. Indeed, the whole story of Hollywood and the mob could be seen as the erosion of any barrier between the two.

As with *The Godfather* and *The Untouchables*, Italian-American groups were quick to jump on *The Sopranos* for blackening their heritage. Several New Jersey towns banned the show from screening, claiming it defamed Italian-Americans. The Chicago-based American Italian Defence Association (Aida) sued Time-Warner, owner of broadcaster HBO, saying the show was grievously offensive to Italian-Americans. *The Sopranos*, complained Aida, depicted Italian-Americans as congenitally inclined to criminality. Aida did not sue Time-Warner for damages; instead, it wanted Time-Warner to acknowledge that the show violated the Illinois constitution's 'guarantee of individual dignity'. Aida chairman Theodore Grippo said that personally he would like to see the show banned for romanticising gun violence. But Chase rejected criticism that *The Sopranos* glorified crime. Rather, he said, the show demonstrated the inner cancer that the Mafia lifestyle causes. Everybody in *The Sopranos* lies to themselves and to each other incessantly; only Tony Soprano's wife Carmela possibly grasps the truth about her situation. All of the characters in the show are going to hell, said Chase, and they know it. Aida's case was thrown out of court.

Chase has attributed the success of *The Sopranos* partly to wish fulfilment. Most people would like to be able to walk into a restaurant and be given the best table like Tony Soprano. And like Soprano most men would like to have affairs with hot young strippers while their wives turn a blind eye. Then there are the lavish dinners and the loafing around in Soprano's bar. Being a made man does not appear to be such hard work; like a pyramid selling scheme, money flows upwards the higher you reach in the organisation. Tony Soprano's work day appears to consist of leafing through model agency books for girls to hire for his strip club. *The Sopranos* also taps into the fantasy of belonging. Soprano's crew is like a surrogate family, whose members care for and support each other. As with every family there are happy moments, estrangements and reconciliations. In an America given over to therapy and self-help, the kernel of whose wisdom boils down to 'follow thy bliss' and forget about responsibility for others, Soprano's role as capo, taking care of his crew, is comforting. Mafia initiates are told they can go to Tony with any problem. Chase has admitted *The Sopranos* occasionally has a saccharine view of This Thing of Ours. For example, Tony and his gang do not deal drugs. But in reality the mob generated an estimated $78 million a year through drug dealing in the 1980s. Today, so-called Sicilian zips courier drugs between Sicily and gangs in New York and New Jersey. In the real world, said Chase, there really is no honour among thieves. As Colombo crime family member Carmine Sessa put it, 'The movie *GoodFellas* explains it well. Meaning, everybody gets killed by a bunch of animals or so-called friends. This thing I thought I respected so much as a young man had no respect at all.' Just when the viewer becomes too sympathetic to Tony's crew, Chase yanks him back to reality with unexpected violence – shooting a shop assistant through the foot for being too slow or murdering a waiter who complains about the size of his tip.

Another comforting illusion in *The Sopranos* is the notion that people who betray us are really the ones who pay. Either they are tortured by guilt or they make a mess of their lives in some other way. When Soprano discovers his best friend, 'Big Pussy' Bonpensiero, has turned FBI informant, the rat is murdered on a fishing trip – although the gang boss is haunted by the killing. But New Jersey organised crime task force member Bob Buccino has pointed out that half of the mob turn informant – and half of those informants sign lucrative book deals. 'The whole thing has become a movie,' said Buccino. The reality is that not only do people betray other people without punishment, but they often go on to bigger and better things, especially in show business.

Indeed, like a Möbius strip without beginning or end, *The Sopranos* shows the links between Hollywood and the mob. Soprano's gang quote or misremember dialogue from *Godfather* movies. In one episode, a Mafia soldier who wants to break into the industry helps a screenwriter make his script more authentic; he comes to realise that Hollywood is even more cut-throat than the mob – at least there is some honour in Tony's gang. Another episode follows a television scriptwriter who loses everything once he is sucked into one of Tony Soprano's high-stakes poker games.

Conversely, one actor who appeared in a couple of episodes of *The Sopranos* took part in a 1992 mob hit in Brooklyn. That actor, Michael 'Big Mike' Squicciarini, was an associate of the De-Cavalcante crime family, the model for the Sopranos. Eyewitnesses identified him after seeing him on the show. Actor Tony Sirico, who plays gang member Paulie 'Walnuts' Gualtieri, has also been mixed up with the real-life mob. Sirico first started acting when he was in prison. He allegedly threatened a New York club owner in 1971, telling him, 'I have an arsenal of weapons and an army of men, and I'm going to use them, and after I take care of [the police] I'm going to come back here and carve my initials on your fore-head.' In December 1998, the Colombo crime family hosted a Christmas party at an Italian restaurant in Little Italy. FBI agents keeping the restaurant under surveillance were surprised to see Sirico show up with Vincent Pastore, the actor who played 'Big Pussy' Bonpensiero in the series. And in December 2005, Lillo Brancato Jr, another actor who appeared in *The Sopranos*, was shot and badly wounded while allegedly burgling a house. Brancato Jr allegedly broke into the house with one Steven Armento, described by authorities as a low-level Genovese crime family associate until he was banished for drug addiction.

Chase has pointed out that show business, like the Mafia, attracts sociopaths. But if somebody goes too far in organised crime at least they face retribution, or even murder. In show business there is no such brake on bad behaviour. Thousands climb over each other's shoulders to struggle on to Hollywood's raft when there is only enough room for a few. Only the most rapacious and hungry make it to the top of the pile. At one point, Soprano blames Hollywood for destroying Cosa Nostra. Grabbing one soldier who has been offered a movie deal by the throat, Soprano says, 'You know how many mobsters are selling screen-plays and screwing things up? The golden age of the mob is gone, it's never coming back – and the mob has only itself to blame.'

By the late 1990s, federal prosecutors in Manhattan and Brooklyn had spent twenty years destroying the five New York crime families. In autumn 1998 the head of each New York crime family was in prison facing years behind bars: John Gotti of the Gambino crime family; Carmine Persico of the Colombo family; Vincent Gigante of the Genovese family; Vittorio Amuso of the Lucchese family; and Joseph Massino of the Bonanno family. According to the FBI, by the end of the century Mafia membership had shrunk to between two and three thousand people out of thirty-five million Italian-Americans. Fifteen years earlier the figure was probably double that. The combined membership of the New York families in 2002 was thought to be 570, down from 634 in 2000 and 940 in 1986. Genovese was the largest family, with 152 members, including nine new recruits. The Gambino crime family numbered 130, having lost 33 members the previous year. The Lucchese family had 113 members, including three new recruits. The Colombo family came next, with 90 members, having lost 26 in the previous year. Smallest was the Bonanno family, with only 85 members in total. As journalist Dave Remnick pointed out, 'once pharaonic earners are sweating over subpoenas; and, in the city, Little Italy dissolves into Chinatown while tourists summon the memory of Crazy Joe Gallo's last supper. It's all on the fade.'

The mob had also been decimated on the West Coast. In 1988 California attorney general John Van de Kamp said that the Mafia was the least of the city's problems compared with street gangs the Crips and the Bloods. Between 1985 and 1988 the Los Angeles Police Department noted a 71 per cent increase in the number of gangs in the city. By 1991 the Crips had thirty thousand members while the Bloods had 9000. Meanwhile, the Medellin Colombian cocaine cartel – which used the Crips and the Bloods as its street dealers – replaced the Mafia as the bogeyman of organised crime. That same year, the FBI launched a final assault on the Los Angeles mob. The FBI's 'Rising Star' organised crime investigation destroyed the Peter John Milano crime family, all that was left of Cosa Nostra in California. Peter John Milano and fourteen other men were indicted on eighteen counts. Attorney general Edwin

Meese III called the prosecution 'the most significant organised crime case on the West Coast for a decade. The indictment, and others to follow, will involve as defendants virtually all of those, the government charges, who make up the membership of the Cosa Nostra organised crime family in Los Angeles.' US attorney Robert Bonner added that the Mafia in Los Angeles had been gutted. Los Angeles Organised Crime Strike Force chief James Henderson told the *Los Angeles Times*, 'I think this puts them out of business for a while. The government does this once more and there's not going to be a La Cosa Nostra in Los Angeles.' Former Milano family enforcer Anthony Fiato summed up his disillusionment: 'The government has too many ways to get you. It's a real mismatch. Whether some of the guys on the street know it or not, it's all over and has been for years.'

Just as the government was killing off what was left of the mob in Los Angeles, so illustrious names from the past were also being killed off. Johnny Rosselli's dismembered torso was found floating in an oil drum in the Florida Everglades. Sam Giancana was shot through the head while preparing himself a supper of pork and beans. Korshak, the *éminence grise*, retreated even further into the shadows. Although he was still respected in Las Vegas, in Hollywood people only care about what you can do for them today. As Hollywood unions purged themselves of links with organised crime, Korshak's influence weakened. In 1976, investigative journalists Seymour Hersh and Jeff Gerth lifted the stone on the squirming underside of Korshak's life in a four-part exposé in the *New York Times*. Hollywood players like Wasserman distanced themselves from their friend. Korshak, wheelchair-bound by now, grew bitter about the way he had been pushed aside. Ironically, for a man whose memory was so prodigious that he had no need to take notes, Korshak developed Alzheimer's disease. He died at his home at 808 North Hillcrest Road in Beverly Hills on 20 June 1996.

Although the big guns had fallen silent, it would be naïve to think that the mob had lost interest in Hollywood completely. There were still skirmishes on the front line between Cosa Nostra and the movie industry.

In February 2004 Steven Seagal's producer was sentenced to eighteen months in prison for conspiring with the Mafia to extort hundreds of thousands of dollars from Seagal. The FBI taped one Gambino family member bragging about how he had petrified Seagal after threatening to hurt him. Seagal's producer, Julius Nasso, pleaded guilty and was fined $75,000 on top of his prison sentence. In a punishment worthy of *The Sopranos*, he was also ordered to see a therapist after his release from prison.

Jules Nasso had been Seagal's producer over a fifteen-year period, from 1986 until 2001. He worked with Seagal on ten films including *Under Siege 2* (1995) and *On Deadly Ground* (1994), which Seagal starred in, directed and produced. Nasso's uncle Julius was connected to the Gambino crime family and his sister-in-law was a Gambino relative. He began his career in the industry working as a runner for director Sergio Leone when he was making *Once Upon a Time in America* (1984). The Leone gangster movie starred Robert De Niro as a character based on Meyer Lansky. Nasso and Seagal first met at Madeo, an Italian restaurant in Brooklyn, in 1987. They became friends and worked together through the highs of Seagal's career in the early 1990s. At one point they became so close that they owned neighbouring mansions on Staten Island. Seagal's eldest son lived with the Nassos for four years as part of the family. Nasso and Seagal's partnership generated more than $1 billion in revenues for Warner Bros, the studio which financed and released all of Seagal's movies throughout the nineties. Seagal's career peaked in 1992 when he made *Under Siege*, in which he played a former Navy SEAL turned chef – one film which Nasso did not produce. Nevertheless, Warner Bros was so pleased with Nasso that the producer had lunch with Warner Bros chief executive Terry Semel at Le Cirque restaurant in New York in 1991. But by 2000 the studio was tiring of the number of court cases being brought against Seagal, all of them involving former female employees of Seagal suing for sexual intimidation. Warner Bros was also becoming exasperated with Seagal's expanding waistline, about which the actor was doing little. The studio even found cookie crumbs next to his weightlifting equipment. By 2000, Seagal's relationship with Warner Bros was effectively over.

Nasso and Seagal decided to go independent. After all, he still had a following in the home-video market. They set about financing and producing a slate of medium-budget movies starring Seagal. One project was to star Seagal as Genghis Khan. Seagal's fee by now had dropped to $2.5 million per movie. But Nasso was growing exasperated by his friend's conviction that he was a reincarnated Buddhist deity. Then Seagal walked away from their first production, *The Prince of Central Park* (2000). Harvey Keitel stepped in to play Seagal's part. Seagal dropped out of the partnership completely. In March 2001 Nasso sued Seagal for $60 million in a breach-of-contract lawsuit.

Meanwhile, the FBI had been investigating Mafia corruption on the New York docks. FBI agents had eavesdropped on conversations between Gambino crime family members. Police in New York and New Jersey arrested seventeen accused mobsters in pre-dawn raids on 4 June 2001. Those arrested were charged with sixty-eight counts of extortion, threats and loan sharking in and around the waterfront of both states. The most high-profile arrest was Peter Gotti, acting head of the Gambino crime family. Gotti was elder brother of John 'Dapper Don' Gotti, who died in prison that same month. Also arrested were several Gambino enforcers, including Anthony 'Sonny' Ciccone, Frank 'Red' Scollo, Primo Cassarino – as well as Jules Nasso.

The following month the FBI released transcripts of some of the 2200 separate recordings they had made of Gambino family conversations. One conversation between Nasso, Ciccone, Cassarinio and Nasso's brother Vincent was about forcing Seagal to kick back $150,000 for every film he made with Nasso. Ciccone told Nasso he should be tougher with Seagal, saying, 'You really gotta get down on him 'cause I know this animal, I know this beast.' Ciccone intimidated Seagal at the Gage & Tollner steakhouse in Brooklyn in 2000, demanding that he continue working with Nasso. Seagal was apparently so shaken by the encounter that he paid out $700,000 to the Gambino crime family. Cassarino was later recorded as saying that Seagal believed 'if he doesn't come up with that thing . . .' Ciccone interrupted the sentence, '. . . that they were gonna hurt him'.

Seagal appeared as a prosecution witness during the first 'Waterfront' trial, which resulted in the conviction of Peter Gotti, his brother Richard V. Gotti and nephew Richard G. Gotti, among others. The Gottis were convicted of racketeering and money laundering relating to their control of Local 1814 of the Longshoreman's Union, the model for the corrupt union in *On the Waterfront*.

It emerged in court that, rather than go to the police, Seagal had turned to an imprisoned Genovese mob captain for help. Angelo Prisco, a capo in the Genovese crime family, was serving a twelve-year sentence for arson and conspiracy to commit racketeering. Seagal admitted giving Prisco's lawyer $10,000 for visiting Prisco and asking for help in the spring of 2001. Seagal wanted Prisco to intervene to 'see if we could settle this like business people instead of like thugs', according to Gotti defence lawyers.

At least Nasso's pleading guilty saved Seagal from being cross-examined about his own history of violence. Seagal pleaded the Fifth Amendment in 1993 when asked whether he had ever solicited murder as part of his videotaped evidence in an assault case. A parking-lot attendant was suing Seagal for roughing him up during a scuffle.

One would have thought that Seagal, given his brush with the Mafia, would have avoided organised crime figures. Not a bit of it. Presumably, like fellow actor James Caan, he had become infatuated with wiseguys – at least this was the argument of the Gotti defence team. Seagal was alleged to be friendly with 'Sonny' Franzese, a convicted bank robber and capo in the Colombo crime family. Franzese and his friend Danny Provenzano allegedly travelled to the Canadian production location of *Exit Wounds* (2000), the last movie Seagal made for Warner Bros. There Provenzano, executive producer of *Vampire Vixens from Venus* (1995), is supposed to have persuaded Seagal that he and Franzese should replace Nasso as the actor's production team. (Provenzano has denied this, saying he would never work with Seagal: 'I don't like people who are disloyal to their friends' – presumably referring to Nasso.) At the time of the alleged Canada visit Provenzano was facing two hundred years in jail. He had been accused of extorting nearly $1.5 million from businessmen through violence, kidnapping and death threats. One of Provenzano's victims was threatened with a baseball bat. Provenzano and eight others had been indicted in May 1999 on forty-four counts including racketeering, conspiracy to commit racketeering, theft by extortion, kidnapping, possessing a weapon for unlawful purposes, aggravated assault, money laundering and terrorist threats. Provenzano was great-nephew of late Teamsters Union boss 'Tony Pro' Provenzano, the man who is thought to have organised the murder of Jimmy Hoffa. In 2003 Provenzano went on national television, somewhat confusedly claiming there was no such thing as Cosa Nostra while at the same time promoting *This Thing of Ours*, a movie he had written, directed and starred in about Mafiosi today. *This Thing of Ours* also featured James Caan and Vincent Pastore (of *The Sopranos*). Some of the scenes in the movie came from Provenzano's own experience, such as mobsters smashing somebody's thumb with a hammer, one of the crimes of which Provenzano was accused. Provenzano's impending court case had not been helped by his bragging on television about the hammer attack. Provenzano eventually pleaded guilty and admitted being an associate of the Genovese crime family. One of the actors in the movie, New Jersey-based Frank Vincent, who appeared in *GoodFellas* and *Casino*, was a character witness during the trial. Despite pleading guilty, the thirty-nine-year-old Provenzano was sentenced to ten years in prison in September 2003. Summing up, Superior Court judge William Meehan said that Provenzano could not decide whether his life was a movie or movies were a way to support his life. New Jersey state prosecutor Vaughn McKoy said later that Provenzano had used the court case to promote *This Thing of Ours*. 'The guy might be a talented filmmaker, but the fact is he used his criminal case to sell his movie,' McKoy said.

Seagal's intimidation by the Mafia and his own friendship with other organised crime associates generated a lot of press coverage. The actor was supposed to have warned off one journalist digging too closely into his private life by faking a Mafia death threat. Seagal was thought to have hired private investigator Anthony Pellicano, whose clients included Arnold Schwarzenegger, Elizabeth Taylor and Michael Jackson, to intimidate *Los Angeles Times* reporter Anita Busch. The private investigator is supposed to have hired drugs dealer Alexander Proctor to smash the windscreen of the reporter's car. Proctor admitted to *Vanity Fair* magazine to placing a dead fish on the smashed windscreen with a rose on it and a note saying, 'Stop'. He said the idea behind the fish and the rose was to make it look like a Mafia death threat, rather than coming from Seagal. Seagal's lawyer responded that Proctor's allegations were untrue and read like a bad screenplay. The FBI subsequently cleared Seagal of any involvement in intimidating Busch.

In July 2004 Nasso tried to get his eighteen-month jail sentence reduced for helping the FBI investigate a threat made against another reporter who had written unflattering things about Seagal. Nasso told the FBI through a private detective that one of the men in a car that had pulled up alongside journalist Ned Zeman and pointed a gun at his head was John Christian Rottger, a former Navy SEAL who was a bit player in Seagal's movies. The authorities were unmoved by Nasso's civic-mindedness. He served one year in prison for his part in the Seagal extortion scheme. Following his release, Nasso announced that he was building an editing and sound facility in Staten Island called Cinema Nasso Film Studios. The first projects to use the post-production facility would be his own, such as *King of Sorrow* starring Chazz Palminteri and Michael Madsen (*Reservoir Dogs*). For Nasso it appears that Hollywood, like the Mafia, is easy to fall into and difficult to get out of.

In April 2006, two New York policemen, Louis Eppolito and Steven Caracappa, were found guilty of playing roles in eight mob slayings, as well as bribery, money laundering and drug-dealing. Caracappa and Eppolito, the eleventh most decorated policeman in

New York's history, even worked as hitmen for the Lucchese crime family. After retiring from the NYPD, Eppolito – who acted in *GoodFellas, Bullets Over Broadway* and *Predator 2* – reinvented himself as a movie producer. Based in Las Vegas, Eppolito conned two elderly women out of $65,000, promising he would turn their memoirs into movies. One of Eppolito's victims, sixty-one-year-old Jane McCormick, was a former call girl at the Sands casino during the 1960s and 1970s who said she had sex with Frank Sinatra. One crooked accountant giving evidence during the trial said Eppolito was desperate to finance his movie project – and didn't care where the money came from to make it. Eppolito had written a screenplay and needed help in raising $1.5 million to finance it. 'He didn't care about the source of the money, he just wanted the money,' accountant Steven Corso told the jury in Brooklyn Federal Court. Eppolito used to hold meetings in his office surrounded by pictures of himself and Hollywood players including Robert De Niro and Martin Scorsese.

Meanwhile, the *New York Post* reported that mob war had broken out between Hollywood studios desperate to turn Eppolito's story into a movie. One Brooklyn prosecutor was talking to Hollywood agents before the trial even began. Universal, Warner Bros and Columbia were all developing their own versions of the 'Mafia cops' story. Columbia pitted *GoodFellas* screenwriter Nicholas Pileggi against the team at Warner Bros that produced Mafia movies *Donnie Brasco* and *Analyze This*. Sitting in their prison cells, Eppolito and Caracappa were talking about developing their own movie project about their case.

Despite isolated incidents such as the Seagal case, for the most part the Italian Mafia had middle-classed itself out of existence by the turn of the century. Today's crew bosses spend huge amounts of money educating their children. They send their sons to the best private schools. They give them every possible advantage to help them avoid a life of organised crime. Mob bosses do not want their children to join This Thing of Ours – the whole fucking life, as Joey O put it, is not for them. In *The Sopranos* Tony Soprano's son Anthony Jr is soft in comparison to his father and still needs his mother's physical protection at the age of eighteen. Instead, children of Mafiosi go on to become accountants, doctors and lawyers. But just as nature abhors a vacuum, so other, hungrier immigrant groups have moved into the space which the Mafia once occupied. In popular imagination, the Russian Mafiya has replaced Cosa Nostra as a criminal conspiracy of almost occult power. As Los Angeles deputy district attorney Anthony Colannino put it, 'The Italian mob has gotten fat and lazy just like the rest of us Americans, but they [the Russian Mafiya] are used to hardship. You throw them in prison, they're living better than they were before.'

The proper name for the Russian Mafiya is *Vory v zakonye*, or 'Thieves within the Code'. With the collapse of the Soviet Union at the end of the 1980s, the Mafiya extended hands across the water, aligning itself with the Colombo, Lucchese and Genovese families of New York. Organised crime as well as legitimate business embraced globalisation. In December 1991 the Mafiya held an Atlantic City-style summit during which gangsters discussed how to increase their money-laundering business. The meeting also decided that Vvacheslav Ivankov – known as Yaponick or Little Japanese because of his Asian appearance – should oversee the Mafiya's US operations. Born in 1940, Ivankov, who was based in Vladivostok, was leader of one of the most powerful gangs in eastern Russia. He was infamous for taking an oxyacetylene welding torch to the rectums of his victims. Ivankov emigrated to America in 1993 under the guise of starting up a Russian film company in New York. He set himself up in the Russian enclave of Brighton Beach, New York. Ivankov soon became involved in drug dealing, money laundering and extortion. He was arrested in 1995 and sentenced to nine years in prison in 1997.

By 1998 Russian crime syndicates were washing money in London and the other European capitals on a grand scale. Money flowed in through drugs, fraud, prostitution and extortion, often with the participation of former KGB officers. In London, money was frequently laundered through the property business. At the time Mafiya money laundering involved a three-stage process known as placing, layering and integration. First, cash would be funnelled into a small firm; second, it would be mixed with clean money and finally moved into totally clean stocks or a larger property. By the end of the process the Mafiya's money would be shining white. By 2000, an estimated $200 billion had been taken out of Russia illegally.

It has often been said that the movie business also provides an ideal way to launder money. Unlike a factory, which takes time to set up and equip, movies need large amounts of cash at short notice. According to Hollywood lobbyist the Motion Picture Association of America (MPAA), the average movie costs $96 million to produce and to publicise. Movies also repay investors comparatively quickly. Providing you are at the top of the revenue cascade, a movie takes less than two years to repay its cost plus a premium. First a movie is released in cinemas, then four months later it appears on DVD followed by pay-television, free television and other ancillary windows.

Most movie budgets are sewn together through a patchwork of pre-sales, subsidy and equity investment. But sometimes it is necessary to start filming before all the money is in place – Tom Cruise might only be available for three weeks in August, for example. This is where so-called gap finance comes into play. A bank lends the producer the portion of the budget that has yet to be closed, under the reasonable expectation that sales of the finished film will more than repay its loan. During the 1990s, however, a lot of films were financed this way, not because of scheduling problems but because filmmakers had run out of places to turn to. In the late 1990s a new wrinkle was added to gap financing – insuring the loan so that an insurance company would step in to repay the bank should the film flop. If a film failed to repay the bank within two years, then the insurance company would reimburse the lender, at least in theory. It was a development that left some scratching their heads; if a bank was so unsure about getting its money back that it took out insurance, why make the loan in the first place? Insurers waded in, attracted by the premiums on offer. By the end of the decade insurance companies had underwritten an estimated $3 billion of film finance, generating about $400 million in premiums.

Organised criminals will typically pay around 30 per cent of illegal capital to have it washed clean, a ratio similar to the cost to the film producer of borrowing insurance-backed gap finance. For every $1 million borrowed, typically about $700,000 ended up on screen. The emergence of insurance-backed gap finance at the end of the 1990s provided an ideal opportunity to launder money. This, together with the ease with which film finance can front financial schemes, may explain why rumours began circulating about money laundering in Wardour Street, the home of the British film industry once described as being the only street in London with shadows on both sides.

Rumours circulated about one company in particular. Flashpoint was an offshore company that had interests in two cinemas in Russia. In the late 1990s it ignited the afterburners on insurance-backed gap finance, raising $250 million to fund sixty different films and television series including the Academy Award-winning *Gods and Monsters*. Indeed, Flashpoint was so overwhelmed by its one success that it took out full-page advertisements at great cost in national newspapers trumpeting its good fortune. It seemed as if it could not spend money fast enough. According to one source, the producer of *Gods and Monsters* had to tell Flashpoint to stop throwing money at his production. Millions were lent to obscure US independent production companies. It bought two Los Angeles-based sales companies and a post-production facility in Hollywood. There were plans to buy a 110,000-square-foot studio in Montreal and a talent agency in Los Angeles. But the company would never explain where the money came from. Perhaps it was Wardour Street adding two and two together and coming up with five, but the mystery as to where Flashpoint got its cash from only fuelled gossip.

In October 1999 Flashpoint held a party in London to launch Alchymie, its new production and distribution business. Flashpoint was ploughing another $250 million into the movie business through Alchymie. Their party was held at the Oxo Tower restaurant, which at the time was charging £30,000 a night just to hire its dining room – a sum which, as *Insurance Insider* magazine pointed out, excluded the cost of so much as a solitary, pitted olive. Magnums of champagne embossed with the company logo flowed freely. Wardour Street parties are usually pretty samey affairs, as caste conscious as rural India. But this party was different. Tough-looking young Slavic men sat at the bar next to bored Eastern European models. And there to give his blessing to the launch was the then British government culture secretary, beaming for the photographers. Even as the minister was speaking, guests were exchanging looks that said 'he is going to regret this'. Money, and where Alchymie was getting it, was the main topic of conversation.

An offshore film financing company like Flashpoint, ran the argument, could be financed with illegitimate funds. Through an associated film production company, such as Flashpoint's in-house production company, Prosperity Films, it could produce films. The quality might be appalling but as long as the source of the cash was prepared to fund production (dependent, of course, on an insurer) then the scheme would succeed. The insurer – who wrote the risk on the back of the advice of a 'risk manager' (which in Flashpoint's case was Flashpoint) – would ultimately be faced with a claim for revenue failure. The paid claim is then legitimate money – with the duped insurer acting as an unwitting agent in laundering money – or so the argument went. Meanwhile, the insiders in the deal – the broker and risk manager – would cream off huge fees, typically 15 per cent of the sum insured.

It is thought that the majority of Flashpoint's money derived from insurers underpinning securitised loans from investment bank Crédit Suisse First Boston. Securitisation involves a bank making loans to a company based on future revenue streams, in this case how much films were going to earn in the future. But legitimate money could have been mixed with dirty money and then insured. 'In the end nobody cared where Alchymie was getting the money, just as long as it was being spent on their film,' said one producer.

Then, just as quickly as it had arrived, Flashpoint disappeared. Privately, producers gave Alchymie a lifespan of two years before going under, which is the usual way of things in Wardour Street. Four months later Alchymie fired most of its staff, not having enough money to fund a single film. Flashpoint went into administration in March 2001. The High Court revealed that Flashpoint had misappropriated nearly $9 million of funds earmarked for film production. It never explained what the money was used for – just that it had been spent. The High Court judge described Flashpoint as having 'opaque' and 'wholly obscure' records on multimillion-dollar deals. None of its film productions performed as predicted; one slate of films towards which Flashpoint lent $16.4 million only generated $1.6 million, leaving a shortfall of $14.8 million. Another slate of films fared even worse, raising only $829,000.

Despite the dubious nature of Flashpoint's productions, Australian insurance company HIH paid out $50 million-worth of claims because it hoped to recover the vast majority from reinsurers – other insurance companies with which it had spread its risk. HIH attempted to sue Flashpoint's insurance broker, JLT Risk Solutions, for fraud but the case was dismissed in 2006. Other insurance companies that HIH had hoped would cover its own exposure to Flashpoint refused to pay out, arguing that Flashpoint had not produced the volume of movies it was contracted to make. HIH was Australia's largest corporate collapse with debts estimated at around A$5.3 billion, some of which came from its exposure to the movie industry.

In America what passes for the Mafiya is thought to be hundreds of thousands of small criminal enterprises, connected by blood, religion, ethnicity or plain expediency. In Los Angeles, for example, the Russian-speaking community has grown to almost 500,000, based in Glendale, Hollywood and West Hollywood. Los Angeles, home to an estimated eight hundred Eastern European criminals, is second only to New York as a centre for Russian mob activity. Organised crime is growing in the expanding Eastern European immigrant community in Los Angeles, said Dr Louise Shelley, director of the transnational crime and corruption centre at American University, Washington, DC. Deputy district attorney Anthony Colannino has said that thousands of former Soviet

Union criminals enter the USA illegally each year, including former KGB officers and Special Forces soldiers.

As yet, the Russian Mafiya has made only small inroads into the movie business. One common way for the Mafiya to extort money is kidnapping. In March 2002, Russian film financier and entrepreneur George Safiev and his producer partner Nick Kharabadze were allegedly murdered by Mafiya gangsters living in the San Fernando Valley. Worse, their ransom of nearly $1 million had been paid but the movie executives had been killed anyway. The decomposed, weighted bodies of Safiev and Kharabadze were hauled out of the New Melones Reservoir near Yosemite National Park on 21 March 2002. Both men had either been asphyxiated or strangled before being dumped in the water.

According to the Grand Jury indictment of the alleged murderers, Kharabadze had been used as bait to get to Safiev. Kharabadze used to run Safiev's Hollywood production company, Matador Media. Safiev, whose wealth has been estimated at $10 million, grew rich introducing computer systems into Russian banks. On 5 December 2001 he was telephoned by Rita Pekler, the accountant at Matador Media. Pekler asked to meet Safiev but he told her he was leaving on a business trip to Moscow and would be unable to hook up. In fact, it transpired that Pekler had been kidnapped and was phoning from one of the gang's houses in Sherman Oaks. Three men had taken her hostage: Iouri Mikhel, of Encino; Jurijus Kadamovas, of Sherman Oaks; and Petro Krylov, of West Hollywood. Mikhel and Kadamovas co-owned an aquarium shop in Sherman Oaks called Designed Water World. Supposedly, their plan was to use Pekler to lure Safiev to a place where they could abduct him. When Pekler failed to set up the meeting, the three men allegedly killed the accountant by suffocating her. Mikhel and Kadamovas drove north to the foothills of the central Sierra Nevada, weighted her body and threw it in the New Melones Reservoir. Pekler's corpse was also subsequently dragged from the water.

Kadamovas then drafted in his girlfriend, Natalya Solovyeva, twenty-six, to try and entice Kharabadze to meet her. Kharabadze was working at the Matador offices on 18 January 2001 when he received several phone calls from Solovyeva. She also left a message on his mobile voicemail to call 'Natalya from Moscow'. Kharabadze drove to the aquarium shop on Ventura Boulevard on the afternoon of 20 January. As soon as he walked in Kharabadze was ambushed. His leg was handcuffed to a chair. According to gang member Ainar Altmanis, forty-five, who later pleaded guilty and cooperated with prosecutors, Mikhel and Kadamovas told Kharabadze not to worry – they wanted Safiev, not him.

Kharabadze was also ordered to telephone Safiev. That night, Safiev too drove to Ventura Boulevard, where he was immediately seized. Kharabadze and Safiev were taken to Kadamovas's home in Sherman Oaks, where they were locked in separate rooms. According to Altmanis, Safiev was forced to telephone London to arrange a ransom payment to be transferred from an account in Singapore to a bank account in Miami. Relatives of previous victims of the kidnapping gang had received faxes from Russia, telling them to send money to bank accounts in Latvia and the USA. Safiev and Kharabadze were told they would be released once the money arrived. Prosecutors later described the accused as displaying wanton indifference to the suffering of their victims.

Safiev did what he was told and his ransom was paid into the Miami bank account. Nevertheless, Safiev and Kharabadze were driven north to the Sierra Nevada on 24 January 2001. Mikhel, Kadamovas and Krylov left Altmanis guarding Kharabadze at a motel near the New Melones Reservoir. The trio then took Safiev to a secluded area where they allegedly strangled him. Then they supposedly weighted his body and threw it over the Stevenot Bridge. After Safiev's body had sunk, they went back for Kharabadze.

The gang was quickly arrested and Altmanis agreed to cooperate with the authorities. The other three are still facing trial for murder, having also allegedly kidnapped and murdered people in Turkey and Cyprus and kidnapped another victim in Idaho. In March 2004, Mikhel, Krylov and Kadamovas tried to escape from their downtown Los Angeles jail. Guards searched Mikhel's cell and found tools and a hole behind a mirror leading to a stairwell. Nine months later a woman who had helped Mikhel launder $50,000 of ransom money was sentenced to twenty-seven months in prison.

In time, it may be that the Mafiya will attempt to control one of the Hollywood unions, like IATSE or the Screen Actors Guild, just as the Outfit and the Syndicate did in the 1930s and 1940s. Just as Russian oil plutocrats have bought European football clubs, so the Mafiya might make a play for a Hollywood movie studio, fulfilling Willie Bioff's dream of owning the action itself. But old industry hands doubt it. Law enforcement agencies have learned from their mistakes. For too long, agencies such as the FBI paid the Mafia little attention as it gained power. This time around, the authorities are not giving the Mafiya time to mature, to get entrenched in Russian neighbourhoods and then infect society at large. *Variety* editor-in-chief Peter Bart does not believe there is any space for organised crime in Hollywood any more. The studios are publicly owned conglomerates bound by corporate governance, scrutinised by regulators. 'There's no organised crime in America any more,' said Bart. 'There's no Mafia any more.'

On the other hand, children of Mafiosi may have grown up to become accountants, dentists and lawyers but, according to former federal prosecutor Richard Stavin, like the undertow of a sinking ship the pull of organised crime is difficult to escape. As Michael Corleone cries out in *The Godfather Part III*, 'Just when I thought I was out, they pull me back in.' To assume that the children of Mafiosi have become the golf-playing middle-class professionals might just be one more thumb-sucking myth. According to organised crime expert James Morton, the dentist son of one mob boss allows his surgery to be used for Mafia business discussions – just as Tony Soprano and his uncle Junior meet in a doctor's surgery. Joseph Pistone, the FBI agent who infiltrated two Mafia families and whose life story was filmed as *Donnie Brasco*, said that the children of the Bonannos and the Colombos were all involved in the Mafia. All of the children of Mafiosi that Pistone encountered undercover knew what their fathers were doing – and none of the fathers ever tried to dissuade their sons from This Thing of Ours. 'Children of Mafiosi are now rubbing shoulders with captains of industry but they don't forget their roots,' said Stavin. 'I have no doubt Mafia corruption of Hollywood is still happening – the question is where and how?'

And so the story of how organised crime has corrupted Hollywood continues to unfold. Perhaps evil is contagious, transmitted from person to person by coming into contact with a carrier. Moreover, like most diseases, some people are more susceptible to evil than others. It is almost as if the carrier is giving the person infected permission to act badly. Therefore, like an insidious version of *La Ronde*, Giancarlo Parretti buys MGM from Kirk Kerkorian, while Parretti's connection Michele Sindona allows porn movies to be shot on Paramount's soundstages; and Sidney Korshak intimidates Kerkorian into giving Al Pacino the lead in *The Godfather*; and Korshak's pal Johnny Rosselli threatens to kill Columbia's Harry Cohn; and Rosselli petrifies Joan Crawford's blackmailers; and Louis B. Mayer warns Crawford that she is finished in movies unless she allows mob relatives on to her set; and there is Frank Sinatra stepping off the plane in Havana on his way to meet Lucky Luciano; and Luciano sitting in his car waiting for Thelma Todd; and Al Capone touring silent movie studios as Luciano and Capone run down the street together as children in the ever-deepening story of Hollywood and the mob.

Bibliography

Books

Allen, Steve, *Ripoff: A Look at Corruption in America* (Lyle Stuart Inc. 1979)

Anger, Kenneth, *Hollywood Babylon* (Straight Arrow Books, 1975)

————, *Hollywood Babylon II* (Arrow Books, 1986)

Bart, Peter, *Fade Out: The Calamitous Final Days of MGM* (William Morrow and Company, Inc., 1990)

Bergreen, Laurence, *Capone: the Man and his Era* (Macmillan, 1994)

Best, Katherine and Katherine Hillyer, *Las Vegas Playtown USA* (David McKay Company Inc., 1955)

Biskind, Peter, *Down and Dirty Pictures: Miramax, Sundance and the Rise of Independent Film* (Bloomsbury, 2004)

————, *Easy Riders, Raging Bulls: How the Sex-Drugs-and-Rock'n'Roll Generation Saved Hollywood* (Simon & Schuster, 1998)

————, *The Godfather Companion* (HarperCollins, 1990)

Block, Max with Ron Kenner, *Max the Butcher: The Life and Times of Max Block* (Lyle Stuart, Inc., 1982)

Brashler, William, *The Don: The Life and Times of Sam Giancana* (Ballantine Books, 1977)

Bruck, Connie, *Master of the Game: Steve Ross and the Creation of Time Warner* (Simon & Schuster, 1994)

————, *When Hollywood Had a King: The Reign of Lew Wasserman, Who Leveraged Talent into Power and Influence* (Random House, 2003)

Carpozi Jr, George, *Bugsy: The Godfather of Las Vegas* (Everest Books, 1976)

Clarke, Gerald, *Get Happy: The Life of Judy Garland* (Random House, 2000)

Cohen, Mickey, *Mickey Cohen: In My Own Words* (Prentice-Hall, Inc., 1975)

Cowie, Peter, *The Godfather Book* (Faber and Faber, 1997)

Cummings, John and Ernest Volkman, *Mobster: The Improbable Rise and Fall of John Gotti and his Gang* (Warner Books, 1996)

Davis, Mike, *City of Quartz: Excavating the Future in Los Angeles* (Verso, 1990)

Decharne, Max, *Hardboiled Hollywood: The Origins of the Great Crime Films* (No Exit Press, 2003)

Demaris, Ovid, *The Last Mafioso: The Treacherous World of Jimmy Fratiano* (Corgi Books, 1981)

Dickie, John, *Cosa Nostra: A History of the Sicilian Mafia* (Hodder & Stoughton, 2004)

Didion, Joan, *After Henry* (Simon & Schuster, 1992)

Edmonds, Andy, *Hot Toddy: The True Story of Hollywood's Most Shocking Crime – the Murder of Thelma Todd* (Avon Books, 1989)

Evans, Robert, *The Kid Stays in the Picture* (Aurum Press, 1994)

Exner, Judith, *Judith Exner: My Story* (Grove Press, Inc., 1977)

Finstad, Suzanne, *Warren Beatty: A Private Man* (Aurum Press, 2005)

Fisher, Eddie, *Been There, Done That: An Autobiography* (St Martin's Paperbacks, 1999)

Ford, Luke, *A History of X: 100 Years of Sex in the Cinema* (Prometheus Books, 1999)

Fox, Stephen, *Blood and Power: Organized Crime in Twentieth Century America* (William Morrow and Company, Inc., 1989)

Friedrich, Otto, *City of Nets: A Portrait of Hollywood in the 1940s* (Harper & Row, 1986)

Gabler, Neil, *An Empire of Their Own: How the Jews Invented Hollywood* (Crown Publishers, Inc., 1988)

Gage, Nicholas, *The Mafia Is Not an Equal Opportunity Employer* (Corgi Books, 1973)

Giancana, Antoinette and Thomas C. Renfer, *Mafia Princess: Growing up in Sam Giancana's Family* (William Morrow, 1984)

Giancana, Sam and Chuck, *Double Cross: The Story of the Man Who Controlled America* (Macdonald & Co., 1992)

Goodman, Ezra, *The Fifty Year Decline and Fall of Hollywood* (Macfadden Books, 1962)

Guiles, Fred Lawrence, *Joan Crawford: The Last Word* (Pavilion Books, 1995)

Hanna, David, *Sinatra: Ol' Blue Eyes Remembered* (Gramercy Books, 1997)

Higham, Charles, *Merchant of Dreams: Louis B. Mayer, MGM and the Secret Hollywood* (Sidgwick & Jackson, 1993)

Hill, Henry, *Gangsters and Goodfellas: Wiseguys . . . and Life on the Run* (Mainstream Publishing, 2004)

Hiney, Tom and Frank MacShane, *The Raymond Chandler Papers: Selected Letters and Non-fiction 1909–1959* (Hamish Hamilton, 2000)

Horne, Gerald, *Class Struggle in Hollywood 1930–1950: Moguls, Mobsters, Stars, Reds and Trade Unionists* (University of Texas Press, 2001)

Jacobs, George and William Stadiem, *Mr S: The Last Word on Frank Sinatra* (Sidgwick & Jackson, 2003)

Jennings, Dean, *We Only Kill Each Other: The True Story of the Life and Bad Times of Bugsy Siegel* (Arrow Books, 1969)

Kashner, Sam and Jennifer Macnair, *The Bad and the Beautiful: Hollywood in the Fifties* (Little, Brown, 2002)

Knoedelseder, William, *Stiffed: A True Story of MCA, the Music Business and the Mafia* (Harper Perennial, 1993)

Kobler, John, *Capone: The Life and World of Al Capone* (Fawcett Publications, 1972)

Lacey, Robert, *Little Man: Meyer Lansky and the Gangster Life* (Century, 1991)

Lait, Jack and Lee Mortimer, *USA Confidential* (Crown Publishers, Inc., 1952)

Lernoux, Penny, *In Banks We Trust: Bankers and Their Close Associates the CIA, the Mafia, Drug Traders, Dictators and the Vatican* (Anchor Press/Doubleday, 1984)

Levy, Shawn, *Rat Pack Confidential: Frank, Dean, Sammy, Joey and the Last Great Showbiz Party* (Fourth Estate, 1998)

Lovelace, Linda, *Ordeal* (Berkley Books, 1980)

——, *Out of Bondage* (Berkley Books, 1986)

Lunde, Paul, *Organised Crime: An Inside Guide to the World's Most Successful Industry* (Dorling Kindersley, 2004)

McCarthy, Todd, *Howard Hawks: The Grey Fox of Hollywood* (Grove Press, 1997)

McClintick, David, *Indecent Exposure: A True Story of Hollywood and Wall Street* (William Morrow, 1982)

McDougal, Dennis, *The Last Mogul: Lew Wasserman, MCA and the Hidden History of Hollywood* (Da Capo Press, 1998)

McNeil, Legs, *The Other Hollywood: The Uncensored Oral History of the Porn Film Industry* (Regan Books, 2004)

Marx, Samuel and Joyce Vanderveen, *Deadly Illusions: Who Killed Jean Harlow's Husband?* (Century, 1991)

Messick, Hank, *The Beauties and the Beasts: The Mob in Show Business* (Pyramid Books, 1973)

Messick, Hank and Joseph L. Nellis, *The Private Lives of Public Enemies* (Dell Publishing, 1973)

Morgan, John, *Prince of Crime* (Stein and Day, 1985)

Morton, James, *Gangland International: An Informal History of the Mafia and Other Mobs in the 20th Century* (Little, Brown, 1998)

Munn, Michael, *The Hollywood Connection: The True Story of Organised Crime in Hollywood* (Robson Books, 1993)

Nielsen, Michael, *Motion Picture Craft Workers and Craft Unions in Hollywood: The Studio Era, 1912–1948* (University of Illinois, 1985)

Pearson, John, *The Cult of Violence: The Untold Story of the Krays* (Orion Books, 2001)

Puzo, Mario, *The Godfather* (William Heinemann, 1969)

Rappleye, Charles and Ed Becker, *All American Mafioso: the Johnny Rosselli Story.* (Doubleday, 1991)

Roemer, Jr, William F. *Accardo: The Genuine Godfather* (Donald I. Fine, 1995)

Ridley, Philip, *The Krays* (Methuen, 1997)

Rose, Frank, *The Agency: William Morris and the Hidden History of Show Business* (HarperCollins, 1995)

Russo, Gus, *The Outfit: The Role of Chicago's Underworld in the Shaping of Modern America* (Bloomsbury, 2003)

Sancton, Thomas and Scott MacLeod, *Death of a Princess: An Investigation* (Weidenfeld & Nicolson, 1998)

Scaduto, Tony, *Lucky Luciano, the Man Who Modernised the Mafia* (Sphere Books, 1976)

Scheim, David E., *Contract on America: The Mafia Murder of President John F. Kennedy* (Shapolsky Publishers, Inc., 1988)

Schlosser, Eric, *Reefer Madness and Other Tales from the American Underground* (Houghton Mifflin, 2003)

Schwarz, Ted, *Joseph P. Kennedy: The Mogul, the Mob, the Statesman and the Making of an American Myth* (John Wiley & Sons, Inc., 2003)

Shapiro, Harry, *Shooting Stars: Drugs, Hollywood and the Movies* (Serpent's Tail, 2003)

Shulman, Irving, *Harlow: An Intimate Biography* (Bernard Geis Associates, 1964)

Simon, David, *Tony Soprano's America: The Criminal Side of the American Dream* (Westview Press, 2002)

Smith, Greg B., *Made Men: The True Rise-and-Fall Story of a New Jersey Mob Family* (Berkley Books, 2003)

Smith, John L., *The Animal in Hollywood: Anthony Fiato's Life in the Mafia* (Barricade Books, 1998)

Stuart, Mark A., *Gangster: The Story of Longy Zwillman, the Man Who Invented Organized Crime* (W.H. Allen, 1987)

Summers, Anthony, *Goddess: The Secret Lives of Marilyn Monroe* (Victor Gollancz, 1985)

Summers, Anthony and Robbyn Swan, *Sinatra: The Life* (Doubleday, 2005)

Thompson, David, *Levinson on Levinson* (Faber and Faber, 1992)

Thomson, David, *Showman: The Life of David O. Selznick* (Alfred A. Knopf, 1992)

Van Meter, Jonathan, *The Last Good Time: Skinny D'Amato, the Notorious 500 Club, the Rat Pack and the Rise and Fall of Atlantic City* (Bloomsbury, 2003)

Vizzini, Sal with Oscar Fraley and Marshall Smith, *Vizzini: The Secret Life of America's Most Successful Undercover Agent* (Futura, 1974)

Wallace, David, *Hollywoodland* (LA Weekly Books, 2002)

Wilson, Earl, *The Show Business Nobody Knows* (Bantam Books, 1973)

Yablonsky, Lewis, *George Raft* (McGraw Hill, 1974)

Yacowar, Maurice, *The Sopranos on the Couch* (Continuum, 2003)

Yallop, David A., *The Day the Laughter Stopped: The True Story Behind the Fatty Arbuckle Scandal* (Hodder & Stoughton, 1976)

Zollo, Paul, *Hollywood Remembered: An Oral History of its Golden Age* (Cooper Square Press, 2002)

Acknowledgements

First, I realise this book is just adding a grain or two on the great silo of published material which already exists on the links between Hollywood and organised crime. This book is a modest attempt to drill deeper into ground already covered by many writers, including multiple biographers of Al Capone, John F. Kennedy, Marilyn Monroe, Lucky Luciano, Bugsy Siegel and Frank Sinatra. It struck me that the one thing that connected these fascinating and legendary figures, like letters through a stick of rock, was the Mafia and the movies. In particular, I would like to single out the work of Connie Bruck, Shawn Levy, David McClintick, Dennis McDougal and the late Hank Messick as being especially helpful.

And I would like to thank my fellow Bloomsbury author Gus Russo for his help and his exemplary history of organised crime in Chicago, *The Outfit: the Role of Chicago's Underworld in the Shaping of Modern America*.

I would like to give special thanks to authors Anthony Summers and Robbyn Swan for reading manuscript chapters and pointing out inaccuracies. To my mind, Summers – biographer of Richard Nixon and J. Edgar Hoover – is the doyen of investigative biographers. I am deeply grateful to both of them for allowing me to go through their files, asking boring and pedantic questions. Both of them have showed me how this book should have been written.

Second, I would like to thank everybody in Los Angeles who agreed to be interviewed for this book, including Peter Bart, editor-in-chief of *Variety*; former *Hollywood Reporter* journalist Dave Robb; and Richard Stavin of law firm Stavin & Associates, who spoke frankly about his investigation into the Mafia's corruption of Hollywood in the 1980s.

Separately, former Metro-Goldwyn-Mayer chairman and chief executive Alan Ladd Jr was most forthcoming about his experience running the studio during the early 1990s.

Author Peter Cowie, who wrote *The Godfather Book* – the guide to Francis Ford Coppola's Mafia trilogy – and organised-crime expert James Morton, whose many books include *Gangland International* and *Gangland Today*, were generous in suggesting people I should talk to and sources I must consult.

I am also grateful to author Peter Evans for allowing me to quote from a previously unpublished interview with Ava Gardner.

Jonathan Davis, strategy adviser to the UK Film Council and European polyglot, suggested avenues in Italy I might explore.

Staff at the British Library, the British Library Newspapers collection and the British Film Institute library – in particular chief librarian Sean Delaney – have gone out of their way to be helpful.

As for picture research, Kristine Krueger at the Margaret Herrick Library, Academy of Motion Picture Arts and Sciences in Beverly Hills, has been assiduous in finding photographs for me.

At Bloomsbury I would like to thank my editor Mike Jones for his close reading of the manuscript and for pointing out the right path when I became hopelessly lost in the forest. Bloomsbury editor Victoria Millar deserves praise for her copy-editing, polishing my copy into something readable.

Also, I would like to thank my London agent, Laura Morris, for her unflagging enthusiasm for this project; my translation agents Jessica and Rosie Buckman of The Buckman Agency; and my US agent Susan Crawford – all of whose support has been helpful during the writing of this book.

Finally, I would like to give a thank you of sorts to the late film critic of the London *Evening Standard*, Alexander Walker, who warned me when I first broached writing *Hollywood and the Mob* that doing justice to the subject would take ten years and a team of researchers. Being arrogant, I blithely ignored his warning. In hindsight, he was probably right.

Index